New Encyclopedia of
SCIENCE

NEW
ENCYCLOPEDIA OF
SCIENCE

VOLUME 1
Abacus - Arctic

RAINTREE PUBLISHERS
Milwaukee • Toronto • Melbourne • London

Consultant Editor: Tony Osman, MSc, BSc, ARCS
Executive Editor: Vivian McCorry
Scientific Editor: Christopher Cooper, BSc, ARCS
Editorial Director: Brian Innes, BSc, MIOP, ASIA
Assistant Editor: Jennifer Sullings, BA
Scientific Consultant, sixth edition: Geoffrey C. Crockett, PhD

Printed and bound in Spain
by Graficromo, S.A. — Cordoba

ISBN 0-8172-5000-X

How to use this encyclopedia

As you will have noticed, this Encyclopedia is organized alphabetically. This makes it simple to find major topics without having to turn to the Index volume. Also, within each article you will find cross-references in italic type (*which looks like this*) directing you to other topics that are related to the one you are reading. Cross-references that occur within the article refer to topics relating to each point as it is raised. Cross-references at the end of an article refer to other entries that relate to the article in general.

The Index is to help you to find all the material in the Encyclopedia that has been dealt with under other titles because the topic was not important enough to merit an entry in its own right. Using the Index you should be able to find anything scientific, no matter how obscure.

The Study Guides are to help you plan a project, or course of study.

Study guides

Science is knowledge, which makes it a pretty big topic. That is why we split it up into various areas of study, or subjects. If you say that someone is a scientist, this does not tell us very much. But if you say that he is a physicist, then we know much more about what he is interested in – we know that he studies matter and energy, rather than psychology or disease or geography. There is another good reason why we split up science into subjects. Few of us would hope to learn everything there is to know; there is too much. So we usually concentrate on one branch of knowledge.

The way in which science is divided up into 'the sciences' is quite logical. For instance, everything on Earth can be divided into two groups: living things and non-living things. We call the study of living things 'biology'. We can split up the study of living things still further into plants (botany) and animals (zoology). We can specialize even further with the study of particular aspects of plants or animals. We may be interested in the growth of plants for food. This is called agriculture or horticulture. Or we may want to study how living things work – how they feed, reproduce, grow and so on. This is the study of physiology. Or we may be particularly interested in the feeding habits of human beings. This is a branch of physiology called nutrition and dietetics. In the same way, the study of non-living things splits into physics, chemistry, astronomy, geography, geology and so forth.

We have seen how science as a whole is split into major fields, and these into specialisations. The study guides follow the same principles. There are five main sections. In each section are listed the subjects that make up that branch of science. Also listed are articles on more specialised aspects of those subjects.

The first section is concerned with **The Earth and its crust.** The second is entitled **Beyond the Earth.** The third is **Living things. Matter and forces** deals with physics and chemistry. **Mathematics and the man-made world** covers maths and technology, which are combined in, for example, the science of computers.

One way of using the guides is to choose a general subject that interests you. Then the study guides will help to plan your reading. They make this easy for you by listing all the subjects that are related to the topic you choose. (We shall discuss other ways of using the study guides later in this introduction.)

Let us suppose that you have chosen plants as your topic of general interest. Which study guide will that be in? The answer is simple: **Living things** (page 233). Directly below this heading you will find a short list of the main articles of interest in that field.

Following this you will find lists of all the articles relating to plants. To make your reading easier, we have split the lists into several subsections on particular aspects of plant science. There are articles listed under Structure, Processes, Plant Environment, Classification and Plant Uses.

You will see that the first few articles in most of the subsections are in **bold type.** These are the major articles in the subsections. So you can pick a subsection and read all of the articles in it. Or you can read just the bold type major articles in each subsection. By the first method you will have read all of the articles on a special aspect of plants. By the second method you will have acquired a good grounding in botany generally.

You will notice that some articles occur in more than one subsection. For instance, **photosynthesis** occurs under both Structure and Processes. **Photosynthesis** is important to both subsections. But this does not mean that if you decided to study both subsections you would read the article **photosynthesis** twice. So if you did decide to read all of the articles under Plants, you would find that the list of articles to be read would be much shorter than it appears when it is split into subsections.

You will also see that throughout all the Encyclopedia articles there are references to other subjects. These are printed in italic type (for example – See: *aerodynamics*). These enable you to pass from one subject to another related one, even when you have not been aware that there is a relationship. For instance, in the course of reading the article on **Earth** you will find references to other related topics: **earthquake, Pythagoras, Copernicus, magnetism, compass, aurora, cosmic ray, chromosomes and genes, evolution, volcano, ozone, dinosaur, astronomy, continent, geology, ocean.** And if you follow up any of these references you will find others – for instance, in the article **evolution** there are references to **reproduction, camouflage,** and so on. You can read as much and as far as you like.

Therefore, starting from one article you may find yourself ranging all over the fields of science, discovering unexpected links.

If you want to pursue your studies in a more orderly fashion, but in a way different to that covered by the study guides, you can use them to invent your own guides. In the course of reading, for example, you may notice a link between two otherwise unrelated facts: birds fly and so do airplanes, but one flaps its wings and the other does not. You will be able to find out which are the related articles by looking in the **Living things** study guide and the **Mathematics and the man-made world** study guide, since birds are living things and airplanes are man-made. These guides will lead you to **birds, comparative anatomy, flying creatures, muscle,** etc. in the field of biology, and **aerodynamics, gravity, glider, weight, air, pressure and airplane** in the fields of physics and technology dealing with airplanes.

If you want to invent your own study guide, the way to decide what to do next is to ask yourself questions about the topic that interests you. Then you should go through the study guide, listing all the entries that might help you to answer your questions. Then you can read those articles in any order you like. Often your own interests are the best guide. And ideas come more quickly when you are interested in a particular topic.

Inventing your own study guide is exciting because it means using your imagination, just as a scientist would. Some of the most useful and wonderful discoveries in science have been made by people who noticed links between things that, at first sight, appeared not to be linked at all. Imagination helps you to see.

A word of advice
There is an important technique to be learned in choosing which parts of an article to read. This technique is known as skimming.

You may not find the answer to your special question all in one place. The information you are looking for will probably be spread through several articles. Suppose you are trying to find out about the absorption and storage and use of energy in plants. You will have to read carefully the whole article on **photosynthesis.** But there is also more information that you need in articles on **oxygen, light,** and **carbohydrate.** Now you do not have to read all of these articles, since they contain further information that you do not need in studying food energy. What you must do is to glance quickly or 'skim' through each article, and pick out the bits that will be useful to you. Then you should read these bits carefully. This technique will help you to save time. And you will not be confused by reading a lot of material that is not going to help you answer your questions. This is a very useful technique to develop.

Finally, remember that using this whole Encyclopedia ought to be fun. If you use it in the ways we have suggested, you will find that learning is exciting. You can find out more

about things that interest you. You can invent your own areas of research and use the Encyclopedia to help you find out still more. And who knows – you might spot something that no one else has ever noticed. You might make a scientific discovery of your own.

The Earth and its crust

Earth, geography, geology

Earth's structure and materials
chemistry, Earth, earthquake, geology, moho, rocks and minerals, solar system, volcano, agate, alchemy, alum, aluminium, amber, amethyst, barium, basalt, calcium, carbon, cave, ceramics, chalk, chromium, coal, continent, copper, crystal, element, fluorine, fossil, gemstones, gold, hydrocarbon, ice ages, lead, magnesium, marble, mercury, metals, mines, nickel, oil, paleontology, platinum, potassium, quartz, radium, ruby and sapphire, salt, sand, silicon, silver, sodium, soil, sulphur, tin, uranium, zinc.

Natural features and happenings
climate, erosion, seasons, aurora, cave, cloud, coal, cold, coral, crater, desert, drought, Earth, earthquake, eclipse, flood, gas, geyser, glacier, gravity, humidity, hurricane, ice, jungle, lagoons and lakes, lightning, monsoon, mountain, oasis, ocean, oil, rain, rainbow, river, sand, snow, soil, stalactites and stalagmites, swamp, tides, time, tropics, tundra, water, wave, weather forecasting, wells, wind, volcano.

Man-made features
agriculture, air pollution, bridge, canal, communication, compass, dam, erosion, fertilizer, fire, fuel, horticulture, hydraulics, hydroelectric power, iron and steel, irrigation, migration, mines, power, railways, reservoir, road, tunnels, wells, windmill.

Earth's products
agate, agriculture, alum, aluminium, amber, ammonia, balsa, bamboo, banana, bean, cattle, cellulose, cereal, cheese, chlorine, chromium, citrus fruits, coal, cocoa and chocolate, coconut, coffee, copper, cotton, dairy farming, fats and oils, fertilizer, fibre, fish, fluorine, food, fuel, gas, gemstones, glass, gold, horticulture, hydrocarbon, hydrogen, iron and steel, magnesium, marble, mercury, metals, milk, mines, nickel, nitrogen, oil, oxygen, paints and pigments, palm, paper, plastics, potassium, potato, quartz, radium, resin, rice, rubber, salt, sand, silver, sugar, sulphur, tin, tobacco, vegetables, wheat, wine, wood, zinc.

Earth's history
continent, Earth, geology, paleontology, Archaeopteryx, archeology, coelacanth, Cretaceous period, Darwin, Devonian period, dinosaur, earthquake, evolution, fossil, glacier, ice ages, Jurassic period, mountain, Ordovician period, pterodactyl, rocks and minerals, Silurian period, Tertiary period, Triassic period.

Places
Africa, Antarctic, Arctic, Asia, Australasia, continent, Europe, latitude and longitude, North America, ocean, South America, time zones.

Beyond
the Earth

astronomy, solar system, universe, Copernicus, Einstein, Galileo, space exploration.

Bodies in space
asteroid, comet, constellation, Earth, galaxy, Jupiter, Mars, Mercury, meteor, Moon, nebula, Neptune, Pluto, pulsar, quasar, satellite, Saturn, solar system, star, Sun, unidentified flying objects, universe, Uranus, Venus.

Observing space
astronomy, universe, calendar, cosmic ray, day and night, eclipse, gravity, light, meteor, Moon, observatory, planetarium, radiation, radioastronomy, relativity, satellite, solar system, space exploration, Sun, telescope, time, Van Allen belts.

Living things

air, biology, carbohydrate, carbon, cell, growth, life, oxygen, water.

Plants
agriculture, botany, horticulture, plant.

Structure
Visible structure
comparative anatomy, flowers and fruits, seeds, annual ring, cellulose, fibre, leaf, Mendel, paleontology, reproduction, rhizome, soil, trees.

Microstructure
cell, fibre, microscope, photosynthesis, carbohydrate, disease, protein, root, spores, textile, transpiration, wood.

Processes
botany, carbon, osmosis, photosynthesis,

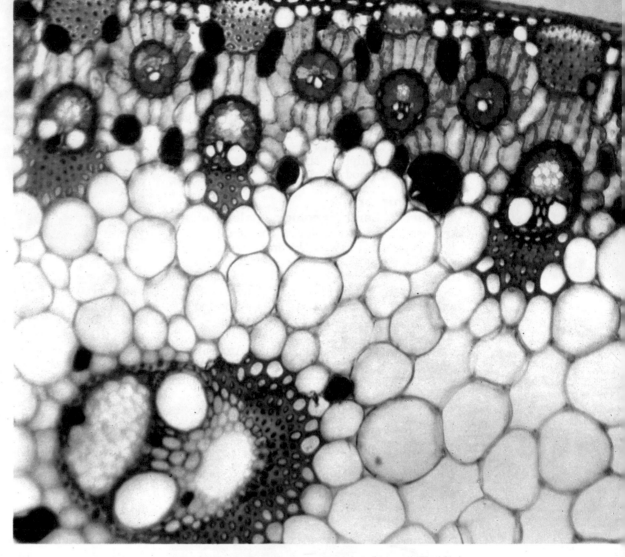

transpiration, absorption in living things, agriculture, air, amino acids, angiosperm, bee, carbohydrate, cell, cellulose, cereal, chemistry, chromosomes and genes, diffusion, ecology, energy, excretion, fertilizer, flowers and fruits, food chain, fungus, growth, gymnosperm, horticulture, hydrocarbon, leaf, legume, life, nitrogen, oxygen, pollen, protein, rain, reproduction, root, saprophyte, soil, spores, symbiosis, trees, vegetables, vegetation, weeds.

Plant environment
adaptation, agriculture, climate, desert, ecology, food chain, jungle, tropics, vegetation, Africa, aquarium, Asia, Australasia, conservation of nature, drought, Earth, erosion, Europe, geography, geology, horticulture, irrigation, mountain, North America, oasis, rain, ruminant, seaweed, soil, South America, swamp, symbiosis, trees, tundra, vegetables, water, weeds, wild flowers, wood.

Classification
algae, angiosperm, botany, evolution, fungus, gymnosperm, lichen, Linnaeus, plant, saprophyte, trees, vegetables, vegetation, weeds, wild flowers, balsa, bamboo, banana, banyan, bean, cactus, cocoa and chocolate, coconut, coffee, comparative anatomy, cotton, grape, grass, moss, orchid, palm, parasite, plankton, potato, rice, rose, rubber, seaweed, sequoia, sugar, tobacco, tomato, wheat.

Plant uses
agriculture, botany, food, horticulture, balsa, bamboo, banana, bean, bee, carbohydrate, cattle, cellulose, cereal, coal, cocoa and chocolate, coconut, coffee, conservation of nature, cotton, drugs, energy, fertilizer, fibre, grass, herbivore, hybrid, insecticide, narcotics, paper, rubber, wheat, wood.

Animals
animal, biology, zoology, evolution, life.

Structure
anatomy, comparative anatomy, evolution, Leonardo da Vinci, taxidermy.

Frameworks
skeleton, bone, bird, cat, crustacean, evolution, fish, insect, joint, mammal, reptile, rickets, shell, turtle, tortoise and terrapin, vertebrates.

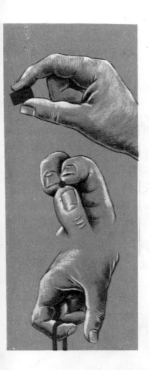

External parts
hair and fur, skin, adaptation, arm and hand, beak, bird, butterfly, camouflage, carnivore, cat, cattle, dog, ear, elephant, fish, flying creatures, hoofed animals, horn, insect, lizard, mammal, marsupial, metamorphosis, monkeys and apes, mouth, nails and claws, reptile, rhinoceros, teeth.

Sense organs
ear, eye, finger, nervous system, senses, taste, adaptation, antenna, bat, bee, behaviour, bird, blindness, cat, colour vision, evolution, mammal, nocturnal creatures, pain, reptile.

Internal organs and muscles
anatomy, comparative anatomy, medicine, abdomen, adenoids, adrenal glands. appendix, Bernard, biology, blood, brain, cell, circulation of blood, digestion, excretion, gland, head, heart, kidney, life, liver, lung, muscle, nervous system, pathology, pineal gland, reproduction, respiration, spleen, stomach, surgery, thyroid, tonsil, veterinary medicine, zygote.

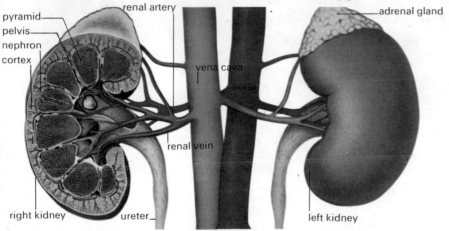

pyramid, pelvis, nephron, cortex, right kidney, renal artery, vena cava, aorta, renal vein, ureter, adrenal gland, left kidney

Processes
biology, medicine, physiology, absorption in living things, adaptation, aging, air, amino acids, bioluminescence, birth, blood, brain, breathing, breeding, calcium, carbohydrate, carbon, cell, chemistry, chromosomes and genes, circulation of blood, co-ordination, dehydration, diffusion, digestion, dreams, drugs, ear, energy, enzyme, excretion, eye, food, food chain, gestation, gland, growth, head, health, heart, heat, hermaphrodite, hibernation, immunity, inflammation, instinct, intelligence, kidney, Koch, life, liver, lung, lymph, memory, metabolism, milk, mouth, muscle, nitrogen, nutrition, osmosis, oxygen, pain, pineal gland, pituitary, protein, reflex, regeneration, reproduction, respiration, senses, skin, sleep, stomach, sugar, thyroid, veterinary medicine, vitamins, water.

Animal environment
adaptation, ecology, food chain, Africa, air, air pollution, algae, Antarctic, aquarium, Arctic, Asia, Australasia, camouflage, cave, climate, cold, conservation of nature, Darwin, day and night, deep sea creatures, desert, Europe, evolution, hibernation, homing, jungle, lagoons and lakes, life, migration, mountain, North America, ocean, parasite, Pavlov, pollution, races of man, radioactivity, reflex, river, seasons, soil, South America, swamp, symbiosis, tropics, tundra, underwater exploration, veterinary medicine.

Classification
animals, evolution, heredity, zoology, amphibian, Audubon, bird, carnivore, crustacean, fish, herbivore, hybrid, insect, Linnaeus, mammal, marsupial, primates, races of man, reptile, taxonomy, worms, zoo.

Mammals
anatomy, anteater, antelope, armadillo, aurochs, baboon, bat, bear, beaver, bison and buffalo, camel, cat, cattle, chimpanzee, deer, dog, dolphins and porpoises, elephant, flying creatures, gorilla, guinea pigs and hamsters, hedgehog, hippopotamus, hoofed animals, horse, hyena, jaguar, kangaroo, koala, lemur, lion, monkeys and apes, mouse, opossum, otter, panda, platypus, porcupine, rabbit, rat, reindeer, rhinoceros, rodent, ruminant, seals and sealions, sheep and goats, sloth, squirrel, tapir, tiger, walrus, weasel, whales, wolf, zebra, zoology.

Insects and anthropods
ant, bee, beetle, butterfly, centipedes and millipedes, locust, mosquito, scorpion, spider, termite, wasp.

Fish and shellfish
barnacle, barracuda, coelacanth, eel, lungfish, mollusc, octopus, piranha, salmon and trout, sea horse, shrimps, squid, sturgeon, swordfish.

Amphibians and reptiles
alligator, anaconda, chameleon, cobra, dinosaur, frogs and toads, iguana, lizard, newts and salamanders, pterodactyl, python, snake, turtle, tortoise and terrapin.

Birds
albatross, Archaeopteryx, auk, eagle, humming bird, kiwi, ostrich, owl, parrot, poultry, vulture.

Man
comparative anatomy, geography, health, medicine, anthropology, evolution, intelligence, races of man.

Structure
abdomen, addiction, adenoids, adolescence, adrenal glands, aging, air, arm and hand, behaviour, birth, blood, bone, brain, breathing, chromosomes and genes, circulation of blood, colour vision, co-ordination, digestion, dreams, ear, energy, enzyme, excretion, eye, finger and fingerprint, Freud, gland, growth, hair and fur, head, heart, heredity, hypnosis, instinct, lung, memory, metabolism, migration, mouth, muscle, nervous system, nose, pain, physiology, pineal gland, pituitary, psychology and psychiatry, reflex, reproduction, respiration, senses, skeleton, skin, sleep, speech, spleen, stomach, teeth, thyroid, tonsil, vegetables, vitamins.

Health and disease
disease, health, medicine, acne, addiction, aging, air, allergy, anemia, anesthesia, antibiotics, antihistamine, antiseptic, arthritis, artificial limb, aspirin, asthma, bacteria, Bernard, birth, blindness, blood, bone, brain, breathing, cancer, carbohydrate, cell, colour vision, co-ordination, Curie, death, dehydration, diathermy, digestion, doctors, drugs, dwarfs and giants, ear, excretion, eye, first aid, Fleming, food, head, heart, hemophilia, heredity, hormone, hospital, immunity, incubator, inflammation, influenza, Jenner, life, Lister, malaria, metabolism, narcotics, nervous system, nutrition, obesity, pain, paralysis, Pasteur, pathology, pharmacy and pharmacology, plastic surgery, pneumonia, poison, poliomyelitis, pollution, psychology and psychiatry, rabies, radiotherapy, rickets, shock, smallpox, stimulants and tranquillisers, sulpha drugs. surgery, tonsil, transplants, tuberculosis, typhoid, typhus, ulcer, vaccination, virus, vitamins, wounds and healing, X-rays, yellow fever.

Medicine
medicine, drugs, pharmacy and pharmacology.

Human behaviour
adaptation, ecology, evolution, food chain, geography, psychology and psychiatry, anthropology, archeology, behaviour, climate, cold, communication, conservation of nature, ergonomics, food, Freud, hypnosis, instinct, intelligence, narcotics, nervous system, oxygen, parasite, Pavlov, pollution, programmed learning, senses, shock, sound, space exploration, speech, telepathy, underwater exploration, vitamins, water.

Races of man
Aborigine, Africa, anthropology, Asia, Australia, Eskimo, Europe, geography, migration, North America, races of man, South America.

Microscopic life
bacteria, microscope, virus, ameba, diatom, hydra, paramecium, parasite, plankton, yeast.

Matter and forces

atom, chemistry, light, matter, physics, Sun.

Structure of matter
matter, air, atom, crystal, Dalton, element, gas, ion, liquids, metals, microscope, qualitative and quantitative analysis, solids, valence.

Forces, movement, work and machines
energy, machine, work, acceleration, accelerator, aerodynamics, ballbearing, ballistics, balloon, bicycle, boats and ships, boomerang, bridge, building, centrifuge, diesel engine, dynamo, Earth, Einstein, elasticity, electricity, elevators and escalators, engine, engineering, equilibrium, feedback, friction, fuel, gear, glider, gravity, gyroscope, hydraulics, jet engine, liquids, metals, motion, navigation, Newton, parachute, pendulum, perpetual motion, propellant, pump, relativity, rocket, root, screw, speedometer, springs, steam engine, supersonic flight, tides, turbine, Wankel engine, water, weight, wheel, windmill.

Pressure
air, liquids, pressure, aerodynamics, aerosol, anemometer, barometer, cell, cloud, cold, deep sea creatures, deep sea diving, density, Dewar, Earth, explosion, fuel, gas, geyser, glider, hurricane, hydraulics, hydrofoil, hydrometer, jet engine, locomotive, lung, mercury, osmosis, pump, rocket, submarine, supersonic flight, surface tension, thermometer, turbine, underwater exploration, water, weather forecasting, weight, whales, wind tunnel, Wright Brothers.

Energy
energy, carbohydrate, coal, electricity, engine, explosion, fuel, heat, hurricane, metabolism, nuclear energy, nutrition, oil, power, propellant, radiation, rocket, steam engine, water.

Waves
light, radio, radioastronomy, sound, television, wave, communication, Doppler effect, electronics, Hooke, Marconi, motion, ocean, radar, radiotherapy.

Sound
sound, acoustics, antenna, communication, density, Doppler effect, ear, Edison, electronics, lightning, phonograph, radio, radiosonde, senses, sound recording, speech, tape recorder, telegraph, telephone, walkie-talkie.

Heat
heat, coal, diathermy, energy, explosion, fire, friction, fuel, ice, oil, radiation, thermometer.

Light
light, absorption of light, after-image, aurora, bioluminescence, colour vision, crystal, day and night, Doppler effect, eclipse, Edison, electricity, energy, eye, glass, heat, heliograph, kaleidoscope, Kepler, laser, lenses and mirrors, lighthouse, lightning, mirage, microscope, motion picture, optical instruments, paints and pigments, photography, photosynthesis, polarized light, quantum, radiation, rainbow, spectrum, stereoscope, Sun, telescope, television, wave.

Magnetism
magnet, compass, Earth, gravity, metals.

Electricity
electricity, Ampère, battery, dynamo, Edison, energy, engine, Faraday, heat, hydroelectric power, ion, light, lightning, machine, nuclear energy, Ohm, power, telegraph, transformer.

Chemical materials and processes
Chemical materials
chemistry, element, abrasive, acetic acid, acetylene, acids and bases, aerosol, albumin, alcohol, alloys, amino acids, ammonia, arsenic, Bessemer, calcium, carbohydrate, carbon, cellulose, chalk, chromium, colloid, copper, crystal, Curie, Dalton, Davy, drugs, enzyme, fluorine, fuel, gas, gold, helium, hydrocarbon, hydrochloric acid, hydrogen, iodine, lead, magnesium, mercury, metals, nickel, nitric acid, nitrogen, oil, oxygen, ozone, paints and pigments, plastics, platinum, poison, polymer, potassium, Priestley, radium, resin, rocks and minerals, rubber, ruby, Rutherford, salt, silicon and silicones, silver, smoke, sodium, sugar, sulphur, sulphuric acid, uranium, water, wax, zinc.

Chemical processes
biochemistry, chemistry, element, acids and bases, adsorption, atom, catalyst, cold, colloid, crystal, dehydration, density, Dewar, distillation, elasticity, equilibrium, fire, fluorescence, heat, ion, magnet, nuclear energy, osmosis, pressure, propellant, radiation, radioactivity, solutions and solvents, technology, valence.

Chemical analysis
chemistry, qualitative and quantitative analysis, absorption of light, alchemy, Archimedes, atom, Boyle, centrifuge, chromatography, crystal, Curie, distillation, drugs, element, ion, Lavoisier, matter, measurement, microscope, Priestley, radiosonde, solutions and solvents, spectrum.

Mathematics and the man-made world

algebra, arithmetic, geometry, mathematics, measurement, trigonometry, abacus, anemometer, barometer, binary number, calculator, chromatography, compass, computer, Geiger counter, graph, laboratory, latitude and longitude, lenses and mirrors, map making, microscope, number systems, Ohm, optical instruments, qualitative and quantitative analysis, radiosonde, scientific method, set theory, slide rule, spectrum, speedometer, statistics, surveying, symmetry, telescope, thermometer, time zones, tools, topology, valence, watches and clocks, weight, wind tunnel.

Technology
engineering, technology, automation.

Construction
acoustics, air conditioning, bridge, building, canal, dam, elevators and escalators, heating systems, hydraulics, iron and steel, machine, moho, plastics, reservoir, road, robot, sewage, tools, tunnels, welding.

Transportation
aerodynamics, air cushion vehicle, airplane, airship, automobile, ballbearing, bathyscaph, bicycle, boats and ships, bridge, canal, diesel engine, elevators and escalators, engine, fuel, gear, gyroscope, helicopter, horse, hydrofoil, jet engine, lighthouse, Lindbergh, locomotive, map making, migration, motorcycle, navigation, parachute, Piccard, propellant, railways, river, road, rocket, space exploration, speedometer, steam engine, submarine, supersonic flight, tunnels, turbine, underwater exploration, Wankel engine, wheel, Wright Brothers.

Industry
abrasives, acetylene, adhesives, aerosol, alloys, antenna, automation, Bessemer, catalyst, cellulose, ceramics, cereal, cheese, coal, cocoa and chocolate, cosmetics, dehydration, distillation, drugs, etching, fibre, food, gear, glass, iron and steel, locks and keys, lubrication, machine, metals, mines, motion picture, optical instruments, photography, plastics, polymer, printing, pump, radio, refrigeration, resin, rubber, salt, screw, sewage, silicon, siphon, soap, soldering, solutions and solvents, springs, steam engine, telephone, textile, tyres, tools, typewriter, valve, wood, xerography, yeast.

Nuclear physics
accelerator, atom, Bohr, Curie, Einstein, element, energy, explosion, fuel, Geiger counter, geology, hydrogen, ion, nuclear energy, radiation, radioactivity, radiotherapy, radium, Rutherford, Sun, uranium, X-rays.

Electronics
electronics, Baird, calculator, communication, computer, engineering, gyroscope, hi-fi and stereo, ion, laser, light, microphone, microscope, navigation, quantum, radar, radio, robot, satellite, tape recorder, television, transistor, valve.

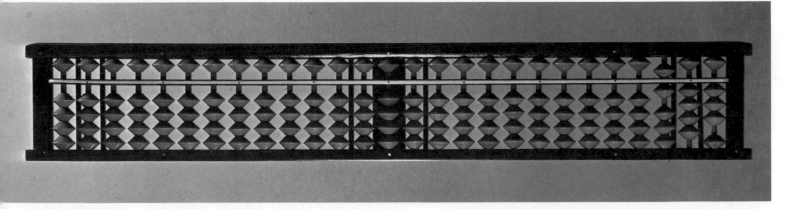

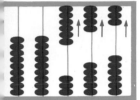

▽ To set up 643 on the ordinary abacus, 3 beads are moved up the first rod, 4 up the second and 6 up the third
\ On the Japanese abacus, 3 and 4 are set in the same way. To set the 6, move 1 lower bead up the third rod, and move the upper bead down. (1+5=6)

A Japanese businessman finds that the abacus is still the best instrument for some calculations

abacus

Some years ago, a competition was held in Tokio between two champions, one from the US Army, and one from the Japanese Post Office. The American soldier used the most up-to-date electric adding machine available; the Japanese expert used an abacus, in a design that has hardly changed in 2000 years.

All sorts of arithmetical calculations were performed. In addition and subtraction, the abacus operator was an easy winner; in division he was just ahead; only in multiplication was he slightly slower than the adding machine.

The abacus is a framework of rods and movable beads, and the beads can be moved up and down the rods to represent columns of figures. The principle of the abacus was first used thousands of years ago, but many shopkeepers and businessmen in China and Japan still use it to work out their accounts.

So many discoveries and inventions — such as paper, gunpowder, silk, printing, rocket propulsion, to name only a few — seem to have originated in China: it is surprising to find that the Chinese apparently adopted the abacus from the Romans, 1400 years ago.

The first abacus was much older than this. It was probably a table covered with fine sand in which calculations could be drawn with a finger or a stylus. Early civilizations did not have very good systems for writing down numbers, and they were also short of writing materials. So a sand table that could be used over and over again was very useful.

Later, the sand table became replaced by a board with grooves in it; counters or small pebbles could be moved along the grooves. The Roman word for pebble was calculus; and this is how we get our word 'calculation'.

When Europeans adopted Arabic numerals. and as parchment and paper became more easily available, the abacus gradually went out of use. Nevertheless, in skilled hands (as the competition proved), it is still a very rapid calculating machine.

There are several different kinds of abacus. A simple one has nine beads on each rod. Those on the first rod are used to add up units, those on the second to add up tens, those on the third to add up hundreds, and so on.

To show numbers on the abacus, beads are moved to the top of the rods. So if three beads are moved up the units rod, four up the tens rod, and six up the hundreds rod, the number shown is 643. To add another number, move up more beads corresponding to the number. To subtract, move the beads down.

Sometimes you will find you have not enough beads at the bottom of a rod for the number you want to add. Say you have the number six already on the units rod, and you want to add seven. But there are only three beads left to move. It is still easy. Start by counting: 'One. . . Two... Three...' as you move up these last three. Then move all nine beads down, and push up one bead on the tens rod, counting: 'Four'. Then go back to the units rod and continue: 'Five... Six... Seven', as you push beads up. Now read off the answer at the top. One bead on the tens rod and three on the units rod makes 13.

The Chinese abacus has a bar across the rods, with five beads below the bar on each rod, and two above. Each bead above the bar is equal to five below. You can see how this is related to the Roman method of counting in fives and tens, fifties and hundreds, and so on.

The Japanese abacus, called a soroban, is similar, but it has only one bead above the bar and four below. Before you begin a calculation, all the beads above the bar are at the top of the rods, and all those below the bar are at the bottom of the rods.

As you begin counting, you move the lower beads up to the bar: 'One... two... three... four'. At 'five', you move the four beads back to the bottom, and move the upper beads down to the bar. Then you go on moving up the lower beads again for 'six... seven... eight... nine'. For 'ten' you clear all the beads on the first rod — the upper one to the top and the other four to the bottom — and move one bead up on the next rod.

Subtraction is carried out by taking away beads instead of adding them. Multiplication and division are also possible. For instance, in an ordinary multiplication you multiply by the hundreds, by the tens, and by the units; then you add all the products together. The procedure is exactly the same on an abacus. Some of the rods are used like columns of a notebook in which you can note the numbers you are multiplying together, and other rods are used to add up the results.

See: *arithmetic, number systems*

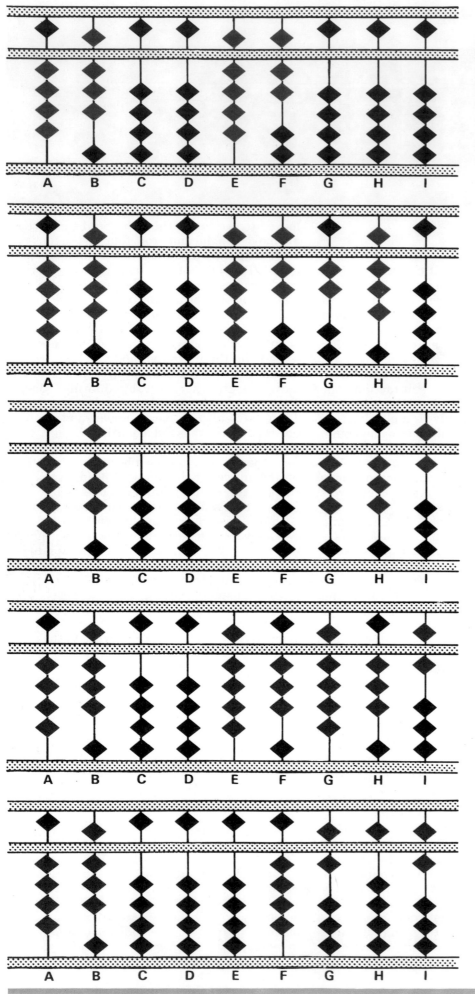

Find out by doing

You can buy a Japanese abacus in many shops, or you can make one for yourself by drawing the bar and the rods on a sheet of card and using coins or small pebbles for the beads.
Try some simple addition first. Write down the numbers you want to add below the rods, just as if they were in the units, tens and hundreds columns of an addition sum. Remember that you have to start from the right-hand column, just as in a written sum. After this you can try multiplication.

To multiply 97 x 48.
Step 1: set up 48 on two rods, which we will call A and B. Set up 97 on two other rods two spaces to the right; we will call these E and F.

Step 2: multiply the 7 by 4; this gives 28, which you set on rods G and H.

Step 3: multiply the 7 by 8; this gives 56, which you add to rods H and I. Clear 7 off rod F. Adding to the 28 on G and H, you now have a total of 336 on GHI.

Step 4: multiply the 9 by the 4; this gives 36, which you set on FG. This makes a total of 3936 on FGHI.

Step 5: multiply the 9 by the 8; this gives 72, which you add to rods G and H. Clear the 9 off rod E. The total, on rods FGHI, is 4656.

Aborigine

A member of any race of people that have lived in the same country for the whole of their known history. It is used especially for the native black people of Australia. They were already living there when the first European explorers arrived.

The origins of the Australian Aborigines are not clear. They tend to be small people. Their hair is curly and varies in colour from being sometimes blond in children to red or dark brown in adults.

The ancestors of the Aborigines probably arrived in Australia about 12,000 years ago. They may have traveled by canoe from Southeast Asia or India. There are people there who are physically similar.

When Europeans discovered Australia in 1770 the Aboriginal population was estimated to be 275,000. Now there are only 30,000 true Aborigines and 50,000 of mixed blood. Traditional life and culture can be seen only in the very remote areas.

Walking fifty miles a day

The Aborigines were 'nomads', or wanderers who lived in small groups. They never settled in villages, and did not build permanent huts. Because they were nomadic they kept very few possessions. They would carry only those necessary for hunting and food gathering. Most of the possessions were carried by the women so that the men could be on the alert and ready to hunt. Aborigines were able to walk great distances, as much as fifty miles in one day.

The Aborigine was very well acquainted with nature. He knew the land, the animals and plants, and the seasons. He studied the resources of the land and was careful not to waste them. He even set aside nature reserves to allow animals to breed.

The men were hunters and fishermen, and very skilful at disguises and tricks to catch certain animals. They hunted kangaroos, opossums and emus with spears and clubs, by setting snares and nets or by digging pits. Wombats and other small mammals were caught by smoking them out of their burrows. Aborigines who lived along the rivers or coastal areas hunted turtles from rafts or bark canoes, using spears.

The Aborigines ate not only roots, young shoots, nuts, and berries, but also edible insects such as witchetty grubs, honey ants and grasshoppers. The women gathered these.

The Aborigine could make fire by two

Australian Aborigines are excellent artists and craftsmen. They paint on rock and bark, and carve the objects they use in everyday life. Here a snake coiled round its eggs has been painted on bark. The snake's markings are clearly shown and make a beautiful design

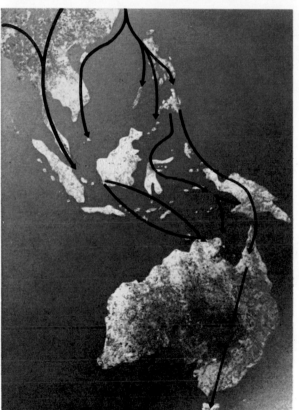

△ A corroboree, or group dance. Here only men are performing

◁ Aborigines first settled in Australia and Tasmania after migrating from South-east Asia

▽ Aborigines paint these patterns on themselves only on ritual occasions

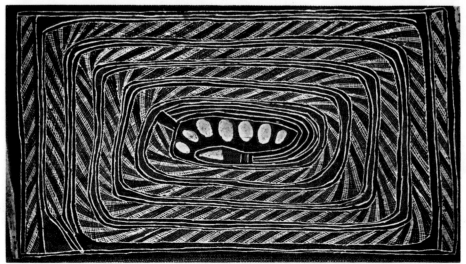

4 Aborigine

High on the rocky hillside
above their spacious
hunting grounds, Aborigines
keep a watch for kangaroos
and other animals to
provide food for the tribe.
They are armed with long,
sharp spears and spear-
throwers in preparation
for the chase

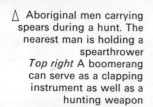

△ Aboriginal men carrying spears during a hunt. The nearest man is holding a spearthrower
Top right A boomerang can serve as a clapping instrument as well as a hunting weapon

A hunter about to spear a fish with the aid of a spear-thrower. In his other hand he holds two hunting boomerangs

methods. He could twirl a stick very rapidly between his hands with one end pressed against a small pit on a log. This generated heat and ash would form. The smoldering ash was tipped onto tinder, such as dry hair, leaves or fur, and the fire-maker would blow on it to make a flame. Or he could strike flint and ironstone together and allow the sparks formed to fall onto tinder.

Most food could be cooked on small fires, but large animals were cooked in a pit lined with hot stones and covered with bark or soil. Hot stones were also placed inside the body of the animal.

The boomerang, a curved throwing stick, was used as a weapon. Most boomerangs were not designed to return to the thrower, but simply to hit the target. The returning boomerang probably developed as a plaything. In some areas the boomerang was used only as a musical clapping stick (see: *boomerang*).

Clapping sticks were the main type of musical instrument. In Northern Australia the didjeridu was also used. It was a hollow tube about ten feet long, which was blown to make a droning note.

Many examples of aborigine art survive. There are cave paintings and drawings. They show people, animals and scenes of hunting. Utensils were decorated in bright colours and paintings were also done on bark. For engraving they used sharp stones; for paint-brushes they used twigs, bird feathers or their fingers. They made colours from natural dyes.

A young Aborigine would be prepared for adulthood at about age thirteen. In preparation he or she learned all the sacred laws of the people. When a boy had learned all this he would usually marry, and was considered a full adult when his wife had a child.

Aborigines lived in tribes. The tribes were different in appearance, language and customs. Each tribe was divided into clans or totems. Clans had their own rules about marriage. Wives were always obtained from another clan. Some rules said which person a man must marry; for example, it might have to be a mother's brother's daughter. When a girl married she left her clan and joined her husband's. Her brothers and their wives remained in the clan she left.

Old people in Aboriginal society were respected for their wisdom. They were never neglected and were fed by their family. They taught the younger generation the mysteries of their religion, which treated all members of a tribe as relatives. Tribes even adopted certain types of animal as members and would not hunt them except at times of drought and starvation. Even then they had to perform elaborate rites before they could kill these protected 'tribe members'. And the old men knew the procedure.

Nearly every Aboriginal tribe practised magic. An object such as a bone was pointed at an enemy for a curse. The victim believed so strongly in the power of the sorcerer that he might die or go blind from fear.

Tribes also had a healer who extracted 'evil' blood or a piece of bone from the painful part of the body. The affected area was massaged and the wound smeared with clay or blood. These practices, too, were often successful because of the complete faith of the patient in the healer.

In the past European settlers treated the Aborigines very badly. They also brought disease and the Aborigines had little or no resistance to them. This reduced their numbers drastically. If Aborigines are to take their rightful place in society in the future, it will be necessary for other Australians to accept them as equals and to respect their way of life.

See: *anthropology, Australasia, races of man.*

abrasives

In the home, sandpaper may be used for shaping wood and removing paint. Emery cloth may be used for removing rust and polishing metal. Scouring powders are used to clean baths, sinks and cooking vessels. Toothpaste acts as a gentle polish. All of these are abrasives.

In industry, abrasives are used for grinding, drilling and polishing. Often they are used in the form of grains bonded to a wheel or drill. Tiny pinhead-sized drills can be used to shape very small machine parts. Huge ones, five feet across, are made for grinding logs into pulp to make paper. Diamond-tipped drills are used to bore through solid rock for oil.

Grinding wheels are often inconvenient for fine work such as cleaning stonework on buildings. Powerful jets of compressed air can then be used to blow a stream of abrasive particles hard against the object to be cleaned. The most important abrasives are man-made. They include synthetic diamonds and carborundum. See: *carbon.*

Fine particles of sand in a powerful air jet have a strong abrasive effect. Here the dirt of centuries is being cleaned from stonework

Find out by doing

Smear toothpaste on a clear piece of perspex, and rub with your finger for a few minutes. The perspex will appear misty when you wash the toothpaste off. Look at the surface with a magnifying glass. Why does it appear misty?

To think about

How many different abrasives are used in your household?
Why is it possible to scratch glass with a diamond, but not with an iron point?

absorption
in living things

To grow, all living things must take up materials from outside themselves. Plants need water and minerals from the soil, and gases from the air. Animals need to take in food and water, and they need oxygen from the air. The process of taking in these substances is called absorption.

Plants absorb water from the soil through tiny hairs on their roots. The water is attracted through the walls of the plant cells by large molecules of chemicals inside the cells. The chemicals inside the cells are also attracted by the water outside, in the soil. But the cell walls have special properties: they are 'semi-permeable'. This means that they will let only small molecules like water pass through. So water and small molecules will be absorbed from the soil, but the larger molecules inside the plant stay in the cells. This is called 'osmosis'.

In animals, water is easily absorbed by the cells in the lining of the intestine. But food material that an animal eats has much larger molecules. First this food must be broken down into smaller molecules. Then special 'carrier' molecules in the cell walls link with the food molecules. They take them into the bloodstream. See: *digestion, osmosis.*

Find out by doing

Place a raisin or a prune in water. Notice how its size increases by osmosis.

Put some freshly cut flowers into water with red ink added. After a while the red will show in the petals. Cut through a stem to see the cells through which the ink has passed.

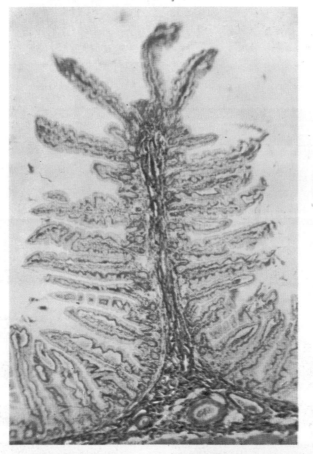

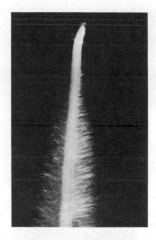

◁ Food is absorbed through these branched 'villi' in the wall of the human intestine, here enlarged 50 times

△ The large area of the spiderwort's root hairs can absorb water rapidly

▽ A prune kept in water will swell as the liquid flows into it

absorption of light

Light from overhead passes through a small thickness of air *(bottom)*. Light from the horizon has much more air to penetrate and is made redder *(top)*

When light passes through a vacuum there is nothing to stop it: nothing for it to bump into. However, when light passes through anything else it will collide with the molecules, or tiny particles, that make up the substance. And any light ray which does strike a molecule will give up some of its energy to that molecule. The energy will be absorbed by the molecule. If all of the light energy is absorbed the light will no longer be visible. But if some light is reflected off a molecule, only some of the energy is absorbed.

Even substances which appear to be transparent, such as air or clear glass, absorb energy from any light passing through. Even a highly polished mirror absorbs energy from light reflected off it. Every time light strikes anything, some of its energy is absorbed.

The amount of energy absorbed from light depends on three things: the wavelength of the light, the sort of molecules it strikes, and how the molecules are arranged.

White light is a mixture of all the colours. Each colour has its own wavelength. If the colours are arranged according to wavelength, we have what is called a spectrum. Towards one end of the spectrum is violet light, which has short

waves. Towards the other is red light, which has long waves. Waves longer than red light are called infra-red waves. They are not seen as light but felt as heat.

At the other end of the spectrum, and even shorter than violet light waves, are the ultra-violet rays. In very small doses they are good for us. When absorbed by the skin they build up vitamin D in the body. They also give us a suntan. In larger doses, however, they can cause blistering and skin damage.

Sunlight contains a lot of ultra-violet rays. However, because they are very short waves, which are most easily absorbed by the ozone in the atmosphere, we do not suffer. This is why some scientists are worried by airliners like Concorde, which would fly in the upper atmosphere and might burn up all the ozone.

The sun appears redder than usual when seen through a haze. This is because there are more particles in the air. These absorb more of the shorter, bluer, wavelengths. The longer, redder, wavelengths are less affected. So if we see sunlight through haze it is redder than on a clear day.

Sunglasses filter the sunlight by absorbing light energy. Even the very best sunglasses will alter slightly the colours we see. But they do give valuable protection from the sun's harmful ultra-violet rays.

Astronauts who walk in space or on the Moon do not have the protection of the atmosphere to absorb the intense heat and ultra-violet rays in sunlight. This is why they wear reflective suits in space.

Infra-red waves are used by doctors to treat rheumatism. They can also be used to cook food. Both the rheumatic tissue and the food absorb heat energy from the infra-red waves. Although infra-red waves are not visible, they can be used in photography. Aerial photography can use infra-red techniques to detect patterns on the land's surface which are not apparent in ordinary light. This can help archeologists to choose sites for excavation.

We see things as coloured because they do *not* absorb particular wavelengths. For instance, a piece of green paper appears green because its molecules have absorbed all the colours in white light *except* green. Light passing through red glass is red because the energy of all the other wavelengths is absorbed by the molecules in the glass. Anything which absorbs light of all wavelengths appears black. Anything which reflects visible light of all wavelengths appears white. If its molecules are arranged to form a very flat surface, it will act as a mirror.

Energy which has been absorbed from light does not just vanish. It may have been lost to the light but it survives in some other form. Usually it is turned into heat in the substance absorbing the energy. Sometimes it is given out again as light of a different colour. This is called 'fluorescence'.

Absorbed light energy can also start chemical reactions. An example is in photosynthesis. This is the process by which green plants use sunlight to make their food. We are able to see

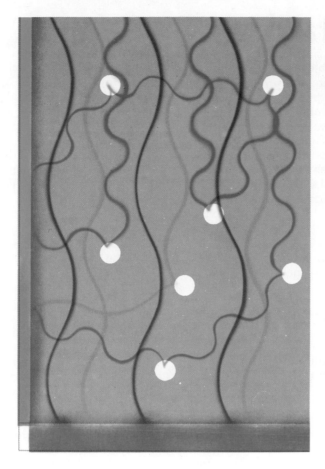

▷The tiny molecules of the gases in the air scatter the short blue waves of light and make the sky look blue. The longer red and yellow waves pass through the air more easily

Far right: an object of any colour absorbs light of other colours. The middle picture picks out the red parts of the beach scene. The red boat and the sand seem bright, but the blue sky and sea seem dark. Below, the blue parts of the picture are shown. Now the red boat and the beach are dark

When light is absorbed by an atom it knocks an electron to a higher orbit. When the electron falls back more light may be given out

because of another chemical reaction started by light energy. When light passes into the eye it lands on the retina, the screen at the back of the eye. There its absorbed energy starts chemical reactions. These send nerve impulses, or electrical messages, to the brain. The brain can then form a picture of what is being seen.

Dark objects absorb more light and heat energy than lighter-coloured objects do. They also give out the energy more rapidly. So a house with a dark roof will be hotter in summer than one with a white roof. This also explains why houses in hot sunny climates tend to be painted light colours.

The ability of molecules to absorb light is used in the laboratory to identify substances and to determine their concentration. This technique is called colorimetry. A sample in liquid form or in solution is placed in a clear-sided container and held against an illuminated screen. The amount of light absorbed in passing through the liquid depends on the concentration of molecules. And the type of molecule will determine what kind of light is absorbed and what allowed to pass through.

See: *colour, fluorescence, light, photosynthesis, radiation.*

Find out by doing

To demonstrate that dark materials absorb and radiate more light and heat energy than lighter coloured materials: wrap a piece of white cloth around the bulb of a thermometer and place it in sunlight. Note the temperature after five minutes. Then do the same with black cloth. Look at the sky through red cellophane, such as a candy wrapper, on a day when there are clouds as well as clear sky. Can you explain why the contrast between cloud and blue sky is greater? (Clue: *clouds reflect white light.*) Use a sun lamp to show how ultra-violet rays cause fluorescence in some materials. Place some commonplace objects in the beam of the lamp and note which ones seem to develop an unusual glow. Suggested items: a cigarette pack, some pictures in this book, a shirt washed in detergent, a glass of quinine tonic water. *Important Warning: never look directly at the lamp. Ultra-violet rays can damage your eyes.*

To think about

Why do people wear light-coloured clothes in the tropics?

acceleration

If the Earth's gravity were to fail the Moon would travel away along a straight path *(dotted line)*. But it is constantly dragged towards the earth by gravity and forced to travel in a circular orbit. So it is always 'falling' inwards

When the speed of an object increases, it is said to accelerate. For example, suppose a car is traveling at 40 fps (feet per second). If it speeds up to 50 fps, it has accelerated by 10 fps. If it does this in two seconds, its rate of acceleration is 5 feet per second per second.

An object accelerates only when a force is applied to it. Otherwise it remains at rest or continues at its original speed. When a bullet is fired, it accelerates from rest until it reaches the end of the gun barrel. It then has maximum speed. After it leaves the muzzle, no further force is applied behind it. Air resistance slows it down, and gravity drags it to the ground. If there were no air resistance or gravity, the bullet would move at constant speed in a straight line for ever.

A rocket's engine continues to fire for a long time after take-off. The rocket keeps on accelerating as long as the engine is firing. If the thrust could continue long enough, the rocket would eventually accelerate until it reached the speed of light.

If there were no air present to resist the motion, a feather and a cannon ball would fall at the same rate. The force that causes them to fall is gravity. The acceleration due to gravity is 32 fps per second. A falling object reaches a velocity of 32 fps after one second, 64 fps after two seconds, and so on. This rate of acceleration is called one gravity, or simply 1g.

It is possible for the speed of an object to *increase* in one direction while it *decreases* in another direction. For example, suppose a car is traveling at 50 mph (miles per hour) due north. It then goes round a bend at constant speed so that it is now traveling eastward at 50 mph. Its eastward speed has increased from zero to 50 mph, so that it has accelerated in an eastward direction. Its northward speed is now zero, so it has decelerated by 50 mph.

This means that whenever a moving object changes direction, an accelerating force is needed to make this change.

An object which travels at constant speed in a circle is always changing its direction of

motion toward the center. In other words, it is constantly accelerating toward the center.

A force is required to maintain this acceleration. If a stone is whirled in a circle on a piece of string, the pull on the string provides the force. The Moon is held in its orbit by the force of the Earth's gravity, which is always directed toward the center of the Earth.

We have all felt the sensations that acceleration causes in our bodies. An elevator that is beginning to rise makes its occupants feel heavier than normal. When it starts to descend they feel lighter, and perhaps have a moment of sickness.

Fighter pilots and astronauts have serious problems with the effects of acceleration. When a plane is in a tight turn, its pilot may feel an acceleration of 4g or 5g for several seconds. It is difficult for his heart to pump blood to the upper parts of his body. He may lose his vision for a few seconds because the blood supply to his eyes is reduced. At higher accelerations he may lose consciousness.

The G-suit is designed to help his heart. It applies pressure to parts of his body at the right moments and forces the blood upwards.

Astronauts lie flat during the launch, thus giving their hearts less work to do. They may experience accelerations up to about 10g.
See: *ballistics, centrifuge, gravity.*

Find out by doing

Gravity acts upon falling objects so that they tend to accelerate at the rate of 1g, or 32 fps per second, regardless of weight or size. However, air resistance does affect some falling bodies more than others. You can demonstrate this with a sheet of aluminum foil and a pebble, or similar spherical object. Hold up one in each hand and let them go at the same moment. The pebble will land on the floor before the foil. Now screw the foil up into a small hard ball and repeat the experiment. This time the objects will land at the same moment. This is because the foil meets less air resistance the second time.

To think about

Look at the water from a faucet that is dripping fairly rapidly. Why do the drops get farther apart as they fall?

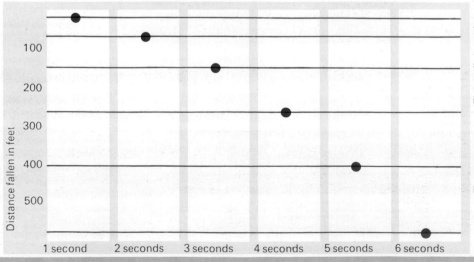

Distance fallen in feet

100
200
300
400
500

1 second   2 seconds   3 seconds   4 seconds   5 seconds   6 seconds

The distance fallen by an object is proportional to the square of the time it has been falling (ignoring air resistance). In the first second it falls 16 ft. After 2 seconds it has fallen 64 ft, and after 3 seconds it has fallen 144 ft

▷ Testing the effects of acceleration on the human body. This machine, used by the US Air Force, can produce accelerations many times greater than gravity. Astronauts and airplane pilots must be able to stand stresses of up to 10g for several seconds

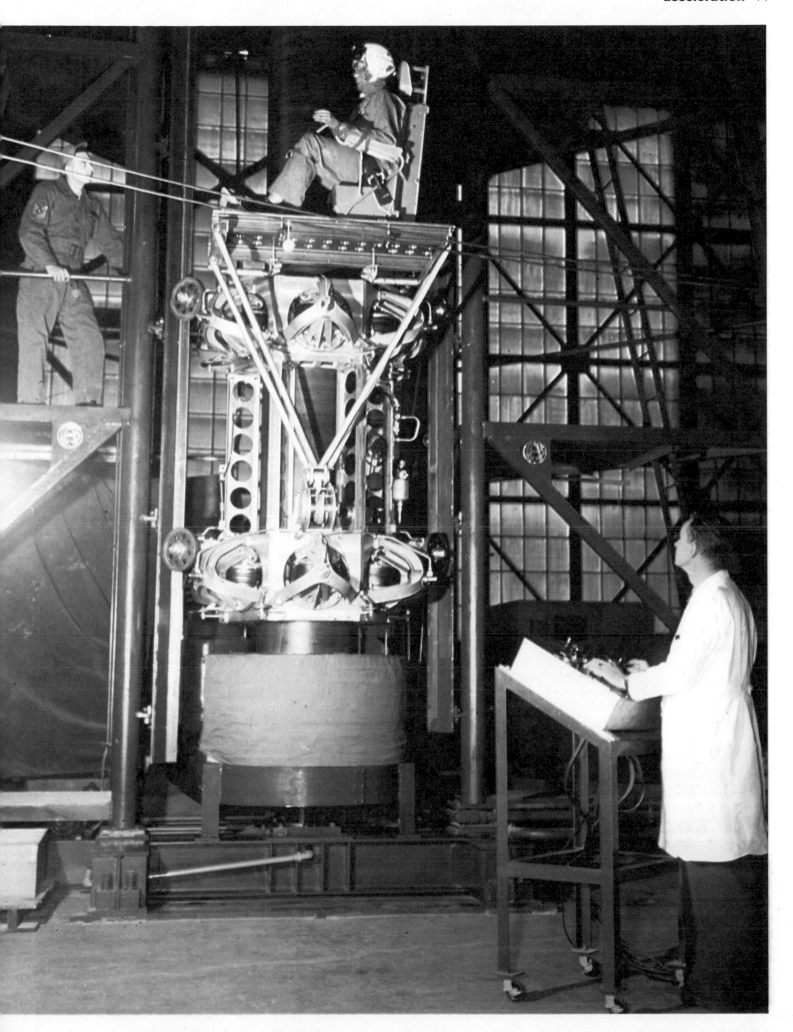

accelerator

Machines that can make atoms or particles smaller than atoms travel at high speeds are called accelerators.

Some accelerators are used in medicine and industry. The fast-moving particles they produce can be used to change atoms of ordinary substances into radioactive atoms. The strong radiations these atoms send out have many uses. The intense beams of electrons and protons produced in accelerators are now being used widely in medicine. Allowed to strike suitable targets, the beams will produce radiation such as X-rays. This has been found useful in the diagnosis and treatment of various types of cancer (see *X-ray*). Beams of other subatomic particles produced in accelerators have also been found useful for such treatments, and patients now sometimes have to make their way to the remote laboratories where such treatments can be given. Radioactive isotopes produced in accelerators play an important part in identifying illnesses too (see *radioactivity*).

Discovering the structure of atoms

The largest and most complex accelerators are those used in physics. Physicists have discovered the structure of atoms by bombarding them with fast-moving particles.

In the early days of research into the interior of the atom, physicists used the fast particles given out naturally in radioactivity. They would allow the particles to strike samples of elements like gold and see what kind of atoms were produced in the collisions. But they soon felt that they needed to be able to produce particles of exactly known energies whenever they wanted them. They wanted even faster particles as well. Modern accelerators are the result of this need.

In some ways a beam of very small fast particles is similar to a beam of light, and can act as a probe. It can be 'shone' on other particles in the same way as the beam of a torch. The faster the particles, the smaller the details that can be caught in the beam when it hits its target.

Alternatively, two beams produced in the accelerator can collide. This causes dramatic changes in the particles which can be observed.

In the most modern accelerators scientists can detect particles a thousand times smaller than even the protons and neutrons that make up the atom (see *atom*). Already they have shown that protons and neutrons may in themselves be made up of even smaller building blocks called quarks.

There is much new information too about the forces that hold the tiny particles together in ordinary matter. These forces are 'carried' by yet another set of 'particles' which can be created independently only in accelerators with beams of very high energies.

Charged particles

Only particles with an electric charge can be accelerated. The particles most often used in accelerators are electrons and protons. Some accelerators are built specifically to produce beams of ions from heavy elements. Electrons are negatively charged and are found in the outer regions of all atoms. When an electric current flows, it is due to the movement of electrons. Protons are positively charged, and found in the centres of atoms.

Charged particles are acted on by electrical forces, and the strength of the force is measured by a voltage. Voltages can be positive or negative. A particle that has a positive charge like a proton is pushed away from an object with a positive voltage. It is pulled toward a negative voltage. And negatively-charged particles do the opposite.

Objects that have a high voltage can be thought of as being like places that are raised above ground level. Then a positively charged particle is like a ball rolling downhill. The ball is moving away from higher places toward lower places.

Negatively charged particles move away from negative voltages towards positive voltages. They are like bubbles in water that try to move

▷ The Cockcroft-Walton particle accelerator. This converts a supply of electricity into an extremely high voltage — 750,000 electron volts — to provide a first giant kick to charged particles such as protons. After leaving this accelerator, protons may be further speeded in a linear accelerator on their path to a synchrotron

▽ The linear accelerator *Top:* a positively charged particle leaves a drift tube at a moment when the tube has positive voltage. It is kicked toward the next tube by the electric field *(arrows). Middle:* it leaves the next tube just as the voltages and fields have reversed and receives another kick. *Bottom:* the process is repeated after another reversal. Each tube must be longer than the previous tube because the particle is going faster each time

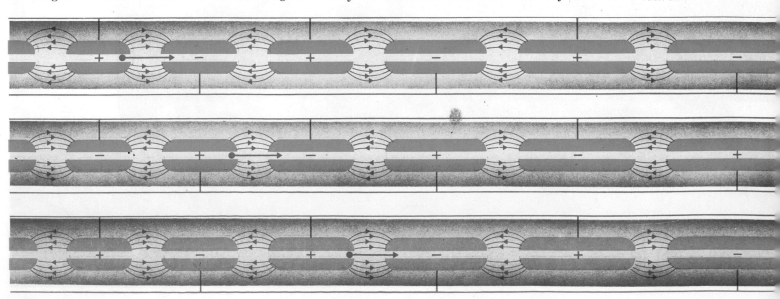

towards the highest places.

A TV picture is made by a beam of electrons striking the inside of the tube. The negatively-charged electrons are given a high speed by being attracted by a high positive voltage.

Some accelerators use very high voltages. The Cockroft-Walton machine turns the small voltage supplied by ordinary home electricity supplies into a large voltage. It then accelerates particles in the same way that a TV picture tube does.

But the highest voltage at which charge can be stored in a machine at ordinary pressure is about a million volts. Charges at higher voltages leak away. If the machine is surrounded by gases at high pressure, charge can be stored at ten million volts. Physicists need even faster particles than these voltages can provide.

To make a thing travel fast it is not necessary to give it just one big push, as the Cockroft-Walton machine does. Smaller voltages can give the particle a series of small pushes.

This is the principle of the linear accelerator, or 'linac' in the diagram on page 4. It consists of a series of hollow metal 'drift tubes'. At every moment each tube has an opposite voltage to its neighbours. This means that a charged particle in the space between each pair of tubes feels a force. But the voltages reverse several billion times each second. The direction of the forces reverses accordingly.

Suppose a positively charged particle drifts slowly down the first tube. If the second tube has a negative voltage when the particle comes out of the first tube, the particle will get a strong pull toward the second tube.

The voltages reverse in the time it takes the particle to travel along the tube. So when it reaches the end of the second tube the electrical force on the particle will be in the right direction to give it another push. These increases add up to a very large final velocity.

The linear accelerator needs very long tubes and the electric fields reverse at very high frequencies. The linac at the Stanford Linear Accelerator Center (SLAC) in California is two miles long. The voltages it uses change their directions nearly six billion times every second.

The Cyclotron
The cyclotron consists of two hollow semi-circular metal chambers called 'dees'. Together they form a horizontal disc-shaped chamber. The two dees are always at opposite voltages. But the voltages are constantly reversing.

A strong constant magnetic field passing vertically through the dees forces the particles to move in curved paths.

Charged particles produced at the centre of the machine drift into the gap between the dees and receive a kick from the voltages between the dees there. The particle then enters the other dee. Its speed does not change, but the magnetic field makes it continue to move in a circle.

When it crosses the gap between the dees again, the voltage on the dees reverses so all the kicks work together to accelerate the partic-

le. It moves ever faster in larger and larger circles.

The Synchrotron
An advanced form of the cyclotron called the synchrotron forces the particles to travel in orbits of constant size. The electromagnets only need to be built along the path the particles follow. They can therefore be much smaller than in an equivalent cyclotron.

Synchrotrons cannot accelerate particles from rest. The particles are first raised to high speeds in a linear accelerator. Then they are 'injected' into the synchrotron.

It is possible to bring about reactions at even higher energies. Two beams which have been accelerated in an ordinary machine are led into two 'storage rings'. They keep circulating, in opposite directions, until the numbers of

◁ Drift tubes of the proton linear accelerator of the Lawrence Radiation Lab at Berkeley, California. All air is pumped out of the tunnel when the accelerator is operating, so that the protons can move freely

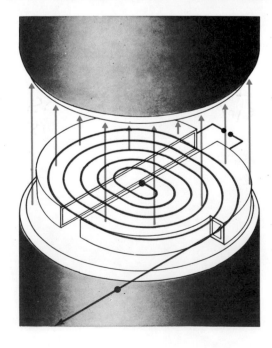

◁ The cyclotron. The charged particles are generated at the centre. A vertical magnetic field causes the particles to move in circles. Between the 'dees' the particles are accelerated electrically and spiral outwards

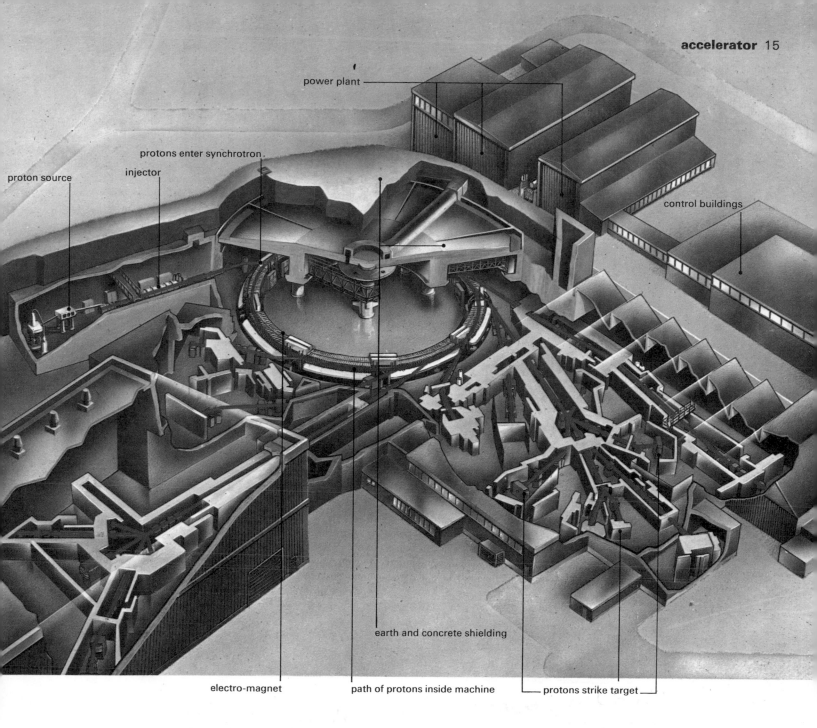

power plant

protons enter synchrotron

proton source

injector

control buildings

earth and concrete shielding

electro-magnet

path of protons inside machine

protons strike target

△The former synchrotron at Harwell, England. Named NIMROD, the machine accelerated protons along a circular track 150 feet across. The proton beam could be allowed to escape at different points, so that experiments could be carried out.

▷ The cosmotron, a proton synchrotron at Brookhaven, NY. Protons are injected at the left and are extracted after whirling round the machine about a million times

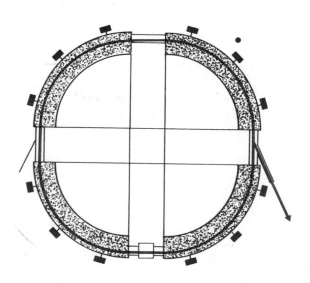

particles in them have built up. Then the beams are allowed to collide head-on. The next advances in our knowledge of matter will probably come from storage rings.

This development is important because it means there is much greater energy in each interaction – the difference between two cars colliding head on and one car driven into a stationary wall. Another step forward is the use of a more powerful type of magnet based on materials whose properties change dramatically at temperatures near absolute zero. Today, particles can be given energies equivalent to acceleration through 500 billion volts.

The physics made possible by accelerators continues to capture the imagination of the world's best physicists. It holds out the promise of answering the most fundamental questions about the nature of matter.

See also *atom*, *electricity*, *magnet* and *radioactivity*.

acclimatization

A suntan protects the skin from the ultra-violet rays in strong sunlight. The man on this Spanish beach has clearly been enjoying the sunshine longer than the woman

Man can survive almost anywhere on earth. But when he goes from one climate to another – from hot to cold, into desert or swamp, for example – or from one time zone to another, his body must have time to get used to the change. These are examples of acclimatization.

Clothes are an important part of acclimatization. In the Arctic, a thick parka and fur hat stop the loss of heat. In the desert, white robes prevent the skin burning, and reflect heat away.

Athletes who have competed at high altitudes have suffered from the lack of oxygen in the air. They needed about four weeks for their bodies to adjust to the different atmosphere.

Because London lies to the east of New York and the sun moves from east to west in the course of the day, time is five hours later in London than it is in New York. Jet-travellers find that it takes about twelve hours to get used to sleeping at the new time. Mealtimes and appetite are also out of step at first.
See: *blood, breathing, cold, heat.*

acetic acid

Vinegar contains acetic acid. Although the acid is greatly diluted, it still gives vinegar its breath-catching smell and sour taste. Acetic acid is a powerful preservative. This is why vinegar is used to pickle fruits and vegetables. Concentrated acetic acid is a clear liquid which is very corrosive and can cause severe skin burns.

Acetic acid is also used widely in industry to make plastics, aspirin and the cellulose film that photographs are printed on. Pure acetic acid has a high freezing point. It will solidify like ice in cold weather and is called glacial acetic acid.

Acetic acid occurs naturally in vinegar by a process of fermentation. The name vinegar means 'sour wine'. If wine ferments for too long, acetic acid forms turning the wine into the sour liquid we know as vinegar. All fruits and vegetables can be fermented to make vinegar and each produces a different flavour, although the acetic acid in each is the same.
See: *acids and bases, alcohol.*

acetylene

A colourless, inflammable gas. In its pure form it has a slight, pleasant smell. However, it usually contains impurities that give it an unpleasant smell. It has a wide range of uses in industry: to make solvents for dry-cleaning; to make neoprene, a synthetic rubber; to make plastics; and in oxyacetylene burners. Mixed with oxygen, acetylene burns with a very hot flame that can reach as much as 3,000°C. This can be used for cutting and welding metals.

Acetylene can be made by the reaction of calcium carbide with water. At one time artificial light was made by lamps that burned acetylene gas produced in a tank containing carbide and water. They were used as bicycle and automobile headlamps and by mineworkers. This type of lamp is still sometimes used by cave explorers.

When acetylene is stored in its gaseous form it is highly combustible and likely to explode. A cylinder of acetylene is like a bomb. However, it can be stored relatively safely in liquid acetone, which can dissolve 300 times its own volume of the gas. In this way it can be transported in bulk.
See: *welding.*

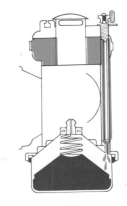

△ An acetylene lamp. Water *(blue)* dripped onto calcium carbide *(black)* making acetylene gas. This traveled up the coiled pipe to a jet where it burned with a bright smokeless flame

◁ Oxyacetylene welding. Oxygen and acetylene are fed into the burner through the two tubes at the left

acids and bases

Ants, automobile batteries and vinegar all have something in common. They all contain acid. Ants make formic acid in their bodies. When they want to inflict a sting they inject the acid into the skin of their victim. The acid irritates the victim's flesh. Car batteries contain sulphuric acid. This acid burns holes in clothes and eats into metal if spilled. Vinegar contains acetic acid in very small quantities. Even such a weak solution of acid has a breath-catching smell.

The properties just mentioned are typical of strong acids. That is, they have a sour taste and pungent smell; they attack metals, giving off hydrogen; and they burn the tissues of animals and plants. They can also react with carbonates, releasing bubbles of carbon dioxide gas. Some acids have these properties more strongly than others.

Acids form one of the most important of the chemical classes. Another important class is their chemical opposites, the bases. Bases that will dissolve in water are called alkalis. This name comes from the Arabic words meaning 'the ashes', because alkalis were once prepared from the ashes of plants and wood. A typical alkali will have a bitter or unpleasant taste and, in concentrated solution, will have a soapy feel. It will burn the skin. Examples are washing soda, caustic soda and potash.

Salts

When an acid and a base are mixed in the correct amounts they neutralize each other and new substances are formed. For example, when hydrochloric acid is mixed with sodium hydroxide caustic soda they neutralize each other to form the harmless substances water and sodium chloride, which is common table salt.

The substance produced in any reaction between an acid and a base is called a salt, even though it might not be common table salt. We can make the simple statement:

acid + base → salt + water

Chemists have a simple way of detecting acids and bases. They use coloured substances called indicators. When a small quantity of acid or alkali is added to an indicator it changes its colour. One natural indicator is called litmus. This is produced by plants called lichens. It is blue, but turns red on contact with an acid. An alkali will turn it blue again. Litmus paper is produced by soaking strips of paper in litmus solution and drying them.

Acids abound in nature. Probably the best known is citric acid, which gives the sharp tang to citrus fruits such as oranges and lemons. It is malic acid that makes unripe apples taste sour. The unpleasant taste of sour milk is caused by lactic acid formed when the sugar in milk, lactose, is broken down. Tannic acid is found in tea leaves. It gives the bitter taste to tea that has been allowed to stand for too long.

Such acids are relatively harmless to the body. But many acids are highly poisonous. Prussic acid, or hydrogen cyanide, is notorious.

Bronze coins lose their shine because the copper in them combines with oxygen in the air. Sulphuric acid cleans them by dissolving the oxygen compounds and leaving bright copper behind

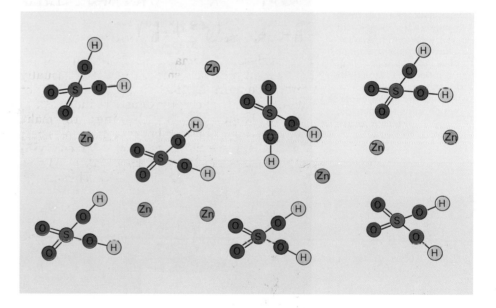

▽The smallest particles of sulphuric acid are molecules containing atoms of hydrogen (H), sulphur (S), and oxygen (O) When atoms of zinc (Zn) react with the acid they replace the hydrogen in the molecules, forming zinc sulphate. Hydrogen gas bubbles off

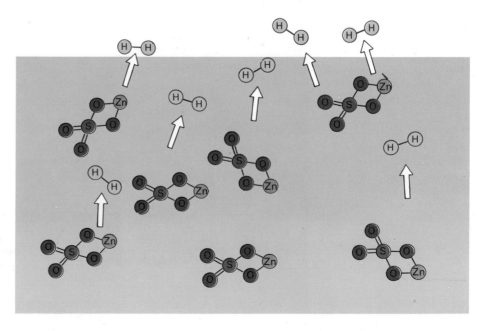

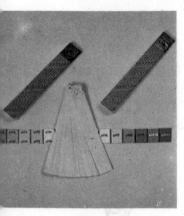

Chemists get a rough measure of how acid or how alkaline a liquid is by using indicator paper

△ Universal Indicator is yellow before use. In a neutral liquid, like pure water, it stays yellow. The colour of the paper can be compared with a scale

▷When dipped in a weak acid the paper turns orange. In a stronger acid it turns red. In a weak alkali the paper becomes olive; in a stronger alkali it becomes blue. *(Far right)* a cruder distinction is given by litmus paper, which turns red in acids, blue in bases

WEAK ACID

STRONG ACID

WEAK ALKALI

STRONG ALKALI

Less than two thousandths of an ounce will kill a man in seconds. Faint traces of this acid are found in bitter almond. Rhubarb leaves contain a poison, too, oxalic acid, although it is by no means so deadly as prussic acid.

Another group of acids, called amino acids are found in all living matter. They are the 'building blocks' from which proteins are formed (see: *amino acid, protein*).

Hydrochloric acid in the stomach plays a vital part in digestion. Overproduction of this acid gives the familiar condition known as 'acid stomach'. The whole body in fact is very sensitive to acid and alkali balance.

Plants cannot thrive if the soil becomes too alkaline or too acid. Acid soils can be neutralized by treatment with slaked lime, calcium hydroxide, which is a weak alkali.

There is acid present even in the air. During thunderstorms the intense heat of lightning flashes causes nitrogen in the air to combine with oxygen. The new substance then dissolves in raindrops to form a weak solution of nitric acid. The sulphur in the air in industrial towns forms substances which dissolve in rain to form sulphuric acid. The acid corrodes metal structures and attacks stonework.

We use quite a few acids and bases every day in the home. Citric acid is an ingredient of many lemon-flavored drinks. It also appears with Epsom salts and sodium bicarbonate in laxative preparations. Tartaric acid is another organic acid often included. It is obtained as a by-product of wine-making. To keep the kitchen clean, housewives once used carbolic soap which contained carbolic acid.

For a general cleansing agent the weak base ammonium hydroxide is still widely used. It is better known under the name of 'household

ammonia'. Many oven cleaners contain caustic soda, which has a powerful action in removing grease.

The medicine chest reveals a host of further examples. There is milk of magnesia, or magnesium hydroxide, to neutralize and soothe an upset acid stomach. There is boric (or boracic) acid, used in ointments as a general antiseptic. There is aspirin, the universal painkiller, known to chemists as acetylsalicylic acid.

Sulphuric acid is probably the most important chemical in industry. Great Britain alone produces nearly 3½ million metric tons a year. Much of it is made into fertilizers, such as ammonium sulphate. It is also used for cleaning, or 'pickling', iron before plating or painting. So is hydrochloric acid.

An interesting acid belonging to the same family as hydrochloric acid is hydrofluoric acid or hydrogen fluoride. It is the only acid that can eat into glass.

As for bases, by far the most important are the alkalis caustic soda and caustic potash. Caustic soda is important to the paper and rayon industries, for it is used to dissolve the cellulose from wood fibres.

Bases can be used in electrical batteries instead of acids. An example is the NiFe battery, which contains sodium hydroxide (base) and plates of nickel and iron. Vast quantities of caustic soda are used in soap making (see: soap). The caustic soda is mixed with fats and oils, which are made of fatty acids combined with glycerine. Salts are formed, just as in other reactions between acids and bases. These salts are what we know as soaps. Caustic potash can be used in soap making as well.

These are only some of the many ways in which acids and bases play an important role in our lives. But, it should always be remembered that strong acids and bases are dangerous chemicals. They must always be handled with great care. If an accident does happen you must act very quickly. The part of the body that has been burned should be held under running water. This will dilute the action of the acid or alkali. If the skin is badly burned call a doctor. See: *chemistry, soap.*

Find out by doing

To make your own acid-base indicator, boil a medium-sized red cabbage in two pints of water for quarter of an hour. Allow it to cool and strain the red liquid into a jar. This is your acid-base indicator. Bases will turn it blue, and acids will turn it back to red. Use it to find out which of the following things are basic and which acid: ammonia, lemon juice, carbolic soap, baking powder, cola, crushed nettle leaves.

Squeeze a lemon, mix the juice in a cupful of water, and add a spoonful of bicarbonate of soda. Can you explain the result? (Incidentally, you have made yourself a refreshing drink.)

Here's how to get a hard-boiled egg into a bottle whose neck is smaller than the egg. Soak an egg in vinegar for several days. It will fizz as calcium carbonate is dissolved from the shell and carbon dioxide is given off. The shell will become soft and the egg can be pushed into a bottle whose neck is smaller than the egg.

The last step is to make it hard again by pouring bicarbonate of soda into the bottle and leaving it for a day. You can then show your friends a very solid egg rolling around in a bottle it can't get out of.

You can do a similar demonstration with chicken bones and strong vinegar. When the bones are soft you can twist them into odd shapes or tie them in knots.

△ Rain in cities contains acids made by lightning strokes. The restored stonework at the left shows what it looked like before it was eroded by many years of rainfall

A bone soaked in vinegar for some days becomes soft enough to tie in a knot

acoustics

The study of sound and how it travels from place to place. A knowledge of acoustics is of value in designing buildings and streets so that they have desirable sound effects.

Sound is made by vibrating air. The faster the air vibrates, the higher the pitch of the sound. Noise is any sound that is unwanted.

Sound vibrations radiate in all directions. The farther the listener is from a source of sound, the weaker the sound he will hear. This is because the sound energy is spread thinly over a large area. Sound energy is absorbed by any matter in its path. Even the air absorbs some sound energy as it transmits sound. Walls and furniture can absorb sound strongly.

In a room sound waves are reflected back and forth from the walls. They may last for several seconds before dying away. The sound waves going direct to the listener are heard first, followed by waves reflected from the walls. This is called reverberation. Reverberation adds richness to sound. A certain amount of reverberation is desirable for orchestral music and even more for organ and choral music in church. Less reverberation is desirable for speech because echoes can make it hard to understand. The preacher in a church has to speak slowly so that the echoes can die between each word. Otherwise there would be a jumble of new sounds mixed with old ones still reverberating.

Fortunately we can control the reverberation in a room. If a room is designed so that its surfaces are sound absorbent, echoes will die quickly. We call such a room 'dead' as opposed to a 'live' reverberant, room. The 'reverberation time' of a room is the time it takes for a sound to die away to one millionth of its original loudness. For speech, the reverberation time should not be more than one second. For orchestral music two seconds is better. In some churches it can be five to ten seconds.

Rooms and concert halls should be shaped to distribute sound correctly. There should be a direct line between sound source and listener. The first reflection to reach the listener should arrive only a short time after the direct sound. They cannot be distinguished from the direct sound and serve to reinforce it. Reflections arriving later only confuse more recent direct sounds. In large concert halls reflectors hung from the ceiling can help to shorten the path of the first reflections. The reflectors should be convex to spread the sound over the auditorium. Concave reflectors would tend to focus reflections on just a few seats.

Side reflections

In a concert hall, reflections from the side walls are also important in determining the quality of sound. They add to the feeling of space. Without good side reflections, listening to an orchestra can be like listening to music through a single loudspeaker. With good side reflections, however, it is like listening on a good-quality stereo system. In fact, of course,

the sound heard in a well-designed hall with fine acoustics is far superior to the sound that can be produced by any stereo system.

Fan-shaped halls are not ideal for orchestral music because the side walls do not bounce much sound back into the audience. Rectangular rooms are generally better. The side reflections are strongest if the room is fairly narrow, perhaps no more than 20 metres (21 yards) or so in width. Some of the world's best concert halls are indeed narrow, rectangular rooms that were built in the nineteenth century, without any scientific knowledge of acoustics.

In the twentieth century, however, architects have wanted to break away from these well-tried designs. They have also wanted to seat larger audiences, and to build halls which can be used for anything from a poetry recital to a rock concert. This produces a challenge for the acoustical engineer.

The larger a hall is the more difficult it is to make the acoustic effects evenly good. There is also a greater likelihood of echoes. Halls which are used for speech-making and music recitals have to compromise between the requirements of each. Even different kinds of music require different acoustic effects. Think of a string quartet or a full sized choir and orchestra in turn using the same hall. The hall's acoustics would not suit both types of performance.

Systems are being developed to meet this situation. We can reduce true reverberation to the minimum and use artificial reverberation.

The direct sound can be played back through loudspeakers a fraction of a second late and this has the effect of reverberation. The advantage is that the delay can be controlled to suit different needs.

In some halls, the reflecting canopy over the stage can be raised and lowered by motors. There are even halls where the whole ceiling moves up and down. Lowering the ceiling has the effect of reducing reverberation, so speech

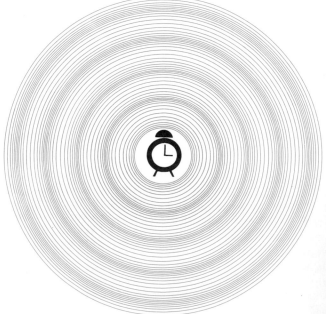

◁ Sound waves spread out from their source in all directions. In a sound wave the air vibrates backward and forward in the direction the sound is travelling. The air molecules at each place become first more crowded, and then further apart

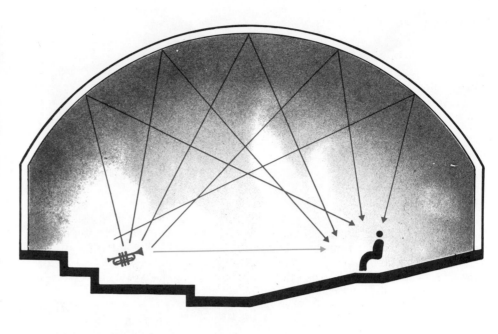

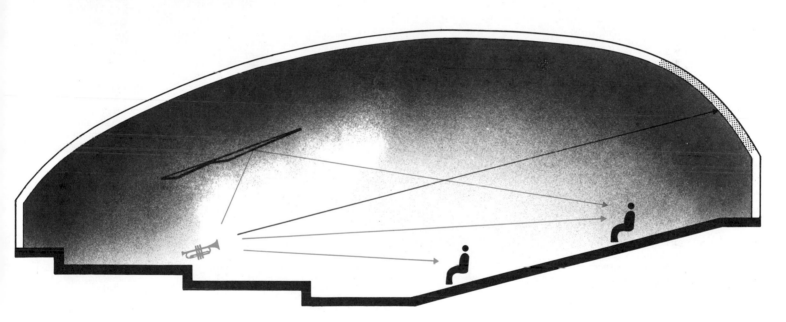

△ A reflector can shorten the path of reflected sound so that it reinforces the direct sound. The hall's rear wall should be absorbent to get rid of serious echoes.
(Top left) Reflectors shaped like mushrooms hang from the roof of a London concert hall. They have greatly improved the acoustics of the circular theatre.
(Top right) A badly shaped theatre roof can cause echoes when the path of reflected sound is much longer than that of direct sound

can be clearly heard. With the ceiling raised, there is more space for the sound to bounce around in. This added reverberation, however, would be wanted for an orchestral concert.

Another way to adjust the acoustics of a multi-purpose hall is by adding or removing areas of sound-absorbing material. This can be in the form of heavy retractable banners hung from the ceiling.

When an auditorium has been successfully designed for its internal acoustics there is still noise from outside or from adjoining rooms to be considered. To counteract this we use sound insulation. Heavy walls are very effective in stopping sound. They do not vibrate very readily when sound waves strike them and therefore do not carry the vibration through to the air on the other side. Low-pitched sounds are transmitted more readily than high-pitched sounds, because the wall can take up the slower vibrations more

easily. Two thin walls separated by a gap are more efficient at shutting out sound than one wall of the same weight of material. However, this insulation is spoiled if there are any holes such as windows or ventilators in the wall. Even minute cracks will spoil the insulation.

Ordinary windows transmit more sound than a brick wall even if they are kept shut. This is because glass is much lighter than brickwork and so vibrates more easily. Windows can be improved by making them double, with a space of about six inches between the layers.

Mechanical ventilation will be required if windows are kept shut. This creates more problems because noise can enter through the ducts. Also, the motors which move the air make noise which can travel along the ducts.

To reduce this noise, mufflers have to be inserted in the ducts. They will also catch external noise coming in through the ducts. The

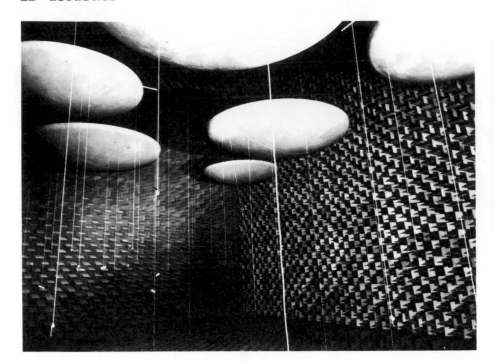

△ Anechoic chamber and a close-up of part of its special wall. Sound reflectors for use in a concert hall are being tested. The blocks in the walls are made of material that absorbs most of the sound, and they are shaped to scatter the rest

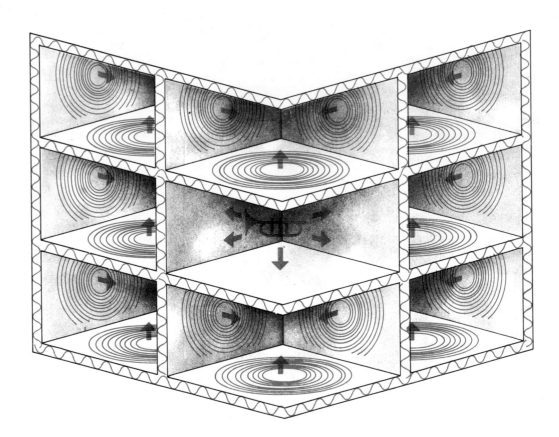

△ When a noise is made in a building, it sets the walls and floors in motion. This motion is transmitted through the building and creates sound in other rooms. The effect is especially strong if the original sound is made by machinery attached to the floor

mufflers absorb the noise energy by passing the incoming air through vanes, called 'splitters', made of sound absorbent material.

Sound does not travel between rooms by direct routes only. All the walls, the floor and the ceiling vibrate and so sound energy can reach the next room by side routes. This is called 'flanking sound'. Quite often as much sound is conveyed by flanking paths as by direct transmission.

A special form of flanking transmission occurs when machinery is fixed to a floor and vibrates the structure of the building directly. The remedy is to 'isolate' the machine on resilient mountings. Footsteps on a floor have the same effect. They can be softened by carpeting, or the floor itself can be isolated – that is it can be constructed on a resilient layer. The characteristics of a floor can be measured using a standard impact generator known as a 'footsteps machine'.

Architects and town planners have to consider the levels of noise in cities. Concert halls and theatres can be protected by heavy walls and roofs and they can be ventilated with air conditioning. Buildings such as hospitals and office blocks need large windows for daylight, thus tending to let in noise. The windows can be made double and kept shut, provided mechanical ventilation is acceptable.

Acoustical oddities

Some of the world's famous buildings have acoustical oddities. High above the floor of St Paul's Cathedral in London, just below the great dome, there is a 'whispering gallery'. The smooth, curving wall of this circular gallery has a focussing effect on sound, so that two people standing anywhere in the gallery can hold a conversation in low voices as if they were standing side by side. The sound actually travels along the wall, and it works best if both speaker and listener hold their heads close to the wall.

There is an open-air example of a whispering gallery at the Temple of Heaven in Peking, China. It is a popular spot for overseas tourists as well as Chinese families. Standing round the edge of the walled, circular courtyard you can see many people apparently talking to themselves. In fact, they are calling out to their friends or families far away at another part of the wall.

The same courtyard has a famous echo. If you stand on a particular paving stone near the centre and clap, you will hear a single echo. Step forward a pace and clap again and you will hear two distinct echoes. Another step forward and this time you are able to hear three echoes of your clap.

In most buildings, of course, effects like these would be quite undesirable. Acoustic designers are well aware of the echoes and focussing effects in circular and elliptical buildings and generally try to avoid designing such shapes.

Town-planners try to site houses, apartments and schools as far away as possible from main roads and other noise sources. It is also sensible to build houses facing away from roads rather than onto them. Planning should take account of prevailing winds, because noise travels more readily downwind than upwind. Belts of trees do not provide much noise protection unless they are very wide and dense. Barriers (including other buildings in which quietness is not important) can help to prevent noise from spreading to housing sites.

As machinery becomes more widespread and powerful in every sphere of life, noise increases everywhere. It should be regarded as a form of pollution. Excessive noise can cause discomfort, pain and even deafness in people who are exposed to it for long periods. In consequence, much more attention is now being given to research into noise control – how to make machines quieter, how to stop noise from travelling far, how to insulate buildings more effectively and more cheaply. In most countries certain minimum standards of sound insulation or noise control are already legally enforced.

Sound against sound

One new method of noise control is to fight sound with sound. A sound wave has peaks of high pressure and troughs of low pressure. A second wave, with peaks where the first has troughs (and vice-versa) is able to cancel out the first. So-called 'anti-sound' that is fed to an airplane pilot's headphones can protect him from the deafening noise in his cockpit.

The levels of noise and the behaviour of sound at various sites can be studied with instruments carried in specially-equipped vehicles. The acoustic properties of materials, and of buildings planned for the future, are best studied in the laboratory. The 'anechoic' chamber is a room lined with blocks of acoustically absorbent material. The blocks are shaped so that the small amount of sound reflected is not directed into the body of the room. It is reflected to fall on the walls again so that further absorption quickly takes place. The noise output of sound sources can be measured in such a chamber. The 'reverberant' chamber, on the other hand, has walls of highly sound-reflecting material, and sounds linger for a long time. The sound absorption properties of various specimens of materials can be measured in such a chamber.

Reverberant and anechoic chambers are also used to test the quality of sound recordings and reproduction equipment. For instance, a recording played in an anechoic chamber will display only the reverberation qualities recorded during the original performance. Because there are none in the chamber, the quality of the recording can be assessed.
See: *sound*.

Find out by doing

Demonstrate that a concave reflector can focus sound waves. Set up two umbrellas as shown in the picture. You will be able to hear the ticking from a distance of three or four yards.

To show that materials of different weights absorb sound differently: place a balloon in front of your radio loudspeaker so that it touches. Put your ear against it and you will find that you can hear the radio as clearly as if nothing were in the way. Now do the same with a cushion of the same thickness as the balloon. The sound will be heavily muffled. A heavy book in front of the speaker will dampen the sound much more, even though it is not as thick as either the balloon or the cushion.

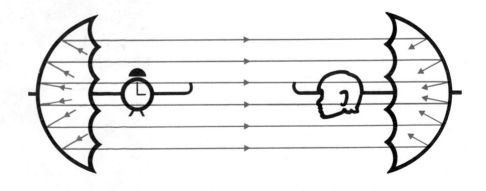

Umbrellas are good curved surfaces for focusing sound. The ticking of the clock can be heard very clearly at the right point near the second umbrella

adaptation

If a person goes bare-foot for several days, the skin on the soles of his feet will become thick and tough to protect them. Over millions of years a breed of animal can change into a completely different form with different habits. Both of these are examples of adaptation.

However, there is a difference between these two types of adaptation. For instance, if a white-skinned person spends a holiday in the sun he will become tanned. He could become quite brown. But the children of heavily tanned people will still be born white-skinned. In other words, a characteristic that has been acquired during a lifetime will not be passed on.

However, the children of a person who was born with a dark skin will also tend to have dark skin. This is called an inherited characteristic. Although children tend to be like their parents, they are not identical. Small differences occur in each generation. If a change happens to be favourable, then the chances of survival of the individual will be improved. If he is fitter and stronger, then he will probably live longer. And in the course of that longer life he will have time to produce more children.

But someone who was born with a variation which was not advantageous would have less chance to have children. Therefore there will soon be more children with that successful variation. And after many generations only persons with the useful variation would be left. Only the persons best adapted to their surroundings would survive. This is sometimes called 'survival of the fittest'.

Natural selection

This explanation of how creatures adapt to their surroundings is called the theory of natural selection. It was first suggested by the English naturalist Charles Darwin in 1859. It explains how a species can be completely transformed over a period of time, just by the selection of small changes that are useful.

If we think about the very beginning of life on Earth, we can see what a tremendous number of chance variations must have been naturally selected to bring man to his present stage of development. Many millions of years ago life began in the oceans. Before life could emerge from the oceans the organisms had to develop systems that would allow them to survive when not immersed in water. Human blood is chemically very similar to sea water.

Some of the life forms that invaded dry land eventually went back to the sea again. It appears that the ancestors of whales did this. They have bony structures in their fins rather like legs. This would not have happened unless it was advantageous. Legs would only be an advantage on land. So we must assume that the ancestors of whales were land animals.

Another interesting example of an animal adapting for life on land, but then returning to the ocean is the marine iguana. This is a large lizard-like creature found only in the Galapagos Islands. It feeds on seaweed at the water's edge and in the shallow shore water.

Like other lizards, iguanas have adapted for

The golden eagle's beak is designed for tearing the flesh of its prey. It is powerful, sharp and hooked. Although the golden eagle feeds mainly on small rodents it can also deal with hares and rabbits and, some say, lambs

The puffin does not need to tear its prey, because it lives on small fish. It needs to carry some of these back to its young, but its webbed feet are not suitable for carrying. So it has a large beak

The African spoonbill is aptly named. Its beak is specially suited to dredging in shallow water for small aquatic animals. The young have normal beaks and are fed on partly digested food from the parents. The spoon shape develops later

The seeds of the yew tree are surrounded by bright red fleshy coats called arils. These attract birds that eat the seeds. The seeds pass through the bird's digestive tract and are distributed in the droppings

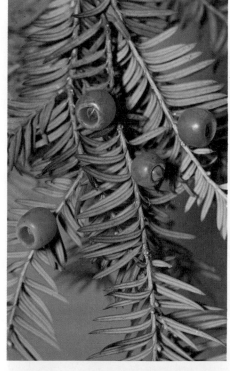

(Far right) Other plants are adapted to different methods of distribution. The dandelion 'clock' has a light fluff attached to the fruit. This enables the fruit to be carried on the wind

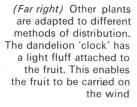

The seeds of the burdock have small hooks which catch on clothing and animal fur. In this way they are distributed

◁ The eagle's talons are large, sharp and strong, being specially adapted for pouncing on animals and carrying them off to the eyrie, or nest. Ducks' feet are webbed, like the feet of most water birds. They make good paddles to propel the bird over water

life on land. They no longer have gills, like fish have, for underwater breathing. They breathe through lungs. However, their bodies have become readapted to swimming for long periods in the sea. They can survive underwater for a very long time without breathing at all.

Charles Darwin, on his trip to the Galapagos Islands, noted that a sailor had tried to drown an iguana in the sea by weighting it with stones. One hour later it was hauled out of the water and was found to be full of life. To have survived so long under water without breathing, its heart-beat must have slowed down almost to a standstill. This is a unique adaptation, which has suited the iguana for part-time marine life.

Plants can also adapt to new surroundings. In dimly-lit places a plant's leaves will grow larger than they would in a good light. In this way they make better use of the little light that is available.

There are limits to the amount by which an organism can adapt. No amount of use can change the size and shape of a bird's beak, or its foot, to any noticeable extent in the course of its life. Nevertheless, the beaks and feet of

birds *have* changed over millions of years, and are among the most striking examples of adaptations to different environments.

Eagles and hawks generally have sharp curved claws which they use to grip their prey, and strong, pointed beaks for tearing its flesh. Ducks, on the other hand, have webbed feet that help them to swim powerfully. And they have flat, blunt beaks with which they can scoop up mud and filter out the small water creatures which they eat. Each kind of bird is clearly adapted to its own surroundings.

Ducks have to find their food by diving under the surface of the water. If they tried to breathe underwater they would drown. If their bodies got wet they would lose heat and might die of cold. If their feathers got soaked with water, swimming would become impossible.

When submerged, the duck lowers its head beneath its body. This automatically stops the bird's breathing. Water cannot penetrate the feathers because they are waterproofed with oil. These features are further examples of the adaptation of ducks to their life in water.

Flesh-eating animals generally have sharp

The swollen stem of this Mexican cactus stores water. The leaves have evolved into spines which protect the cactus and give off no water

▽ *Top:* all kinds of cactus have thick skins and lack broad leaves

Bottom: the colouring of this fawn hides it when it lies still

pointed teeth for biting flesh and, usually, flat grinding teeth for chewing. Grass-eating animals have chisel-like teeth at the front for cropping grass and flat grinding teeth at the back for chewing. The amount of muscle in the jaw is also influenced by the diet. Some snakes can even pull their lower jaw out of joint to swallow a particularly large meal.

Just as animals are adapted to the diet they live on, they are adapted to deal with the animals that feed on them. For example, the armadillo has tough armour-plating and can roll up into a tight ball when attacked. The hedgehog also rolls up into a ball and has sharp spines to protect it. Many animals have speed as their only form of protection. Skunks produce a disgusting smell to deter attackers. And salamanders exude a poison onto their skin for protection.

Perhaps the oddest form of defence is that used by the opossum. This is a furry animal about the size of a rat. If it is cornered by a dog it will turn and snarl and attempt to attack. If, however, the dog manages to get hold of it, the opossum will 'play possum'. That is, it will pretend to be dead. It will roll over with its eyes shut and its tongue lolling out. The dog then usually loses interest. No one quite knows why this should work, but it does.

A similar type of adaptive behavior exists in very young fawns of red deer. When a dangerous animal is near, the mother runs away and leaves the fawn behind. The fawn, which cannot run fast enough, does not try to escape. Instead it just curls up on the ground. Here its colour makes it very difficult to see. It stays absolutely still, and also it no longer gives off its normal scent. So the animal chasing its mother overlooks it completely.

The colour pattern on the wings and body of some moths that spend the day resting on tree trunks makes them very difficult to see. In one such case – the peppered moth – it has been possible to observe an animal gradually adapting to changes in its surroundings. A black variety of the peppered moth has always been known in England and America. But it was rare in country districts compared with the lighter-coloured variety. When factories began to spread in the early nineteenth century, whole areas became blackened by soot. In these areas the dark-coloured moths flourished. Birds that fed on them found them harder to see against the background of darker tree trunks. The lighter variety became rarer in the same areas.

This is an example of adaptive camouflage. But some animals are brightly coloured and very easy to see. Very often they are animals which also have stings, or can bite, or taste bad. Wasps and hornets are bright yellow and black, skunks are black and white. Experiments have shown that toads rapidly learn to associate the bright

△ A wasp beetle *(top)* and a queen wasp compared. The wasp is brightly coloured as a warning to its enemies that it has a sting. The beetle's colouring tricks its enemies into thinking it is a wasp

Black peppered moths have an advantage in areas where trees are blackened with soot *(above)*. They are less noticeable than the lighter varieties, which will soon be eaten by birds. Where trees are not sooty *(right)* the lighter moths have the survival advantage

colours of an insect with its sting or bite or bad taste. Once having learnt, the toad will not attempt to feed on that kind of insect again. Warning coloration, like camouflage, appears to increase the animal's chances of surviving.

Sometimes animals that do not sting, bite or have a bad taste imitate the colouring of animals which do. This is called mimicry. It is confined to insects and plants. Insects that birds find tasty, but which can imitate unpalatable insects, share their protection. Luckily for the mimic, birds very quickly learn not to eat distasteful insects. The mimic need worry only about young inexperienced birds that have not yet learned the lesson.

Warning coloration can be a disadvantage under some circumstances. For instance, in a herd of deer, warning of danger can be passed from individual to individual by flashing a white patch of hair on the rump. But as well as warning other deer of danger, the flash could act as a guide to the enemy. This would destroy the value of the camouflage on the rest of the deer's body. So the white rump patch is normally kept covered by the tail.

Plants have to adapt to their environment just as much as animals. For example, the fruit of the sycamore is carried from the parent plant by wind. The 'wings' of the fruit are obviously a feature that makes dispersal by wind more effective.

Some types of cactus are adapted to hot, dry environments. There are no broad leaves from which a lot of water can be lost. In some species the stem is protected by a thick wax layer which reduces water loss. The root system is just under the soil surface, spreading out widely around the stem. The widespread shallow roots of the desert cactus enable it to obtain water from a wide area before it all evaporates. In zones where water is abundant, the roots of plants go deep to make use of water that is trapped in the soil after rain. The desert cactus stores water in its swollen stem.

Some of the most interesting adaptations occur in the insect-eating plants. The leaves of pitcher-plants form a hollow structure shaped rather like a sort of jug, or pitcher. Around the edges of this pitcher a honey-like substance is produced. There are also bright red and purple patches in the opening. Insects are attracted, and crawl onto the edges of the pitcher to feed on the sweet substance. They then slip and fall into the base of the pitcher. They cannot get out again because there are hairs pointing downwards in the mouth of the pitcher. So they die and are digested by the liquid in the bottom. The plant is able to feed on the juices which are formed.

Examples of adaptation among sea fish are no less remarkable than in the rest of the living world. The flounder feeds and lives on the sea bed. It is therefore convenient for it to lie flat on its side. However, normally this would mean that one eye was looking into the mud, which would not be very helpful. So the left eye migrates as the young fish grows, and ends up on the same side as the right. Both eyes look up from the sea bed. It is always the left eye that migrates. The fins are also adapted so that it can swim across the sea bed in its new skewed position. It is thought that the flounder can take off from the sea bed in the manner of a vertical take-off airplane. It takes water in through its mouth and squirts it out of the gill on the underside. It can thus take off from the sea bed with remarkable speed.

Changes in living conditions usually occur for reasons beyond the control of life forms themselves. Those that can make the necessary adaptations will survive. Those that cannot will perish.

Finding a new environment
Sometimes an animal copes with a changed situation, not by adapting to it, but by moving from it to another location. There it may still have to adapt, but the type of adaptation may be easier.

There are primitive races of man that have attempted to avoid the pressures or changes that civilization brings. They have had to adjust to living in remote or harsh conditions.

Examples are the pygmies of the Congo who have escaped into the thickest jungles which are full of dangers. They have learned to obtain a living there and to cope with the hazards of savage animals.

African bushmen manage to live off the arid

Top: when an insect touches the sundew, it is caught by a sticky fluid *Bottom:* Sharp spines in the pitcher plant prevent insects escaping

◁ Crab spiders lie in wait in flowers for the insects they feed on. There are several kinds of crab spider, and each kind is the same colour as one kind of flower

Kalahari Desert where there is hardly any other life. Life is tough for the bushmen but they are left in peace.

These social adaptations could well lead to biological adaptations over a number of generations, but this is a very slow process and it is unlikely that any one person would be aware of it taking place.

Man has had to adapt to living in a great range of surroundings. The different races of the world are the result of these adaptations.

As man spread over the earth, it was his way of life that first adapted to new surroundings, while his body was still unchanged. Much later, his shape, size and skin colour altered to suit his new home. Possibly this slow change is still taking place in mankind today.
See: *evolution*, *heredity*.

To think about
Match these birds' beaks with their habits of feeding:

golden eagle	dredging water
duck	sipping nectar
humming bird	peeling fruit
parrot	tearing flesh

How are they especially suited to their task?

addiction

A person who uses drugs and finds that he is unable to stop doing so is said to be addicted. An addict in fact suffers severe mental and physical discomfort if he does stop taking his drug. The powerfully addictive drugs are known as narcotics. We sometimes say that a person is addicted to gambling or smoking. But he does not suffer 'withdrawal symptoms' such as a heroin addict suffers.

Some drugs are first used because of the pleasant sensations they bring about. Opium and heroin are of this kind, and they will cause addiction which soon leads to the death of the user. Alcohol, tobacco and even coffee are mildly addictive, and many people depend on one or more of these in their daily life, but in moderation they are harmless and can be beneficial. Nevertheless, like all drugs, they are dangerous if taken in excess. Narcotic drugs should never be taken, even in moderation.

With many kinds of drug, it becomes necessary to take larger and larger doses to achieve the same effect. If the user is addicted, he will have to pay more and more for his drugs, and he may be driven to crime to find the money. The dangerous drugs are regulated internationally, and it is only legal to produce or sell them for medical purposes. But the existence of millions of addicts round the world makes it possible for a huge illegal trade to flourish.

There are three types of narcotic drug. First, there are the ones that have a sedative effect. These include heroin and morphine. Other drugs of this kind are found in many sleeping pills. If these are taken in the correct doses they are harmless. But, in excess, they are addictive.

The second type of narcotic drug are the ones that have a stimulating effect. They make the person feel very lively and excited. The 'amphetamines' are drugs of this type.

'Hallucinogens' is the name given to the third type of addictive drug. They alter a person's perception and thoughts.

Addiction can be cured by gradual reduction of the dose under medical supervision. After cure the patient needs to be further supervised for some time to guard him from the temptation to resume taking the drug.
See: *drugs*.

Find out by doing
Ask a cigarette-smoker why he smokes, if he would like to stop, and if he thinks he could stop easily.

adenoids

Swellings in the roof of the throat, at the back of the nose. If they are very large, they interfere with breathing through the nose.

The swellings are due to enlargement of special glands that fight infection in the throat. These glands are similar to the tonsils, which are on each side of the throat, lower down. A person with inflamed tonsils (tonsillitis) often also has adenoids.

During the ages from seven to ten it is quite normal for the glands to enlarge slightly. After this they usually shrink again. But for some reason they may become very large, and fail to shrink. Fortunately it is an easy matter to remove such adenoids and cure the complaint. See: *glands, tonsils.*

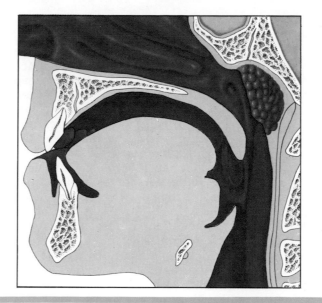

The adenoids are located between the passage leading back from the nose and the pharynx, the top part of the throat. Here they are shown as they appear when they have grown too large

adhesives

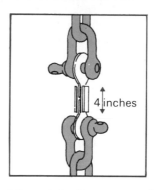

Modern adhesives can have amazing strength. The truck is being supported by the bond between two metal surfaces. The detail at the right shows that the entire weight is being taken by an area of a few square inches

Materials that are used to stick objects together are called adhesives. They are useful in the home, for mending all sorts of broken things, for sticking stamps on envelopes, and making models. They are even more important in industry. Without strong adhesives it would be very difficult to make buildings, furniture, cars, or even roads. For nearly every purpose there is a specially suitable adhesive.

Why should adhesives stick things together? The answer is that whenever two surfaces come into close contact there are atomic forces that make the particles that touch adhere, that is, cling together. These are called 'adhesive forces'. They may be strong or weak. How strong they are depends upon what the surfaces are like, and how closely the particles meet. It also depends upon what substances the surfaces are made of.

Particles of the same material tend to cling together, too. Otherwise everything we know would fall to pieces. However, the forces between particles of the same substance are called 'cohesive forces', not adhesive forces.

Adhesives are materials that have a particularly strong attraction for other substances that they touch. By making a sort of sandwich of the adhesive it is possible to bind solid objects tightly together. Some types are excellent for sticking together certain surfaces, but will not work with others. An adhesive that is useful for sticking pieces of paper, for instance, may be no

The milky fluid that oozes from rubber trees when cuts are made in their bark is called latex. It is a natural adhesive

good for sticking plastics. And one which works with wood may be quite unsuitable for metals.

There are many types of adhesive. There are the natural ones, that have been used since ancient times, and there are the modern synthetic ones. Most of them are liquid when applied. They then set in a firm solid bond.

Among the natural adhesives are starch and dextrin. These are prepared from plants such as corn, tapioca and potatoes. Starch paste is useful for paper and paperboard. It can be used for sticking up wallpaper, for example. Other plant adhesives are the sticky resins and fluids produced by trees. One of these is rubber latex. Natural rubber sticks fast to almost any surface.

From animals come the protein glues. These are made by boiling up animal bones, hide and horn and using the liquid. Other glues can be made from blood, and from the protein called casein in milk. Glues of this sort are useful in woodwork.

Man-made adhesives

Synthetic adhesives are better than natural ones because they are much stronger. There are different kinds. There is the kind that softens when heated, and becomes hard again when cold. These are called 'thermoplastic' adhesives. Another kind is soft to start with and becomes hard when heated. These are called 'thermosetting' adhesives. Once a thermosetting adhesive has been 'cured', or hardened by heat, it is very tough indeed. It will not dissolve in water, and will not melt again. This is because a chemical change has taken place.

The thermoplastic adhesives include complex chemicals called synthetic resins. Vinyl and polyvinyl resins are very resistant to moisture. They are used to stick together layers of glass to make the safety-glass for car windshields, and to make waterproof paper containers. Cellulose cements are very good for bonding wood, paper and plastic, but no good for metal and glass. They are used for assembling plastic model kits, and for general household purposes.

The thermosetting type of synthetic adhesives are often made by mixing two chemicals. When the mixture is heated, a reaction takes place and a different, very tough, chemical is formed. A mixture of phenol and formaldehyde is used to stick layers of wood together to make plywood. The types of resin called epoxy resins are amongst the toughest of all. They are used in aircraft construction. They will stick metals together, and even glass, pottery and stone.

For any adhesive to form a really strong bond, the surfaces must be very clean first. Water, grease and dirt prevent adhesives from touching the surfaces as closely as they should. When metal objects are to be joined, they are often cleaned with acids or alkalis to remove the last traces of grease. Even the grease of a fingerprint or the moisture from a person's breath can stop proper adhesion, and ruin a joint.
See: *cellulose, colloids.*

Find out by doing

Make your own casein glue. You will need a pint of skim-milk and a cup of vinegar. Mix them in a non-stick pan and heat gently. Keep stirring. Lumps will form and settle to the bottom. Pour the mixture into a bowl and let it cool. You will find one large lump at the bottom. Pour off the thin liquid on the top. Now add to the lump a quarter of a cup of water and a spoonful of sodium bicarbonate. The reaction produces a casein glue which can be used for many purposes in the home.

To think about

How many adhesives can you find in and around your own home? Remember that they are used in its construction and repair as well as by its inhabitants.

adolescence

The time during which a child is growing up to be an adult is called adolescence. It is really an overlap period between childhood and adulthood. During this time both the body and the mind are developing very quickly. The person is no longer a child. He or she is by no means young and helpless, but at the same time cannot be called 'grown up'.

The duration of adolescence varies greatly. It can start at age 9 and end at 18 in some people. It can start at 14 and end at 25. Everybody grows up in a different way, and at a different rate.

One of the main things that happens in adolescence is the development of the body so that it is ready to produce children. The stage at which this happens is called puberty. At puberty both girls' and boys' bodies grow rapidly. A girl's hips become wider, and her breasts start to develop. She has her first menstrual period. This is a sign that she is no longer a girl, but a young woman, who can one day have babies. Her sexual organs – the organs of reproduction – are being prepared for the part they will play.

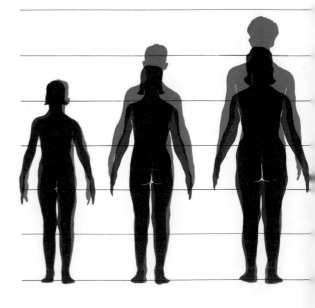

Boys *(blue)* and girls *(red)* change shape as they mature

Pubic hair appears, and hair under the arms.

A boy's voice becomes deeper, as the rings of cartilage in his throat increase in size. His beard starts to develop. His sexual organs, the penis and testes, increase in size. Besides pubic and underarm hair, he may develop hair on his chest.

During this period of growth, young people often feel awkward about the physical changes that are taking place. They may sometimes feel that their arms and legs are growing too fast. They feel clumsy and unsettled. To make things worse, changes in the body's chemistry may lead to the annoying skin condition acne. But all this gradually passes away. Adolescents gain self-confidence as their bodies turn into adult bodies. Their emotions and thoughts become more grown-up. They take on more and more adult responsibilities.

Adolescence can be an unpleasant experience for some people because of the emotional upsets. However, these pass, in some cases quite quickly.

The age at which an adolescent is finally accepted as an adult varies from society to society. In some primitive peoples there is a special ceremony during puberty. One day a young person is treated as a child. The next day he is treated as an adult. In other societies such as our own things take longer. It may be several years after puberty before we are expected to pay taxes, or do military service, or to vote in elections. All of these are different signs of the responsibility of adulthood.
See: *puberty*.

To think about

How many signs of being an adult in our society can you think of? (For example, 'official' ones like being allowed to drive a car, and 'unofficial' ones like actually being trusted with a car.) How is adulthood marked in such different societies as those of the American Indians, African peoples, Pacific Islanders?

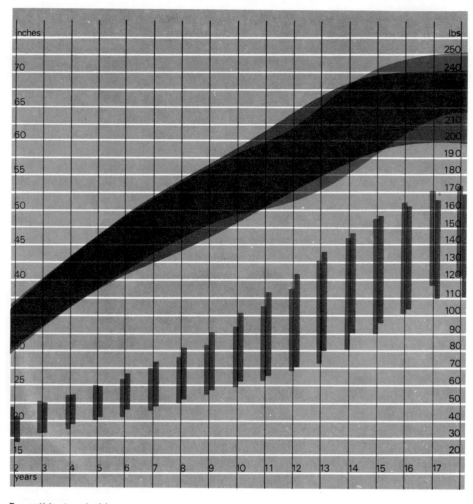

Boys *(blue)* and girls *(red)* grow rapidly during adolescence *(upper graph)*. At each age there is a range of heights; the tallest girls are taller than the shortest boys. Weight *(lower graph)* also increases rapidly. After this age height and weight change very little

adrenal glands

Two small glands that sit like caps on the top of each kidney. They produce a number of different hormones. A hormone is a chemical 'messenger' that travels in the blood and controls some activity in the body.

The adrenal glands are controlled in turn by the pituitary just below the brain. The pituitary controls many of the most important glands in the body.

Each adrenal gland is divided into two parts. The outer part, which is like a kind of nutshell, is called the cortex. The hormones it produces control the growth of the sexual parts of the body, the distribution of water and salt in the body, and the rate at which various foods are turned into energy.

The central part of each gland is called the medulla. It produces a hormone called adrenaline or epinephrine.

Adrenaline has been called the hormone of 'fright, flight or fight'. If a person or an animal becomes aware of danger, and is anxious or frightened, it is adrenaline which prepares him to deal with the situation. A message from the brain tells the adrenal glands to prepare the body for sudden action. Large quantities of adrenaline are then poured into the bloodstream.

As a result the heart beats faster, and the main blood vessels become slightly wider, so that more blood can flow to the muscles and the brain.

At the same time the smaller blood vessels in the skin, which is not so important, become narrower. The skin becomes pale and cold. This allows more blood to be sent to where it is most needed.

The mouth becomes dry. Sweating is increased so that the palms become moist. Breathing becomes faster. Food is converted into energy more quickly. In animals the fur may bristle, to frighten the enemy. In humans the

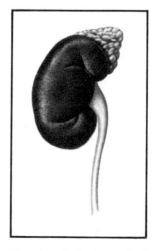

The adrenal glands perched on top of each kidney play a large part in the body changes that are caused by emotional disturbance

The lowered ears and snarl of an angry cat

hair of a frightened person is said to 'stand on end'.

In these ways the body is prepared for the sudden activity that may be necessary, whether it is fighting an attacker, or running away from danger.

Adrenaline is not released only when there is danger at hand, however. It is poured into the bloodstream to prepare the body for any increased activity. For example, there is more adrenaline than normal in the blood of an athlete getting ready for a race, or a football player before an important match. This produces symptoms that resemble those of anxiety.

The many effects of adrenaline are used in medicine. Doctors can give patients injections of the hormone. It can also be applied as a spray. For instance, it may be used in operations to constrict smaller blood vessels, and so reduce blood loss.
See: *hormones*.

To think about
What things do you notice in a frightened cat that are probably due to the action of epinephrine? What changes are there in its eyes, its fur, its claws, and the way it holds its body, as soon as it sees a dog?

adsorption

Brown sugar, dissolved in water and shaken with carbon particles, is poured through a filter funnel *(right)*. The colouring matter is trapped along with the carbon which has adsorbed it. This process is used commercially to make white sugar. Adsorbent substances can be used to speed up chemical reactions *(far right)*. Because the atoms of the reacting substances *(red and black)* cluster around the adsorbent *(grey)* they react more quickly

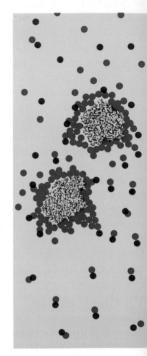

When a substance sticks to the surface of another it is said to be adsorbed by it. For example, when cheese is kept in a refrigerator without being covered, the other foods may take up the smell. The particles in the air that are responsible for the smell stick to the other foods.

When a piece of blotting paper is dipped into water, it soaks it up. The water rises between the fibres of the paper and sticks to their surfaces. The water is adsorbed by the paper.

*Ad*sorption is different from *ab*sorption. When a substance is absorbed by another one, it spreads throughout the absorber. Blotting paper, dry soils and sponges may appear to be absorbent when they soak up water. In fact they are made up of masses of loosely-connected particles and each of these is adsorbing.

A substance will usually adsorb some things more easily than others. This fact can be used in removing impurities from fluids. Adsorption is important in some catalysts. Catalysts are substances that speed up chemical reactions without being used up themselves. Some of them work by adsorbing layers of the reacting substances. Because these are concentrated on the catalyst's surface they react quickly.

Charcoal is commonly used in adsorption

processes. It is made active by heating, which drives off any previously adsorbed substances. It is then cooled to increase its rate of adsorption. Activated charcoal is used in gas masks to remove poisonous gases from the air. When sugar is raw it has a brownish colour which is removed with activated charcoal.

At very low temperatures activated charcoal becomes even more highly adsorbent. It can be used to remove the last traces of gas from a vessel, thus producing a high vacuum.
See: *catalyst*, *chromatography*.

Find out by doing
Buy some barbecue charcoal (or make your own by strongly heating small pieces of wood in a can till they char). Mix a few drops of ink with a lot of water in a glass jar so that the water is distinctly coloured. Sprinkle powdered charcoal onto the surface of the water, shake, and filter. Why is the liquid now clear again?

To think about
Why are adsorbents more efficient when they are finely divided? (*Clue: work out the surface area of a cube with sides 1 cm long. If the same cube were divided into 1,000 cubes with 1 mm sides, what would be their total surface area?*)

aerodynamics

The science that explains what happens when gases move past objects and when objects move through gases. Aerodynamics explains what keeps an airplane flying but it is concerned with many other subjects. Automobile designers must study aerodynamics for it affects fast-moving cars. Architects must keep in mind the effects of winds on the buildings they design. Sailboat designers must use aerodynamics to make sure that sails get the maximum power from the wind.

Some of the forces that air can exert have long been known. Breezes can disturb leaves and hurricanes can destroy buildings. Windmills and sailing-ships put the winds to good work. But only in the eighteenth century did the scientific study of mechanics reveal new ways of harnessing the power of the air.

The most important law to be discovered was called Bernoulli's Principle, after the Swiss scientist Daniel Bernoulli. He studied moving liquids in tubes. The laws that govern these are

▷ Before the importance of correct airfoil shape was known many airplanes were built that would not fly. French designer Octave Gilbert built this machine. With its flat wings it flew like a kite when towed on a rope, but crashed as soon as it was released

▷ Bernoulli's Principle states that air pressure *(red arrows)* decreases when air flow *(blue lines)* speeds up. Here air flowing through a tube is forced to speed up because the tube becomes narrower. The pressure drops in that part of the tube

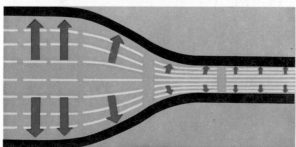

◁A kite is held up by the pressure of the wind *(red arrows)* pushing on the underside. Bernoulli's Principle is hardly used. The wind also exerts a drag *(yellow arrow)*. The cord overcomes the drag and stops the kite from being blown away

▷When an airfoil is at the best possible angle *(near right),* the lift is greatest and the drag is least. At a smaller angle, drag is greater, and there is less lift *(centre)*. At different speeds the best angle for the airfoil is different

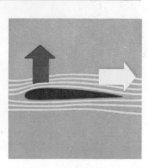

◁When an airfoil meets the airstream at too great an angle *(near left)* it 'stalls'. The flow of air behind the airfoil is broken up and causes a large drag. The lift is reduced. At low speeds the stalling angle is usually very small

similar to those that control moving gases.

If a tube contains an obstruction, or if it becomes narrower at one point, liquid flowing through it has to speed up at that place. Bernoulli found that when the liquid was forced to speed up in this way, the pressure that it exerted in all directions became less.

This general fact about liquids and gases is used in the design of an airplane wing. The shape that would be obtained if a wing were sliced through from front to back is called an airfoil. It is fairly flat underneath, but strongly curved above.

Air that flows over the wing must travel a greater distance than air traveling beneath the wing. This means that it has to travel faster. And by Bernoulli's Principle, its pressure drops.

So the pressure the air exerts on the lower side of the wing is greater than the pressure that it exerts on the top surface. The wing feels an upward force called lift.

The lift that a wing generates overcomes the plane's weight. The lift is greater the faster the plane moves through the air. But the plane also experiences a backward resisting force from the air called drag. This also increases with the plane's speed and puts a top limit to it. The problem of the airplane designer is to get as much lift for as little drag as possible.

Streamlining

Planes, cars and trains are designed with smooth curved bodies. This helps the air flow over them quickly and so reduces drag. This is called streamlining. When the machines are being designed, models are tested in wind tunnels.

If smoke is introduced in a wind tunnel it will show how the air flows around a body in the tunnel. This helps designers to decide whether the body has desirable aerodynamic qualities.

An airplane creates a disturbance that spreads through the air with the speed of sound. This disturbance travels on ahead of a plane that is traveling slower than sound, and makes the plane's flight easier. When a plane travels faster than sound the air has no time to get out of its way.

When a plane reaches the speed of sound it experiences a sudden increase in drag. This resistance is called the sound barrier. Drag continues to increase as speed increases. Supersonic flight has special design problems, which are discussed elsewhere in this Encyclopedia (see: *supersonic flight*)

A car is shaped in such a way that air passing over it has to travel faster than air passing underneath it. This produces a lifting force. The whole car acts as an airfoil. This can be dangerous in a racing car travelling fast because the wheels grip the road less firmly.

Many modern racing cars now have upside-down airfoils mounted on them. These create a downward push on the car at high speed and press the wheels more firmly onto the road.

Low speed aerodynamics applies to sail-boats. It is not so well understood as high-speed aerodynamics, but its broad principles are

△ A model of the Concord supersonic transport being tested. Airflow is simulated in a tank of oil

◁ Architects now have to study aerodynamics. At th power station in England, cooling towers were built too close together. The drop in pressure as wind blew between them cause one to collapse

▷ Wind tunnel experiment with models of offic blocks. Smoke clearl showed air gusts near th ground between the block The space finally had t be roofed ov

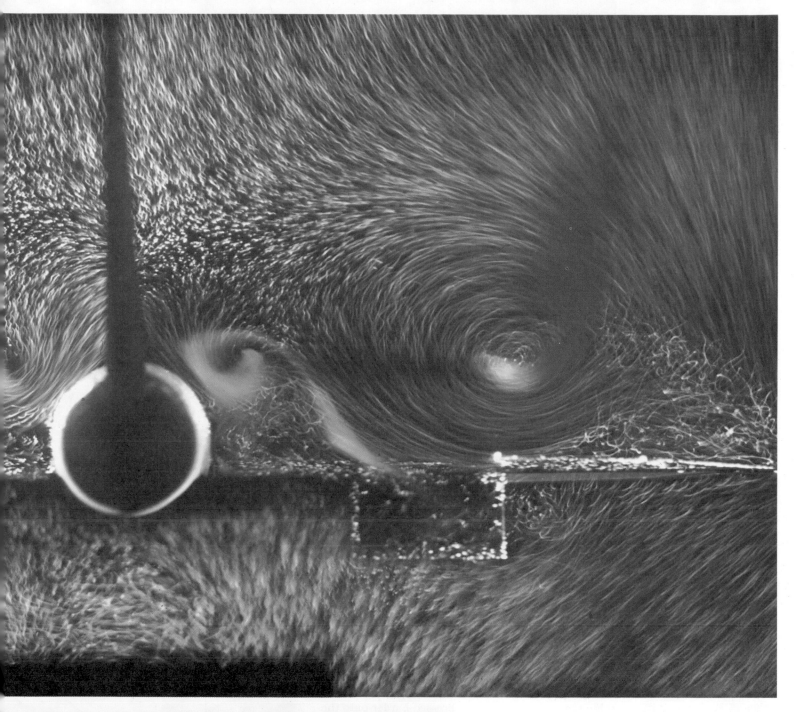

known. A sailboat can let itself simply be pushed by the wind. But when it is sailing into the wind – 'tacking' – Bernoulli's Principle applies.

When the front edge of the sail meets the wind, the sail forms a curve like an airfoil. Air has to go farther round one side than the other, and a force is developed at right angles to the sail. The shape of the hull only permits the boat to move in the desired direction.

Architects have problems with the forces that the wind produces. They have to know how much force winds can exert on tall buildings. When a number of tall buildings are grouped close together, the air is funnelled by the buildings. Strong gusts can be produced at ground level, as well as high stresses on the buildings themselves for brief periods.

See: *airplane, boats and ships, building, supersonic flight, wind.*

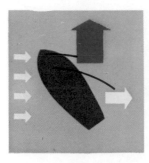

△ How a boat sails against the wind — 'tacking'. The shape of the sail is like that of an airfoil. As the wind travels faster round the curve of the sail it produces a force like the lift of a plane's wing *(red arrow)*. It also creates drag *(yellow arrow)*. The shape of the boat lets it move forward easily, but stops it moving sideways. Instead the boat 'heels over'

△ Racing cars have an airfoil shape that tends to lift them at high speeds. Upside-down airfoils *(red)* are added to keep them pressed to the track

Find out by doing

Put thread through two table tennis balls or attach it to two inflated balloons. Hang them up with a gap of an inch or two between them. Using a drinking straw or rolled-up paper tube, blow a jet of air between them. Make sure the draught doesn't touch either of them. What happens? Can you explain this?

Connect a funnel to a piece of rubber tubing. Hold the funnel upside down just above a table tennis ball standing on a table. Blow along the tubing through the funnel.

The ball will not be pressed harder onto the table; in fact it will jump off. This is because there is air flowing fast over it, while the air beneath it is not moving. So according to Bernoulli's Principle the pressure above the ball will be lower than the pressure below it. The ball is pushed off the table by the pressure difference.

You can make a cricket ball curve in flight by making it spin as you bowl it. This is due to the aerodynamic effect described by Bernoulli.

To think about

Why does the ball stay on the water jet at a fairground shooting gallery? (*Clue: the water in the middle of the jet is moving faster than the water on the outside. So the pressure of the water in the middle is less than the pressure at the outside.*)

aerosol

A cloud of very tiny particles or droplets hanging in the air. Smoke is an aerosol, and so are fog and mist. The smaller and lighter the particles, the more likely they are to remain suspended. They are kept moving in different directions because they are electrically charged. This stops them from settling downwards. The particles which make up tobacco smoke are only between one tenth and one hundredth of a micron across (a micron is a millionth of a meter). An aerosol is one form of colloidal suspension (see: *colloid*).

The word aerosol is now used, often incorrectly, to describe any pressurized canister (an aerosol 'bomb') for producing a spray. Many materials are now available in this form, including insecticides, shampoos, hair lacquers, deodorants, antiperspirants and paints. Only a few form a true aerosol spray. Some form sprays with large droplets, and some form foams.

There are several different types of aerosol can. Simple ones contain a liquefied gas, called the propellant, in which material is dissolved or suspended. Very often the propellant is the gas called Freon. When the valve is opened, the pressure drives the liquid up a tube and forces it through a special spray nozzle. The propellant immediately evaporates. Only very small droplets or particles of material are then left hanging in the air. These droplets themselves evaporate after a time.

Other types of can contain the liquid propellant gas and the material mixed together in the form of an emulsion, or a foam. These are other sorts of colloid. Shaving foam is often dispensed in this way. The size of the particles produced by canisters varies considerably, being between one and about 800 microns.

To think about
Which of the spray cans you use in your household produce a genuine aerosol (as opposed to, say, a foam of some kind)?

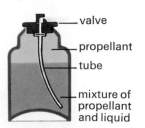

valve
propellant
tube
mixture of propellant and liquid

Aerosol sprays are driven out of the can by the pressure of the propellant gas inside

Africa

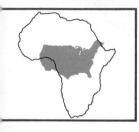

North to South: 5,000 miles
East to West: 4,600 miles
Area: 11,500,000 square miles
Highest point: Mt Kilimanjaro 19,340 ft above sea level
Lowest point: Qattara, Egypt 440 feet below sea level
Average height: 2,460 feet above sea level
Population: 350 million

The second largest of the world's continents, Africa occupies more than one fifth of the Earth's land surface. It stretches 5,000 miles from north to south and 4,600 from west to east. The equator runs across Africa, roughly in the middle, from Gabon in the west to Somalia in the east. Three times the size of the United States, Africa is compact, with a regular outline. It has only 17,000 miles of coastline and few natural harbours. It is also remarkable for its vast expanses of unchanging landscape.

Africa may once have been part of a giant continent called Gondwanaland, including South America, Antarctica, India and Australia. This is suggested by the evidence of rocks, fossils, magnetism, past climates and so on. The theory is that this old continent broke up and the new continents drifted apart.

Most of Africa today is formed from a rocky rigid block, or basement, which is at least 500 million years old. Some of the parts date back 3,000 million years. In some places these rocks are exposed. Elsewhere they have a thin covering of more recent soil and rocks.

The surface of Africa consists mainly of large flat areas, or plateaus, although these occur at different levels. Exceptions are in the extreme north-west (Atlas) and the southern tip (the Cape) where there are mountains. In East Africa there are also numerous peaks, and in the Sahara the Tibesti and Hoggar Mountains.

African game gathers at a waterhole

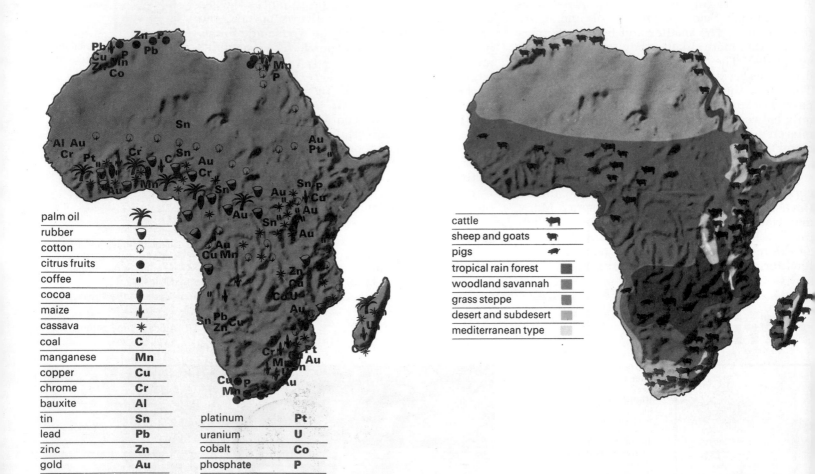

palm oil	![palm]
rubber	![rubber]
cotton	![cotton]
citrus fruits	●
coffee	![coffee]
cocoa	![cocoa]
maize	![maize]
cassava	✳
coal	**C**
manganese	**Mn**
copper	**Cu**
chrome	**Cr**
bauxite	**Al**
tin	**Sn**
lead	**Pb**
zinc	**Zn**
gold	**Au**

platinum	**Pt**
uranium	**U**
cobalt	**Co**
phosphate	**P**

cattle	![cattle]
sheep and goats	![sheep]
pigs	![pig]
tropical rain forest	■
woodland savannah	■
grass steppe	■
desert and subdesert	■
mediterranean type	■

Today the plateaus are separated by escarpments, or rifts, through which mighty rivers flow and fall. At Victoria Falls, for example, the River Zambezi drops 355 feet. This poses great problems in building railroads and highways. It also complicates river transport in that goods have to be transshipped: that is, when one ship has gone as far as it can, the cargo has to be shifted to a boat on the other side of the obstacle.

Africa slopes down towards the north. The continent ranges in altitude from 1,000 feet above sea level in the north to 6,000 feet in the south, with an average of 2,460 feet. These height differences have a very profound effect on climate, population and economy.

In East Africa there is a massive series of 'faults', areas in which some of the land has shifted its level. An example is the Great Rift Valley which runs for 3,500 miles from the Red Sea to Mozambique. It is 25 to 30 miles wide and sometimes as much as 6,000 feet deep. It is here, also, that Africa's greatest mountains are found. There are extinct volcanoes such as Kilimanjaro (19,340 feet) and active ones like the Virunga Mountains (14,660 feet). Most of Africa's great lakes lie in the western arm of the Rift Valley: Lakes Albert, Edward, Kivu and Tanganyika.

Five major rivers carry most of the water flowing from Africa to the sea. They are the Niger (2,600 miles), Nile (4,000 miles), Congo

(3,000 miles), Zambezi (1,600 miles), and Orange (1,300 miles). However, the sea claims only 48 per cent of Africa's rainfall: 12 per cent collects in landlocked basins such as Chad and Okavango where it evaporates in the heat of the sun. The remaining 40 per cent falls on desert. There it evaporates very rapidly and the desert is so dry that no water-flow system is in operation.

The African climate has a complex cycle of seasons which affects everything living there.

Some areas, like the Sahara, receive very little rain (10 inches per year); others, like the Congo Basin, have two heavy rainfalls per year (as much as 400 inches). Only 15 per cent of tropical Africa has no water shortage. 40 per cent is permanently arid or has a serious water shortage.

The variation and interplay of these many factors produce very clear categories of vegetation:

Tropical rain forests develop under conditions of maximum rainfall.

Woodland-Savanna has a wide variety of vegetation including trees and grasses. The variety depends on the amount of rainfall. These areas have marked dry seasons – sometimes up to seven months.

Grass steppe, in which rainy seasons are shorter and grassland is dotted with thorn trees.

Sub-desert and desert, which have more than 10 dry months per year.

▷ Africa's rich variety of peoples. In the north and north-west most are of Arabian stock. East Africans have dark skins, but often with Arabian features. True Negro peoples occupy the forest zones of West and Central Africa. A mainly Negro people called the Bantu live in southern Africa. The center pictures show a pygmy and a woman of the bushman people

(Far right) Yearly rainfall and temperatures. Darker areas receive more rain. Compare the vegetation zones shown on this page. The wettest areas get over 1,000 inches each year, the deserts less than 10. The bars show the average summer and winter temperatures. Each division marks 10°C. Near the equator there is little seasonal difference

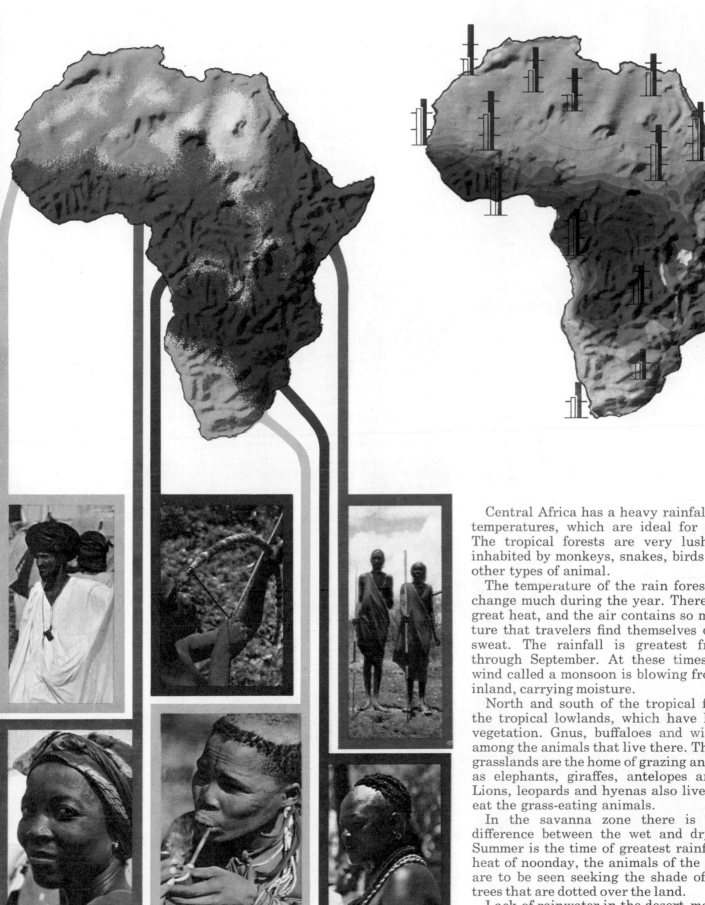

Central Africa has a heavy rainfall and high temperatures, which are ideal for plant life. The tropical forests are very lush and are inhabited by monkeys, snakes, birds and many other types of animal.

The temperature of the rain forest does not change much during the year. There is always great heat, and the air contains so much moisture that travelers find themselves damp with sweat. The rainfall is greatest from April through September. At these times a steady wind called a monsoon is blowing from the sea inland, carrying moisture.

North and south of the tropical forests are the tropical lowlands, which have less heavy vegetation. Gnus, buffaloes and wild pig are among the animals that live there. The savanna grasslands are the home of grazing animals such as elephants, giraffes, antelopes and zebras. Lions, leopards and hyenas also live there and eat the grass-eating animals.

In the savanna zone there is a marked difference between the wet and dry seasons. Summer is the time of greatest rainfall. In the heat of noonday, the animals of the grasslands are to be seen seeking the shade of the small trees that are dotted over the land.

Lack of rainwater in the desert means fewer animals. Only animals that are specially adapted for the climate can survive there. These include gazelles, foxes and hares.

Vast areas of Africa are thinly settled or totally uninhabited. Densely populated areas such as Nigeria and Egypt are exceptions. In a country containing 350 million people, 90 per cent live in the country and the remaining 10 per cent live in towns. This situation is quite different from America where about 30 per cent live in the country and 70 per cent in towns.

The population of Africa is developed from three basic types, the Bushmen, the Pygmies and the Negroes. Two other types of people, called the Semites and the Hamites, also immigrated. Today these two groups have become so mixed that it is easier to trace their origins by studying their languages and culture than observing their physical appearance.

The individual African's position in his community today is deeply affected by ancient tradition and tribal custom. The majority of workers are engaged in agriculture which is badly organized, inefficient and under-productive.

Most farming is restricted to crop-growing, as tse-tse fly prevents cattle-keeping over roughly half of tropical Africa. Oxen cannot survive and tractors are too expensive for most farmers. Many farming tribes are nomads; that is, having gathered a crop they move onto new pastures, leaving the old to grow again. South of the Sahara there is some cattle farming, which is for meat and hide rather than dairy products. In northern Africa the livestock are mainly camels, sheep and goats.

Families in the rural parts of Africa usually grow their own crops and raise their own animals. A few of the peoples, like the pygmies, are still hunters, and also gather berries from the forest for their food. But most of them are either farmers or cattle-raisers.

In the north and the east, in the desert areas, the people get their milk and meat from the goats and camels that they keep. They get plant food from the moist and fertile areas around oases.

Maize is one of the most common foods in many parts of Africa. Women grind the grain into flour, which is mixed with water and boiled in a big kettle. This makes a sort of porridge, which can be eaten with vegetables such as beans.

Many other foods are important in the diet of Africans. Many fruits are grown that are familiar in America and Europe. There are pineapples, bananas, oranges and paw-paws. And there is the yam. Its swollen root is like the potato. It can be boiled or fried, like the potato. Africa also has sweet potatoes, similar to those of America.

Today the task of growing food is being taken over more and more by large farms and plantations, as Africans from the rural areas move into the towns and cities.

While most Africans produce foods for their own consumption, European farms or plantations operate on a much larger scale to produce raw materials for export. These include cocoa, oil palm, coffee, tea, tobacco, cotton, rubber, sugar and sisal.

Africa's rich mineral deposits have provided a boom industry for overseas investment. Minerals include iron, gold, diamonds, copper and petroleum. Other minerals, such as potash and bauxite, have been mined in a smaller way, and these industries can be expected to expand.

Manufacturing industry is underdeveloped in most countries, with a few exceptions such as South Africa, Egypt and Zimbabwe.

Yet Africa has great potential. Numerous mineral discoveries have yet to be developed. Prospects are good for local iron and steel production, fertilizer plants and copper and aluminium refineries.

Water resources may be used for irrigation, hydro-electric power, transportation and fish-farming. Africa has at present only four or five per cent of the world's irrigated land – Egypt and Sudan alone account for half this total. Yet rivers like the Congo and Zambezi are largely wasted in a continent where most of the land suffers from water shortage. Similarly, although Africa has around 40 per cent of world hydro-electricity potential, it has used only 1 per cent of this so far.

Work is under way to make use of this vast potential. In the Congo, in Mozambique, and throughout southern Africa, rivers are being diverted as dams are built.

Forest resources are also considerable, and may be developed to benefit the economy. No other continent has such a range of large mammals. In the savanna, animals that are now hunted for sport could be the most productive 'crop' to harvest there. Tourists are beginning to discover the splendor of Africa's scenery, wild life and human life, and could become an important source of revenue for the African economy.

See: *climate, continents, desert, geology, races of man.*

◁ Many of Africa's vast natural resources are so far scarcely exploited. The Victoria Falls, on the Zambezi River, are nearly a mile wide, but most of the water in this great river goes to waste.
▷Some of the contrasts of the African climate are typified in this photograph. The summit of Mt Kilimanjaro, crowned with perpetual snow, rises above the clouds, while three male buffaloes wander through the acacia trees and grass of the savanna land of Amboseli game reserve

▷The African elephant usually seeks out areas with plenty of water. In the national parks, elephants are now so numerous that they are destroying all the trees on which they depend for food. As a result, protection of elephants has led to a situation in which they are in danger of dying out

after-image

After looking at a reflection on a shiny object, you may have noticed coloured spots floating 'before your eyes'. These are called after-images because they are like pictures of a scene that remain after the eye has looked away.

A bright red object will give a greenish after-image if you look at a sheet of white paper. This is the complementary, or 'opposite', colour to red. When red and green light of the right shades are mixed together, they give white light. A blue object will give an after-image which is orange. Orange is blue's complementary colour.

We see after-images because the retina at the back of the eye becomes 'tired' when it looks at one colour for some time. Suppose that a person looks at a piece of white paper after looking at something red for a few seconds. White light is a mixture of light of all colours. Part of his retina becomes tired by the red object. It cannot respond properly to the red that is included in the white of the paper. But it can respond to all the other colours. These other colours add up to

make green. So the eye tells the brain that there is a greenish patch at that point.

There are other kinds of after-image. Some kinds are the same colour as the object that caused them. These are called 'positive' after-images, and they are formed in different ways from the ones described above. The workings of the retina are very complex and not yet fully understood.

See: *colour, eye.*

▷ Look at the picture in a strong light for a moment. Then look at a piece of white paper. You should be able to see the American flag in its proper colours

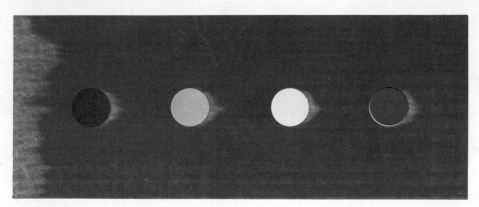

△ The afterimage of these spots will show you the complementary colours

▷ Looking away from this leopard after a moment, you will find him changing his spots

agate

A form of quartz that has beautiful bands of colouring. The bands are usually parallel, and they may be straight, zig-zag or circular. The mineral was formed thousands of years ago in cavities in rocks. The bands developed as layers of different materials were deposited.

Agate is valued for its attractive appearance. But it is also useful because it is very hard. It is often used in the 'knife-edges' which support the weighing beam in a balance.

Onyx is a type of agate with flat coloured layers. It can be cut to make cameos. Moss agate contains pieces of a mineral that resembles moss.

See: *quartz, rocks and minerals.*

The coloured layers that appear in agate are what give it its value as a gemstone

aging

New clothes become worn and shabby in time,
and new cars have worn parts after several
thousand miles. Similarly, our own bodies are
continually wearing out inside and growing
'shabby' outside. This process is aging.

Humans age more slowly than closely-related
animals. For example the large apes live only
about thirty years, and chimpanzees about forty
years. A man or woman can live to over a
hundred years. The favourite pets of human
beings age even faster. Rabbits live only about
twelve years and dogs and cats about twenty
years. Each animal species has its own natural
rate of aging. But an accident or an illness may
prevent an animal or a human being from
reaching its normal 'old age'.

In the human being the different body parts
start growing at birth and go on to the age of
twenty-one. About then the body reaches full
height because the long bones stop growing.
From then on all parts of the body begin to age.

Different working parts of a car wear out at
different times. Similarly, in each human being
the different organs and tissues show different
stages in the wearing-down process. A person's
eye-sight may weaken before his hearing
becomes less clear. His muscles may become
weaker before his joints become stiffer.

Different people age at different rates. This
means that two people of, say, sixty years, may
be very different in their strength and alertness.

Parts of the body change their appearance as
they age. The hair on the head becomes thin and
grey. Men especially may lose their hair and
become bald. The teeth may fall out. The skin of
the face, neck and arms loses its smooth and
soft look and becomes wrinkled and dull.

The lenses of the eye cannot change shape as
easily as they once could. Glasses may be
necessary for reading small print clearly. The
voice changes, becoming roughened and hoarse,
or high and piping. Hearing is less sharp,
especially for the higher tones. Women at about
the age of fifty can have no more children. Their
ovaries no longer produce eggs every month.
(See: *reproduction*).

The lining of bony joints, like the knees and
hips, becomes worn with age. The joints are no
longer well 'oiled'. They become stiffer and less
easily movable. The bones in the spine become
thinner, producing a bent or slightly stooped
appearance. All the bones of the body become
more brittle. An old person has to be very careful not to fall, because it is especially easy to
break a bone.

A very important change affects all blood
vessels in time. The arteries become narrow and
twisting. Their job is to carry blood containing
oxygen and glucose to all the tissues and organs.
Narrow tubes slow down the blood supply and
this causes the tissues they feed to age faster.
This change in the arteries is called arteriosclerosis. It is most serious when it affects the
brain, the heart and the kidneys.

Aging affects the thinking powers as well as

△ The weathered face of an aged Portuguese woman. Sun and wind have added to the aging process

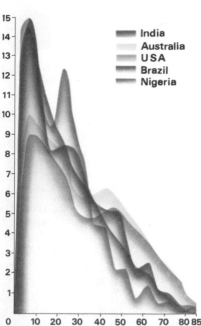
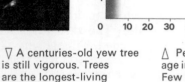

▽ A centuries-old yew tree is still vigorous. Trees are the longest-living things on Earth

△ Percent of population by age in rich and poor nations. Few Indians and Nigerians reach old age

Despite all the changes, Sir Winston Churchill at 80 was unmistakably the same man as the Churchill of 30

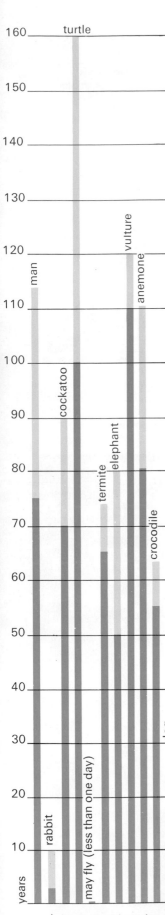

turtle

vulture

anemone

man

cockatoo

termite

elephant

crocodile

dog

rabbit

may fly (less than one day)

years

△ Average and maximum recorded life-spans of a number of animals. The dark blue shows the average and the light blue the record maximum

the working parts. Old people often cannot remember recent events very well. But their memory for people, places and events in the distant past may still be excellent.

Mental arithmetic and similar brain exercises are harder to do. New skills at work or at play are harder to learn. If there is arteriosclerosis in the brain, the mental changes of aging are more severe.

All organs and tissues are made up of cells. As these grow older more and more of these decay and die. They are replaced by 'scar' cells, which are not active. For example, the cells which make up the tissue of the skin decay and die. The skin loses its ability to stretch when needed. This is why it looks wrinkled.

The reason why this aging process takes place over the years is still not properly understood. Some scientists think that aging is controlled by a built-in 'clock' which times the running down process. Even if this is true, we still do not know what is actually happening to make the cells die.

One suggestion is that cells lose the power to reproduce properly. Healthy cells can divide to form two new ones. These replace old cells that have died. It is possible that in old people the new cells made in this way are faulty.

Another idea is that the body loses the power to recognize its own parts. It mistakes its own tissues for foreign intruders, like bacteria. It then tries to destroy them by producing substances called antibodies.

Yet another idea is that aging is due to a lack of chemicals called sex hormones (see: *hormones*). Doctors have unsuccessfully tried to slow up aging by giving hormones as tablets or injections.

Aging brain cells often show large amounts of a material called lipofuchsin. Some doctors have been using a drug to remove the lipofuchsin. The results of this in reducing the aging effects are not yet clear.

We know a lot about how to keep people alive longer by preventing and curing disease. Because of this, old people make up a larger fraction of our society than in the past. But we still know almost nothing about how to prevent the harmful effects of age.

See: *growth*.

Find out by doing

Talk to some of your older relatives. Find out what differences they notice in themselves as they grow older. For example, do they need the same amount of sleep as when they were younger? Does physical exercise seem harder? Does food seem to have less taste and smell than it used to?

Agricola

A sixteenth-century German mineralogist and mining engineer, whose work greatly influenced later geologists. His real name was Georg Bauer, which means George Farmer. He preferred to use the Latin version as a pen-name – *agricola* is Latin for farmer. He studied the mining industry. He described many minerals and suggested ways of locating and extracting them.

In his writings about geology, Agricola explained how wind and water affected and changed the earth's surface. He developed theories to explain earthquakes and volcanoes. He also classified, for the first time, the stones, minerals and gems in the earth's crust. Because of his contacts with the mining industry, Agricola became the first mineralogist to write from first-hand knowledge.

Agricola's great book on mining and metallurgy went into such details as the methods of getting into and out of underground mines. Here men can be seen descending by (A) a ladder, (B) a rope and (C) simply sliding, with a rope to help in climbing out again. Example (D) shows a shallow shaft that can be walked up and down

agriculture

The raising of vegetable crops and animals to provide food, textiles and other materials useful to man. Agriculture is one of the oldest of all human industries.

The first known farmers lived in south-west Asia – Israel, Syria, Turkey and Iraq – ten thousand years ago. Excavation of villages has revealed early grain seeds and granaries. The Egyptians, too, were early cultivators where there was a water supply adequate for planting crops and keeping sheep and goats.

Further to the East, the Indus Valley civilization in north-west India built huge granaries around 2500 BC. From India, men took agricultural science to China along the old trade routes. In China, millet was the primary crop and the hog the most important animal.

Agriculture went to Europe from the Near East. At first, bad farming sapped the fertility of the lands. However, the land was still good for grazing and sheep were introduced, quickly becoming important and popular.

Greek and early Roman farms were small, but when the Roman Empire became powerful, the aristocracy turned agriculture into a commercial enterprise with large farms staffed by slave labour. After the collapse of the Roman Empire in 476 AD, farms in Europe again became small peasant businesses.

Feudalism was the basic economic system in Europe from the 4th to the 13th centuries. A village and its surrounding land would be owned by a lord who, in return for service, often military, allowed peasants to farm the land. The crop land was divided into three main fields, and each was then divided again into strips. Each farmer had strips in each field, with equal amounts of good and poor ground.

Crops were grown in rotation. In one field winter corn, wheat and rye were sown. In the second field, spring barley, beans and oats. The third field was left fallow – giving it a rest from crop production – and used only for grazing. This method was known as the open-field system.

Under this system, village life was economically steady because there was no opportunity for expansion and profit. Each farmer used his crops and animals for himself and his family and there was hardly any trading. This is known as subsistence farming. It was unprogressive and there was little understanding of how to enrich the quality of the fields. Leaving one field fallow helped to replenish the land's resources but also meant a loss in yield.

The change from open-field subsistence agriculture to commercial farming began in England during the 14th century. This new type of farm-

▽ Ancient Egypt's power and prosperity depended on the enormous fertility of the Nile valley, due to the river's yearly floods. These wall paintings from a tomb in Thebes show farm people gathering the harvest of corn, flax (used for spinning linen thread and for making linseed oil), and dates.
(Right) A combine harvester typifies the mechanized farm of today. Combines were one of the first devices to perform the work of several farm workers automatically

Number of people
in millions
working on farms

agricultural
production in US
(per cent of
1957/58)

Scottish farmers on the island of Uist are subsistence farmers. They grow only enough to feed themselves, without any surplus for the market

ing involved enclosures, when the common land became private property farmed by one person, usually the land-owner. Open fields were replaced by closed ones used for sheep grazing rather than crops. Over the years, the enclosure system drove many farm workers off the land because there was no work for them. But at the same time it made many sheep farmers rich, and wool became a major European trade.

Despite these important changes in the way the land was used, there were few improvements in farming methods until the 18th century. During that century the fallow field system was abandoned and replaced by 4-crop rotation. One year, root crops would be grown; the next year, cereals. This would be followed by clover and then cereals in the fourth year. The land was divided into four fields so that all crops were always growing although they moved in rotation.

Although farmers did not understand the scientific basis of what they were doing at

that time, the importance of growing clover lay in the fact that this crop can get the essential nitrogen that it needs for growth from the air. Cereal crops can only get their nitrogen from nitrogen compounds in the soil (See: *nitrogen*), but plants like clover have little colonies of bacteria in their roots which can 'fix' atmospheric nitrogen. So growing clover gave the land a chance to recover some of the nitrogen compounds that the cereals had taken out. And if the soil had been made very poor the clover could be ploughed back in.

Alternatively, the clover – as well as the root crops like turnips – could be used for feeding animals, providing more meat and more manure, which also helped to enrich the soil.

In England, this method was developed by Viscount Charles Townshend, who retired from politics to his farm in Norfolk, and earned himself the nickname 'Turnip Townshend'.

In the 1750s Robert Bakewell, an English

◁ Selective breeding has produced the high beef yield of this Hereford bull *(far left)*. The sacred Indian cow *(near left)* shows how little meat wild cattle have

▷ These early tractors are taking part in an agricultural show of 1919. They were fueled with a mixture of petrol and paraffin. Later the large pneumatic tyre with a deep tread was introduced, enabling the tractor to work on the muddiest ground

◁ The use of machines has allowed more countries to grow more food with the labour of ever fewer people. Farm workers themselves have often preferred the greater ease of the cities. This graph shows the changes that have taken place in America during the last twenty years

▷ Poultry farmers have increased egg and meat output in chickens by strictly controlling their surroundings. The hens in this 'battery' *(near right)* are fed from automatic dispensers, and their eggs are automatically removed. *(Far right)* Spraying from planes is the best way to get insecticide onto this huge cotton crop

farmer, made the first attempt at improving live-stock by selective breeding. This meant using only the best animals for breeding so that their good qualities were maintained in further generations (see: *breeding*).

Farm implements, too, had remained the same since Roman times in Europe: the axe, scythe, sickle, spade, hoe, and horse-drawn wooden plough were the only tools of the European farmer until the beginning of the 18th century.

Farming becomes scientific

In the nineteenth century came mechanization of agriculture and the use of fertilizers which replaced the land's lost nutrients. The introduction of tractors had two effects: it increased the speed of farmwork and also released land once used for grazing work-animals, to be cultivated for human food crops. With the use of fertilizers each acre gave a greater yield. Chemical fertilizers and pest-killers have greatly improved agricultural yield. But many experts now

believe that their use threatens natural food chains and that only 'organic' (animal) ferti-lizers should be used.

As farming has become more scientific and commercialized, there has been a steady move-ment of population away from the land. Farmers and farm labourers have moved to the cities to work in industry. In 1896 over 75 per cent of the population of the United States lived by farm-ing. In 1969 the percentage had dropped to less than 3 per cent. There has been a similar move-ment in all advanced countries. At the same time the number of acres of farm land has doubled.

The increased wealth of workers who have moved from agriculture into industry has the effect of increasing demand for quantity and variety of food stuffs. This forces farmers to increase production. One result is the combine harvester, which speeds harvesting while reduc-ing the number of labourers required. Another is electric milking: just one man can supervise the

◁ Badly eroded land in the Tennessee Valley in the 1930s. The land in the valley was threatened by intensive farming and by regular flooding of the Tennessee River. Since the Tennessee Valley Authority was set up in 1930 to harness the river for power and agriculture, flooding has been prevented

▷ Sheep farming in the American state of Montana has hardly changed over the years. With several thousand sheep in a herd, it is necessary to keep them constantly on the move to find enough grass for pasture. The herds are driven from the valleys to the mountains according to the season

◁ Combine harvesters work throughout the night in the harvest season. The combine reaps the grain, separates the seed from the straw, and throws out the straw from the back of the machine. Later another machine will collect the straw and tie it into bales

▷ Techniques of dairy farming have also become more and more refined. Modern milking machines can deal with many cows at the same time, leaving the dairyman with more time in which to check on the health of his herd

◁ Climate and the nature of the land determine the crop. Tea plantations are found mainly on the hills of India, Ceylon and China

▽ These rice-fields in Indonesia have been made by terracing the hillside. Rice needs a heavy rainfall and a thick clay soil to retain the water, to grow well. Rice is the staple diet of millions of people in Asia

milking of a whole herd of cows. And another is battery poultry farming, in which all attention is focused on the egg-producing process.

But many of these modern methods of farming have brought long-term ill-effects close on the heels of short-term benefits. Intensive farming in the American Midwest caused the soil to become dry and dusty. By the 1930s dust-storms and drifting made agriculture in that area impossible. Similar problems have recently arisen in East Anglia.

The price of food

Farming is economically more important to some countries than to others. And it contributes to the economy in different ways. Poor countries that have little industry have to export farm produce to pay for imports. These countries export crops like coffee, rice, tea, beans and cocoa. The price they get for their exports depends on how keen other countries are to buy them. It also depends on how much of the produce is available on the market.

This makes underdeveloped countries very vulnerable. The situation is even worse when a country restricts its production to only one crop. The Caribbean island of St Vincent, for instance, grows mainly bananas, and the whole crop is sold to one banana trader. In the event of drought or glut or any of a multitude of misfortunes, the whole economy tumbles.

Sometimes, when too much of a certain crop is available, its market value drops. To stop this crops are destroyed. This keeps the market price stable. Thousands of tons of Canadian wheat have been dumped in the ocean following a particularly good harvest. Over-production of milk has also led to dumping. Protests against this apparent waste are usually met with the answer that producers have to be protected from sudden price changes. Also storage or transportation would be uneconomic.

Despite the great advances made in agricultural science over the last 100 years, scientific and commercial agriculture is still only practised in Western Europe, North America and pockets of the rest of the world.

Over half of the world population still makes a living from subsistence agriculture under primitive conditions. The peasants of the Orient, Eastern Europe and most of South America use few scientific aids. The methods of the people of the Amazon basin and areas of tropical Africa are particularly primitive. These people use a method known as shifting cultivation. They sow crops on one patch of land, and as this loses its fertility they move on to another area. And those who live in deserts must herd animals, as their land will not support crops.

Thus there are natural factors affecting the type of agriculture suitable for any one place. The amount of rainfall is a vital factor, although in more advanced countries, irrigation can overcome the scarcity of rain. Latitude and height above sea-level also influence the rate of growth and the length of the growing season. It is these that make people choose one type of agriculture or another.

The amount of agricultural land available in the world is very unfairly distributed. Asia (outside the USSR) has more than half the world population, but less than one third of the usable land. The continent of America, with 15 per cent of the world population, has 30 per cent of the agricultural land. Science in agriculture is therefore going to become of increasing importance.

There are three ways in which world food supplies can be increased. The amount of land being cultivated can be enlarged; the output from existing land can be increased; or the way in which we make use of the food we produce can be improved. Scientists are working on all three. But the great problem remains: will food production be able to increase at a greater rate than the population of the world is increasing?

See: *erosion, food chains, irrigation, soil.*

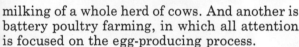

△ Cowboys branding a calf in about 1870. It was important to identify all cattle with the owner's special mark, especially since cattle were taken to market on the hoof. Cattle are now transported in railroad cars. *(Above left)* A harvester climbs a palm tree to cut down the date clusters. Each cluster may contain many hundreds of dates

air

We hardly ever notice the mixture of gases that surround us. We only realize it if there is a strong wind, or when fog or smog cuts off our view into the distance. Yet we depend on the air in many ways. It provides the oxygen that we breathe. Plants, on which all animals depend for food, could not live without the carbon dioxide in the air. And it is a barrier, hundreds of miles deep, protecting us from the burning ultra-violet rays of the sun. Fast-moving pieces of stone called meteoroids are burnt up when they enter the atmosphere from space, before they can reach the ground. And cosmic rays, which are made up of fragments of atoms travelling from distant parts of space, are slowed down before they can do damage.

To the Ancient Greeks, air was one of the four basic elements (see: *elements*). Everything was supposed to be made from mixtures of fire, water, earth and air. The picture has become a little more complicated since then. We know now that air itself is mainly composed of two basic chemical elements, oxygen (about one-quarter by weight) and nitrogen (about three-quarters). There are also small amounts of water vapour and carbon dioxide, along with the 'rare gases' (argon, krypton, xenon, neon and helium).

The air has not always had its present composition throughout the history of the earth.

Early in the earth's development (more than three thousand million years ago) there was no atmosphere at all. The surface of the earth was extremely hot, and gases and steam were produced by volcanic action. They were so hot that when they came to the surface they escaped into space. As the earth cooled down it became possible for these gases to be captured by the force of gravity (see: *gravity*). An atmosphere of nitrogen and carbon dioxide was formed, and the steam condensed to make the first oceans. The development of life, and the process called 'photosynthesis', led to the presence of oxygen in the air (see: *photosynthesis*).

Animals and plants depend on one another to keep the quantities of oxygen and carbon dioxide in the air constant. Plants take carbon dioxide and water from the earth and energy from sunlight. They build up sugars from carbon and water, and they give out oxygen. This is photosynthesis. But animals, including humans, 'burn' sugar in their muscles, and turn the oxygen that they breathe back into carbon dioxide and water.

About seven hundred million years ago the first plants began to manufacture oxygen from carbon dioxide in the atmosphere. Most of the carbon dioxide was used up in about one hundred million years. The new conditions enabled animals as we know them to develop.

Animals and plants breathe in oxygen and use it to burn the foods they eat. Water life takes in oxygen dissolved in seas and rivers. Fires and petrol engines also consume oxygen. The carbon dioxide produced in these different forms of burning is taken in by plants in daytime and used in photosynthesis. This is how plants and animals depend on each other. Nitrogen also follows a closed cycle. Plants 'fix' nitrogen, and are later eaten by animals. They excrete nitrogen in compounds which in turn help plants to grow. Lightning flashes convert nitrogen in the air into nitric acid, which is washed down in rain. Some marine organisms use carbon dioxide in their shells, which fall to the ocean floor to become future chalk beds

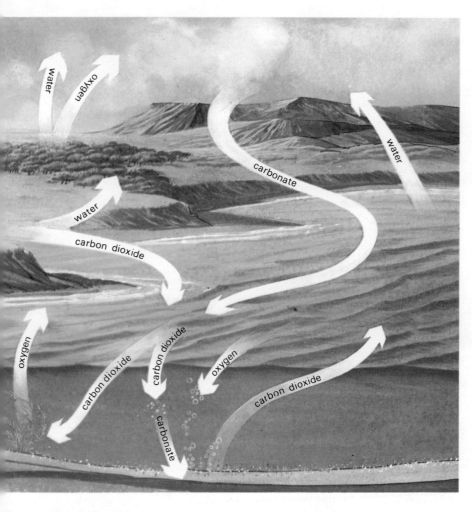

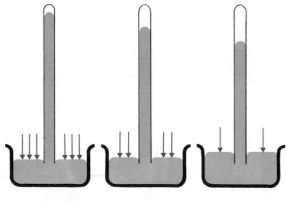

▷ If the air is pumped out of a tube dipping into a bowl of mercury, the liquid rises in the tube. It is pushed up the tube by the air pressing down on the mercury in the bowl. If the pressure of the air gets smaller, it can only hold up a smaller weight, and the mercury in the tube falls

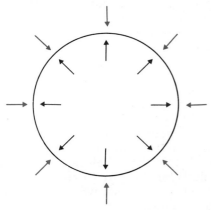

▷ The weight of the air pressing in on our bodies does not crush us. It is balanced by the pressure of the fluids and gases in our bodies acting outwards. The skin of a balloon is held taut by air pressure inside it. The pressure of the air in a diver's suit saves him from being crushed by water pressure

All animals breathe in oxygen and breathe out carbon dioxide. But at the same time fires, automobiles, industrial processes, jet aircraft and so on generate large quantities of the gas. At present the green plants on the earth are able to cope with all this carbon dioxide and keep the proportion of oxygen in the air steady.

The nitrogen in the air is also essential to life. Many of the complicated molecules in living tissues contain nitrogen. Almost all the nitrogen in living things has been part of the air at some time. Most plants and animals can use it only after combining it with other substances to make new chemicals like ammonia or nitric acid. This is called 'fixing' the nitrogen.

Two main 'fixing' processes occur naturally. In a flash of lightning some nitrogen from the air may interact with oxygen and water vapour to form nitric acid. There are also bacteria that 'fix' atmospheric nitrogen into nitrates. Some of these bacteria live in the nodules that you can find on the roots of pea and bean plants. They help peas and beans to form green leaves.

The weight of the air

Air can be very strong when it is compressed. When workmen dig up the roadway they use a drill driven by compressed air to break up hard concrete.

We live under about a hundred miles of air. Why are we not squashed by it? We are not squashed, strangely enough, because our bodies are soft and so everything in our bodies is at the same pressure as the air around us. This causes trouble only if the pressure around us is increased or reduced too quickly. For instance, if we fly in an airplane when we have a head cold, we may get severe pains in our ears. The pressure of the surrounding air is reduced when the airplane goes up. But there is air at ground-level pressure trapped inside our ears, because a head cold blocks the tubes from the nose that let this air flow in and out.

To measure air pressure we use a barometer. A simple barometer consists of a glass tube that has only one end open. If this tube is filled with water or mercury and then held upright with the open end still in the liquid bath, some of the liquid will remain in the tube. It is held there, above the level of liquid in the bath, by air pressure acting on the surface of the liquid.

We can measure air pressure by the length of the column of liquid that it will hold up. In the case of water the length is about 34 ft (1,033 cm) at sea level. Mercury is usually used to measure air pressure. It is much denser than water, and a column only about 30 in (75 cm) high will balance the pressure of air at ground level. This is why we refer to atmospheric pressure in inches of mercury.

Air pressure also varies with the weather. Water vapour is lighter than oxygen, nitrogen or carbon dioxide. So, if the air is damp it weighs less and the air pressure is lower. When a barometer falls, showing that the air pressure is decreasing, it means that the air is growing moister and therefore that rain is likely.

Sound is transmitted through the air because

of the way air can be compressed. A radio loud-speaker is a sort of high speed piston. It pushes and pulls very rapidly, hundreds or thousands of times every second, depending on the pitch of the sound. This first compresses the air nearby, then decompresses it. This air pushes against the air further away, and makes waves from one layer of air to the next, until they reach our eardrums. The waves then push and pull against the eardrum and cause a vibration, which we recognize as sound.

The speed of sound through the air depends on the way one layer of air pushes against the next layer. This is affected by the temperature of the air. Sound travels more slowly in colder air. At normal temperatures the speed of sound is over 700 miles per hour.

In watching moon flights on television you may be surprised to notice how easily the astronauts talk to each other on the surface of the moon. The moon has no air, because its gravity is not strong enough to stop an atmosphere from escaping into space. Sound cannot be carried without air, so that the astronauts must use built-in walkie-talkie radios in their space suits – even when they are standing face to face two feet apart.

But light does behave in the same way both on earth and on the moon. Light is a wave motion too. It is not composed of disturbances in the air itself. Visible light, like radio waves,

radar, X-rays and gamma-rays, is a form of 'electromagnetic radiation'. It usually travels through air as easily as it travels through the vacuum at the surface of the moon. But in mist or cloud there are tiny water drops in the air, which scatter light. These sometimes cause a rainbow, or a 'ring' round the moon or sun.

Dirty air may scatter light too. Fine dust, carried up to the top of the atmosphere, scatters blue light more than red light, so that the sun appears redder (see: *absorption of light*).

Even clean air is slightly different from a vacuum in the way it transmits light: light travels a tiny fraction slower in the air. The speed is also affected by the temperature of the air. This bends the light, as you can see in the shimmering of the air above a hot stove.

Even when the air feels dry it still has water vapour in it. On a dry summer day a bottle that has just been taken out of a refrigerator is soon covered with tiny drops of water. These have been condensed out of the air. When the air contains as much water vapour as it can hold without mist appearing, we say the humidity is 100 per cent (see: *humidity*). Cool air can hold less water vapour than hot air. A block of dry ice (solid carbon dioxide) generates a mist because it cools the air close to it, and causes the humidity of that air to rise above 100 per cent. Clouds are formed when warm moist air rises and is cooled due to its expansion.

△ Water vapour is always present, even in the air of the driest desert. But it becomes visible only when it condenses into water droplets, as in the coastal mist *(top)*. At high altitudes, water exists in the form of ice crystals. These can often cause halos of light, sometimes coloured, round the sun or moon *(top of facing page)*. Sometimes the air itself can become visible. The shimmering blue layer just below the desert horizon in the lower picture is a reflection of the sky. Low-lying air, made hot by contact with the ground, is bending light from the sky towards the camera

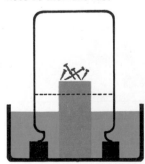

As far as life is concerned, it is only the few miles of atmosphere nearest the earth that are important. Three-quarters of the atmosphere (by weight) lies within seven miles of the Earth's surface and nine-tenths of it is within ten miles of the surface.

The weather is 'made' even nearer the earth. Most of the water vapour, which forms rain-clouds, is contained in the lowest 10,000 feet and half of it is in the lowest 7,500 feet.

The higher you go into the atmosphere the colder it is, but this gradual chilliness stops after a certain height. The point where the temperature stops dropping is called the 'tropo-pause'. The atmosphere below this height is called the 'troposphere'. Above it is the beginning of the 'stratosphere'.

At about 50 miles up the layer is called the 'mesosphere'. Above it comes the 'ionosphere'.

The ionosphere is so called because the air molecules are bombarded by the sun's ultra-violet rays to become electrically charged (ionized). The ionized particles form layers which reflect radio waves back to earth. This is why we can send radio signals round the world instead of the signals going into space.

The very top level of the atmosphere where the air is very rarefied and gases escape into space is sometimes called the exosphere.
See: *aerodynamics, climate, Earth, light, sound.*

Find out by doing

Place a tumbler in a bowl of water right way up. You need to push to make the tumbler go right to the bottom, to overcome the upthrust of the water against the bottom of the tumbler. Next push the tumbler into the water upside down. The force of your push is probably about the same. This time the water is pushing on the air trapped in the tumbler, which is partly compressed.

Lay a tumbler down in a bowl of water so that it completely fills up. Then try and pick it up, bottom first. If you do it carefully you can lift almost the whole tumbler out of the bowl without a bubble getting in. The water is held up inside the tumbler by the pressure of the air on the water in the bowl outside the tumbler.

Invert a glass jar over some wet nails, iron filings, or wire, standing over water, as illustrated. As the iron rusts over a period of days and weeks, it uses up oxygen in the jar. The water will rise to fill the space formerly occupied by the oxygen in the jar.

Pour an inch or two of boiling water into a large square can and screw the lid on tight. Pour cold water over it. The water vapour in the can will condense rapidly, reducing the pressure inside. If the metal of the can is not too thick it will be crushed by the pressure of the atmosphere.

Rising currents of air can be revealed with the paper spiral shown, balanced on a pinpoint. Held over a radiator or a hot kitchen cooker it will begin to rotate as it is driven round by the rising air.

△ A paper spiral that can detect rising air
▽ The water in the jar rises as the nails rust

air conditioning

A means of controlling the temperature, moisture, movement and purity of air. Changes in these affect human comfort. They also affect some industrial processes.

High temperatures and moisture levels are extremely uncomfortable (see: *humidity*). They make us feel hot and sticky. They also make it difficult for the body to control its temperature. Usually sweat evaporates and cools the body. If humidity is high, sweat cannot evaporate.

Man has experimented for centuries with ways of controlling air conditions. There were many ideas, one of the simplest being to hang wet mats over doorways. This cooled the incoming air. But it also moisturized it and that is not always a desirable thing.

None of the many other systems really did the job. It was not until refrigeration techniques were developed that modern air conditioning standards could be achieved.

Temperature and moisture also affect materials like cloth, paper and certain metals. When printing on paper, or weaving cloth, these air conditions must be kept constant. In the manufacture of delicate instruments, such as those used in spacecraft, conditions must be controlled to protect fine metal parts from rusting and corrosion.

Air conditioning can be used either to reduce or to increase heat and moisture. However, it is usually concerned with cooling and drying. That is mainly what we will consider in this article.

In most air conditioning equipment, a refrigeration system is used. A cooling chemical, such as the gas Freon, begins at room temperature. It is condensed by pressure, and this makes it hot. This excess heat is blown away by a fan and the Freon turns into a liquid at room temperature. It is then fed through a fine nozzle into an evaporator where it returns to its gas form. In the course of evaporating it absorbs heat. This process is repeated continually.

A fan blows air over the evaporator chamber. The air loses heat, which it gives up to the evaporating Freon. It also loses moisture, which condenses on the surface of the chamber. The cooler and drier air is then filtered to remove impurities, such as dust, pollen or smoke, and pumped into the room that is to be air conditioned.

Most air conditioners can be adjusted to make air hotter and more moist if required.

The first effective air conditioning machine was invented by Willis H Carrier in 1902. He used it to solve problems that were occurring at a colour printing plant in New York. Paper stretches when it is moist and shrinks when dry. This meant that a sheet could change size between one application of ink and another of a different colour. Thus air conditioning became a necessity rather than a convenience.

Since then air conditioning has become common in cinemas, public buildings, private homes and even in automobiles.

See: *heat, refrigerator*.

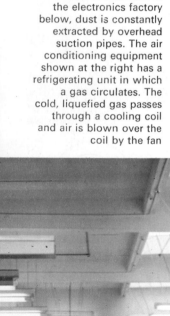

▽ Air conditioning cools, dries and cleans air in homes or factories. In the electronics factory below, dust is constantly extracted by overhead suction pipes. The air conditioning equipment shown at the right has a refrigerating unit in which a gas circulates. The cold, liquefied gas passes through a cooling coil and air is blown over the coil by the fan

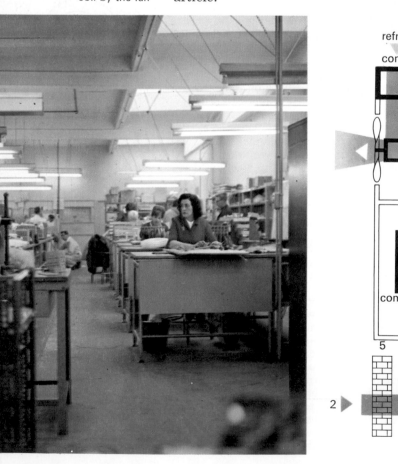

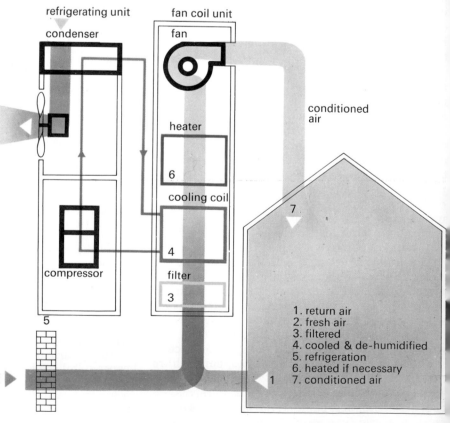

refrigerating unit

condenser

fan coil unit

fan

heater

6

cooling coil

4

compressor

filter

3

5

conditioned air

7

2

1

1. return air
2. fresh air
3. filtered
4. cooled & de-humidified
5. refrigeration
6. heated if necessary
7. conditioned air

air cushion vehicles

Vehicles, sometimes called 'hovercraft', which travel on a cushion of air. The cushion is created by compressing air with a fan to form a 'bubble' which lifts the vehicle off the ground. The vehicle can then be driven and steered by jets or propellers. A principal advantage is the reduction in friction between the vehicle and the surface it travels over. ACVs are also able to travel over land and sea with equal ease.

ACVs were first developed by Sir Christopher Cockerell, in Britain, and were launched in the English Channel in 1959. They have since been used on land and water.

The cushion of air upon which the ACV travels is like a pneumatic tire except that it is continually leaking. The air that leaks out is continually replaced by the powerful fan.

There are various ways of enclosing the cushion. A rigid skirt may be constructed around the base of the craft. However, this trails on the surface and creates friction which slows down the vehicle.

A skirt may be created by high-powered downward air jets forming a curtain around the cushion of air. This limits the height at which the ACV can travel. The jet curtain becomes less and less efficient the higher the vehicle is off the ground.

The third type of skirt is flexible and, although it may touch the ground or water, does not cause much friction.

At sea, ACVs are capable of speeds up to 100 mph. They do not require special docks or landing stages as they can draw up on the beach to land passengers or freight.

In the future we may expect to see 'hovercars' and 'hovertrains'. Cars will travel long distances quickly, smoothly and cheaply. Trains will travel over a rail or track, just a fraction of an inch above the track, at 300 mph or more.

The air cushion principle can also be used to relieve the strain on tyres carrying heavy loads. See: *air*, *airplane*, *pressure*.

An ACV's air-cushion is stopped from escaping by a stream of air flowing out below the edges of the craft *(below left)*. The air for this stream is drawn in above the machine by a powerful fan. The huge ACV at the bottom of the page carries cars and passengers across the English Channel, coming onto land at the end of its journey. The experimental hovertrain below could be developed into a 300 mph passenger train

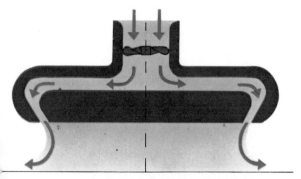

airplane

At the beginning of this century, there were many arguments about what to call the newly-built 'flying machines'. The American inventor Langley called his an 'aerodrome'. The word 'aeroplane', which really meant a wing of an aircraft, was applied in France and England to the whole machine. But since 1907 'airplane' has been used increasingly to describe a heavier-than-air craft driven by engines.

The first planes were made of wood and fabric, and could carry only one man at 30 mph. Today giant airliners made entirely of metal can carry 350 passengers at up to 600 mph. Soon, aircraft will take off from ordinary airfields to travel outside the atmosphere, and there will no longer be a sharp distinction between air travel and space travel.

All man's early attempts to fly were based on copying the birds. The great Italian artist and inventor Leonardo da Vinci was the first to realize that this method is hopeless. Man is not strong enough to lift himself by flapping wings.

The first known flight of a true airplane was by a model glider. It was designed by the Englishman Sir George Cayley in 1804. He based it on the shape of ancient Chinese kites. In 1849 and 1853 he built full-sized gliders, with kite-like wings and adjustable tail surfaces. They carried a boy and a man.

In 1843 W. S. Henson, one of Cayley's admirers, designed the 'Aerial Steam Carriage'. It had fixed wings, a controllable rudder, and elevators. If it had had the right wing shape and a suitable engine, it would probably have flown.

A light but powerful engine was the only thing now needed for powered flight. During the second half of the nineteenth century, the petrol engine was developed. The American brothers Orville and Wilbur Wright adapted this for their experiments with powered planes.

At last, on 17 December 1903, the first true man-carrying powered airplane flight took place. It was made by Orville Wright, near Kitty Hawk, North Carolina. He and his brother Wilbur flew four times that day. Their longest flight covered more than half a mile.

The Wrights' Flyer was designed on the same principles as modern planes. Aircraft depend on the air to support them in flight. Their wings are more curved on the top surface than on the bottom surface. When they are moving forward through the air this shape has the effect of creating a lifting force (see: *aerodynamics*). The Wrights owed their success to their careful study of the forces that moving air can exert.

The air not only lifts an aircraft. It also resists its motion. This resistance is called 'drag', and the engine must overcome it. So in straight and level flight an airplane is under the influence of four forces. The drag is counteracted by the thrust of the engine. The weight is counteracted by the lift of the wings.

The Wrights' achievements were way ahead of those of all other inventors. The first real European flight was made in France in 1906. Alberto Santos-Dumont flew a primitive biplane, the '14 *bis*'. Europe's first practical airplanes were basically box-kite gliders with engines fitted.

But airplane development in Europe began to gather momentum in 1909. This followed a visit by Wilbur Wright in 1908, and was due chiefly to two men: Henry Farman and Louis Blériot. Farman converted an existing biplane and made it much more controllable and efficient. Blériot,

A Hawker Siddeley Harrier of the US Marine Corps makes a vertical take-off. In flight the nozzles of its Pegasus jet engine swivel to point rearwards

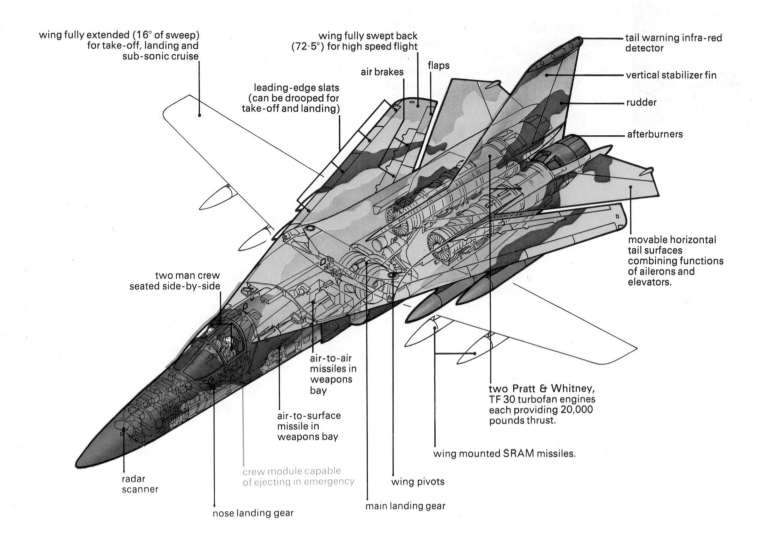

wing fully extended (16° of sweep) for take-off, landing and sub-sonic cruise

leading-edge slats (can be drooped for take-off and landing)

wing fully swept back (72·5°) for high speed flight

air brakes

flaps

tail warning infra-red detector

vertical stabilizer fin

rudder

afterburners

movable horizontal tail surfaces combining functions of ailerons and elevators.

two man crew seated side-by-side

air-to-air missiles in weapons bay

air-to-surface missile in weapons bay

two Pratt & Whitney, TF 30 turbofan engines each providing 20,000 pounds thrust.

wing mounted SRAM missiles.

radar scanner

crew module capable of ejecting in emergency

wing pivots

nose landing gear

main landing gear

The F-111 variable-geometry fighter-bomber, built by General Dynamics Corporation. With wings extended it can take off with large loads from runways of moderate length. With wings swept back it can fly at 1,500 mph

in July 1909, flew across the English Channel in a monoplane of his own design.

At this time America, France and Britain led the world. This was demonstrated at the world's first international flying meeting. It was held in Reims, France, in August 1909. The USA was represented by Glenn Curtiss, who won the speed contest at 52.63 mph in his Golden Flyer biplane. Such events, especially Blériot's cross-Channel flight, made people realize the potential of airplanes.

So far biplanes, and even triplanes, had been more successful than monoplanes. They had a large wing area, which gave a large amount of lift. Consequently designers concentrated on them. A standard form was beginning to emerge, with propellers pulling, instead of pushing, the plane.

A new method of steering the craft was also being developed. The Wright brothers had controlled the Flyer by operating cables that changed the curvature of the wings. This would cause a loss of lift on one side, and the plane would tilt – 'bank' – and turn.

A Frenchman, Robert Esnault Pelterie, pioneered a new method as early as 1904. His system is basically the one used on modern planes.

There are three ways in which a plane can rotate. It can *pitch* – that is, raise its nose to climb or lower it to dive. It can *roll*, lowering one wingtip. And it can *yaw*, turning its direction of flight to left or right.

The pilot of a modern plane can control these three manoeuvres with three different sets of moving surfaces, on the wings, tail fin and tailplane.

When the pilot moves the control stick backwards the 'elevators' are raised. These are flaps on the tailplane. When they are raised the air flowing past the plane pushes the tail down, and the plane begins to climb.

The rudder on the fin is operated by pedals. When it turns to the left the airstream presses on it and pushes the tail of the plane to the right. This changes the plane's course to the left.

When a plane is turning to the left, the pilot has to make it tilt slightly to the left. He does this with the aid of the 'ailerons'. The ailerons are larger surfaces on the main-plane, or wings. When the control stick is moved to the left the aileron on the left wing rises, pushing that wing down. The aileron on the right wing is lowered, pushing that wing up.

During World War I (1914-18) came the air-

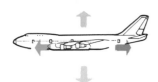

One of Cayley's gliders. With moving tails and wing surfaces, they were the first true airplanes

In level flight at constant speed, *lift* cancels *weight* and *thrust* cancels *drag*

▽ *(Top)* Orville Wright pilots the 'Flyer' on its historic ascent. *(Bottom left)* Blériot's monoplane flew from France to England in 1909. *(Bottom right)* Sopwith Pup fighter of the First World War

plane's first big test as a military weapon. At first airplanes were used simply for observation. Then the pilots began to carry rifles, and later machine-guns and small bombs. Then in 1915 Germany produced the Fokker 'Eindecker' (monoplane). It carried a machine-gun that could only fire forward, between the propeller blades. It was synchronized with the propeller, so that the bullets were timed to pass between the blades and not strike them. To aim the gun the pilot simply pointed the plane at his target.

After the war thousands of surplus war planes became available. Some of them were used by the first airlines to carry a few passengers or mail. Trailblazing flights mapped out longer routes that could be used commercially later.

The Atlantic was first crossed by plane in 1919. A US Navy Curtiss flying boat flew from Newfoundland to Portugal, stopping off at the Azores islands. The first non-stop crossing was in the same year. Alcock and Brown, two British fliers, flew a Vickers Vimy biplane from Newfoundland to Ireland in 16½ hours. They won a $50,000 newspaper prize.

The first solo crossing was Lindbergh's great flight from New York to Paris in 1927. His monoplane 'Spirit of St Louis' arrived in 33½ hours. Lindbergh's prize was $25,000 and he instantly became an international hero.

Winds mostly blow from west to east over the Atlantic. This means that planes are slowed down when flying in the other direction. They have to spend a longer time in the air without mechanical failures and they have to carry more fuel. The first east-west crossing was not achieved until 1928, by a German crew.

In 1926 Richard E Byrd of the US Navy, with a co-pilot, Floyd Bennett, flew over the North Pole. In 1929 Byrd became the first man to fly over the South Pole.

It was in the '20s that the technique of refueling planes while they were flying was first tried. The plane needing fuel flew close behind a tanker plane, which had been sent up to meet it. A fuel line was trailed from the tanker. A crew man on the other plane, standing up in his cockpit, caught the line and made a connection between the planes. The fuel was then pumped across. The US Army kept a plane aloft for over six days above Los Angeles in this way.

Flying was really brought within general reach after 1925. The public were given joy-rides in airplanes like the Curtiss 'Jenny' and 'Avro 504'. 'Barnstorming' displays were popular. De Havilland in Britain produced its first 'Moth' biplane. It was easy to fly and its price was low. With wings folded it could fit in a garage or be towed behind an automobile.

There were competitions for speed and range. The aircraft that won the Schneider Trophy and the Pulitzer Prize were to be developed into the streamlined all-metal airplanes of the '30s.

The age of the monoplane

Biplanes lingered for several years in military service. They began to yield to sleek, well-armed monoplanes during the late 1930s.

In 1933-34 three American airliners – the Boeing 247, Douglas DC-1 and Lockheed Electra – brought a revolution in air travel. These were twin-engined, all-metal monoplanes. They had retractable landing gear and

△ A plane *rolls* using ts ailerons, *pitches* using its elevators, and *yaws* or *urns* using its rudder

Planes grew more reamlined as speeds creased. Swept wings ppeared, then deltas

luxurious interiors. The '30s saw the heyday of the flyingboat, notably the Boeing 314. It began non-stop airline services across the North Atlantic just before the start of the Second World War.

The same year, 1939, saw the flight of the first jet airplane, the German Heinkel 178. Jet engine development continued in several countries during the war.

The war saw the perfection of fighters like the Mustang and Spitfire. In Britain the Spitfire (developed from a winning Schneider Trophy design) and its sister plane the Hurricane were rushed into production. They were just in time to meet the huge air attacks launched by the German Air Force in 1940.

The British fighters were guided to successful interceptions by radar stations on the ground. Later aircraft themselves carried radar. It enabled fighters to find bombers in darkness and in bad weather; and when a bombing target was invisible to the bomber because of cloud, it could still be observed by radar in the plane.

During the war the four-engined bomber grew larger and heavier. Squadrons of many hundreds of Allied bombers flew on missions from bases in Britain. One of the most important of these planes was the B-29 Superfortress. Superfortresses later dropped the atomic bombs on Hiroshima and Nagasaki that marked the end of the war.

The engines that had powered aircraft from the time of the Wrights until the thirties had all used pistons. They used the same principle as the engines that drive ordinary cars. The pistons move back and forth, and drive a shaft round. In a car the shaft turns the wheels. In a plane it turns a propeller, or airscrew. The propeller really does act like a screw. As the blades spin round they throw air backwards. In a similar way the propellers of a ship throw water backwards. This creates a forward force on the aircraft.

The propeller serves to pull the aircraft forward through the air. It does not directly contribute to the lift. It is the motion of the wings through the air that does this.

During the war the gas turbine was developed. It burns kerosene and has two forms, the jet and the turboprop. In the jet engine the hot gas that is produced expands out of the rear of the engine. It pushes the plane forward. It is like a rocket except that it needs to take in oxygen at the front to burn its fuel.

The gas is also used to drive a set of wheels with blades. This is the turbine, and it serves to suck in the air that burns the kerosene. In the turboprop engine, the turbine is used to turn a propeller. There is no push from the exhaust gases.

The first jet airliner was the British Comet of 1952. The first turboprop airliner was the British Viscount of the following year. Jet travel has built up enormously since the Boeing 707 and the Douglas DC-8 were introduced. There are now dozens of kinds of jet airliners.

By 1945 propeller-driven fighters could reach around 450 mph, but not much more. In the

△ 'Spirit of St Louis' made the first solo trans-Atlantic flight

▷ The Macchi 72 seaplane which set a world speed record in 1934

▽ Boeing B-17 heavy bombers flew missions in World War II

△ Spitfire fighters were vital to Britain's wartime defence against bombing attacks

▽ *(Top)* The P-51 Mustang, a wartime escort fighter. *(Bottom)* The F-86 Saber jet fighter

next 15 years the jet engine added another 1,000 mph to that figure. During this period designers had to overcome the so-called 'sound barrier'. Sound travels at about 760 mph at sea level. As a fast-moving airplane approaches this speed, the air becomes compressed ahead of it. This 'shock wave' can throw the airplane out of control. It certainly creates so much drag that it is difficult to pass the speed of sound. (See: *Supersonic flight*.)

The speed at which an aircraft is to fly determines the wing-shape. Up to about 500 mph ordinary straight wings give the best results. At higher speeds these cause excessive drag. Swept-back wings are then used, as in the Boeing 707, for example. Swept wings can be flown at over the speed of sound without losing efficiency. At around 1,400 mph the aerodynamic problems become more severe. Special delta (triangular) wing forms are necessary.

The first airplane to fly level at supersonic speed was the rocket-engined Bell X-1, on 14 October 1947. It achieved 670 mph.

Many military planes now fly at two to three times the speed of sound. The latest supersonic transports (SSTs) are designed to carry passengers at such speeds.

The official world speed record now stands at over 2,000 mph. Unofficial records are much higher than this. The X-15 rocket plane reached 4,534 mph in 1967.

When air flows over an object at these high speeds a lot of heat is generated by friction. The plane must be constructed of special alloys that will not melt at these temperatures. The X-15 has withstood temperatures of 3,000° Fahrenheit (1,600° Celsius).

As aircraft have grown heavier and faster, they need more space in which to take off and to land. Military planes need complex airfields which can easily be damaged by enemy attack.

△ The thin wings of a B-52 bomber flex upwards as it cruises at speed. The main equipment of US Strategic Air Command for many years, they have intercontinental range

The Soviet-designed Tu-144, the first supersonic transport aircraft to fly

▽ A Boeing 707-320B, an advanced version of one of the most successful of all airliners

View from the flight deck of a VC-10 airliner as it makes a night landing. The pilot has been guided to this distance by radio beams from the ground. Since the visibility is good he will now rely on the runway lights to judge his angle of descent. He is controlling the engine thrust by means of the throttles mounted between him and the second pilot

▽ Make a simple paper airplane as shown. Adhesive tapes used where indicated will help to keep it rigid. After a few trial flights, try the effect of folding its wingtips up. Then see where a paper clip has to be fixed to the body to compensate

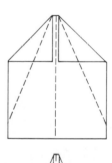

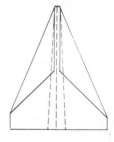

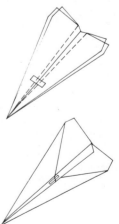

Both military and civilian airports take up huge areas of valuable land. As airliners take off they fly low over residential areas, creating a nuisance with their noise. Designers have long been trying to reduce the distance a plane needs for landing or take-off.

Helicopters have never needed runways. But their forward speed is limited. New types of plane have appeared that will not need long runways. In 1954 Rolls-Royce experimented with their 'Flying Bedstead'. This machine could lift itself vertically by swivelling its jet engines to point downwards. The principle is used in the only vertical take-off aircraft in military operation, the Hawker Siddeley Harrier. This machine is used by the US Marine Corps and the British RAF. It has a single Pegasus jet engine with swivelling nozzles. The USSR has developed a similar plane, the Yak-36.

A different method of getting vertical thrust is used in the American XC-142A and the Canadian CL-84-1. These are propeller-driven planes with their engines mounted on their wings. The wings can rotate so that for landing and take-off the propellers give a direct vertical force. The wings are then turned to their 'normal' position for forward flight.

The kind of wing that is best for supersonic flight is not best for short take-offs and landings, or for lowspeed flight. Planes that can change their wing form are called VG (Variable Geometry) aircraft. The General Dynamics F-111 was the first VG fighter on active service.

At take-off the pilot needs maximum lift. For his he needs wings that are wide from wingtip to wingtip, and that have a large area. The wings are set at an angle of only 16° of sweep. They then measure 63 feet from tip to tip.

Flaps are extended from the forward and rear edges of the wings to increase the area still further. After take-off, these are retracted.

As speed increases, drag increases too. The pilot therefore pivots the wings backwards. When they are fully swept to 72.5 degrees, the wings measure only 32 feet from tip to tip. The wings and tailplane then form a slim delta shape able to fly at supersonic speeds. They can be moved to in-between positions for maximum efficiency at other speeds. They are returned to the fully spread positions for landing.

Supersonic aircraft
The Soviet Tu-144 was the first supersonic transport airplane (as opposed to a combat aircraft) to fly. First to carry fare-paying passengers faster than sound, however, was the 1450 mph Concorde. This aircraft was developed jointly by Britain and France and went into service in 1976. Although it marked a significant advance in transport technology and design it has proved extremely expensive to operate and in its first five years of service lost large sums of money. Civil airplane makers have now abandoned the pursuit of speed. The emphasis is on fuel economy, quietness and automation.

The light alloys used for most aircraft bodies may give place to composite materials, which are lighter and easier to mould into aerodynamic shapes. The Lear Fan 2100 is built almost entirely of graphite-epoxy composite – epoxy resin (a very strong plastic) reinforced with graphite fibres.

The nine-seater Lear Fan is a turboprop, and though not as fast as a jet, it is far more economical with fuel. Its top speed is about 420 mph. Cruising at 350 mph it travels 11 miles on every gallon of fuel. This means that it is comparable in fuel usage to a large limousine.

On long-haul flights, much of an airplane's load-carrying capacity is taken up by the plane's own fuel. Planes could carry more passengers and cargo, or travel further non-stop, if the fuel

△ One of the ground crew guides the pilot to a stop

▷ Controllers direct planes even on the ground

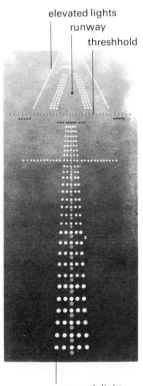

elevated lights
runway
threshhold

approach lights

Airport landing lights are designed to help the pilot judge his distance, angle of approach and angle of descent accurately. Leading up to the runway is a blue centre-line with crossbars, which are shorter the nearer they are to the runway. Red and green lines mark the runway threshold

itself weighed less. This is why future airplanes may be fuelled with hydrogen, a gas which gives more energy per unit of mass than any other fuel. But the practical problems are daunting. Liquid hydrogen boils at minus 253 degrees C, so it must be kept in thickly insulated tanks. The gas is highly inflammable and, when mixed with air, potentially explosive.

In 1981 Steve Ptacek flew a solar-powered airplane, the *Solar Challenger,* across the English Channel. Some engineers believe that commercial planes with solar cells and electric motors may one day fly above the clouds.

In the United Kingdom 2000 commercial flights take place every day. This number does not include military and private aircraft movements. If you could look at a radar display of all these flights at any moment it would look as if many of the airplanes were going to crash into one another. The job of keeping airplanes from colliding with each other is the task of Air Traffic Control.

Some 4000 air traffic controllers are needed to ensure that each flight safely takes off, flies to its destination and lands with the minimum delay. Before take-off the pilot hands in a flight plan to the local control centre. The plan includes the time at which he wants to depart, the route he wishes to follow, the height he wishes to fly at, his destination, and the time he estimates his flight will take.

When the pilot sits down and fastens his seat belt before take-off, he becomes part of a huge and complex system. He and his passengers do not see much of this apart from the airport control tower. But until the flight is completed he is controlled at all times.

When he is ready to go, the pilot receives his first instructions from the ground controller on his radio-telephone. When he has taxied to the correct runway, the local controller gives him clearance for take-off. As soon as he has left the airport he will be told the height, speed and direction to fly. His flight on the airway will be watched on a radar screen at all times.

Each aircraft is given its own airway. No other airplane at that height is allowed within five miles in any direction. Nor are there any aircraft within 1,000 feet above or below him.

As the pilot flies across country he comes under the control of various Air Traffic Control Centres. Each hands him on to the next one on his flight plan. To make doubly certain that Air Traffic Control are tracking the right airplane, they can ask the pilot to alter course. This movement is seen on their radar screens. As an alternative the pilot can operate an electrical device that gives a signal on the radar screen on the ground. The latest devices warn the pilot if he is going to fly near another airplane, so that he can take avoiding action.

The controller's most difficult task is guiding the airplane while it is approaching and landing at its destination. While waiting to land, the plane flies in a set pattern called the holding pattern. This is usually an oval path over a radio beacon. As the airspace below him empties he is told to fly lower. Gradually, a thousand feet at a time, he will spiral down to the lowest level in the vertical stack. Then, when it is his turn to land, he will be ordered on to course for final approach.

The pilot usually depends on his own eyes during the final landing. A pattern of lights guides him to the runway, helping him to judge his distance and angle of approach.

In addition, the pilot may be helped by a Visual Approach Light Indicator. Coloured lights are positioned beside the runway. If the aircraft is approaching too low the lights will appear red

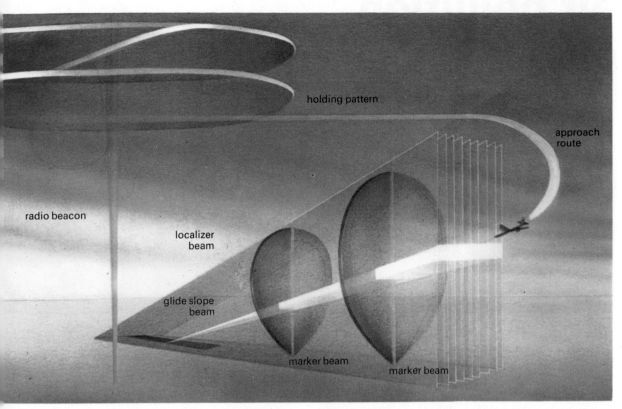

holding pattern

approach route

radio beacon

localizer beam

glide slope beam

marker beam

marker beam

◁ Planes waiting to land fly in oval paths over the airport. When they leave this landing 'stack' they fly to a point approximately over the centreline of the runway. From here they are guided by radio beams that fan out from an antenna at the end of the runway. A tone in the pilot's headphones tells him when he is too far to the left or right of the centreline. He passes over vertical radio beams that mark his distance from the runway. For the final landing he uses his eyes

o the pilot. If he approaches too high they will appear white. When he is on a correct line of approach they will seem half red and half white. This will enable him to adjust his approach.

If the weather is bad, and if the airport is equipped with an Instrument Landing System (ILS) the pilot guides himself by radio beam until the runway is in sight. Two radio beams are transmitted from antennas near the runway. One tells the pilot if he is in line with the runway. The other tells him whether he is at the right height and the proper angle of descent.

Fully automatic landing systems have now been developed. When these are in use the pilot does not have to touch the controls during landing.

Airports normally have a choice of runways, so that planes can land and take off into the wind. In places where the winds are nearly always in the same direction, there may be no need for runways in other directions. For example, Los Angeles International Airport uses only east-west parallel runways, and at London Heathrow Airport the two main runways are also aligned east and west.

The modern airport is large and complex. It has to have radio and radar facilities to control the airplanes in its area. It has to provide refueling, repair, and maintenance, and storage facilities for the aircraft that use it. It has to have passenger buildings, customs, car parks, services such as entertainment and restaurants, and possibly even its own police force and prison cells.

The world's busiest airport is Chicago International Airport at O'Hare Field. It has well over half a million take-offs and landings every year. This represents an average of more than one a minute, day and night. By 1981 it was handling over 60 million passengers a year.

Figures like this give an idea of the important role which the descendants of Orville and Wilbur Wright's frail craft now play in our lives. They will be even more important in the future. We can only guess at the form future aircraft will take.

An airplane making an intercontinental flight may no longer depend on the atmosphere during the whole of its journey. It will accelerate to very high speeds while climbing at the beginning of its flight, and then turn off its motor. It will then 'coast' on an elliptical orbit that will carry it out of the Earth's atmosphere for a short distance. This is called 'ballistic' motion (see: *ballistics*). It was used by spacecraft before complete orbits outside the atmosphere were achieved. So future long-distance travellers may also be travellers in space.

See: *aerodynamics, engine, jet, supersonic flight.*

To think about

All successful early airplanes were multiplanes. That is, they had two or three sets of wings to give more lift. Why do you think they were replaced by planes with only one set of wings?

The speed of sound is about 760 mph. Why could piston-engined aircraft not be made to travel much faster than 450 mph? (*Clue: the speed of the propeller tip is different from the speed of the airplane.*)

As engines become more powerful it becomes possible for airliners to carry heavier loads. Alternatively they can carry the same load, but take off from shorter runways. Which way of using increased power do you think should be chosen?

Aircraft engines can be mounted in the wings, or in pods under the wings, or near the tail. What advantages and disadvantages do you think each design has?

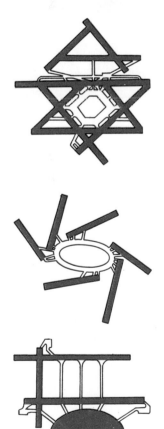

Aircraft take off into the wind. Where winds are variable, runways are built in several directions *(top and centre)*. Where winds are constant, runways need be in only one direction

air pollution

▷ Polluted atmosphere makes a colourful sunset. However, the same industrial wastes are a threat to health and life

Facing page Air pollution produces a heavy pall of smoke over the city of Dallas, Texas. Gases and dust in the air we breathe are not just unpleasant— they are a danger to health

▽ A casual shopper in Japan wears a face mask as protection against polluted air

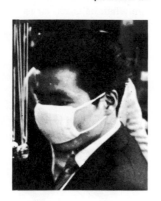

Ever since early man lit his first fire he has been polluting, or fouling, the atmosphere. It is, however, only since the Industrial Revolution, in the last century, that pollution of the air we breathe has reached dangerous levels.

Air pollution arises from modern man's demands for energy – to light and heat his home, to run factories and to power vehicles and aircraft for travel.

Whenever a fuel like petroleum, fuel oil, natural gas or coal is burned, it produces heat, which can be turned into power. But it also produces dirt and dangerous chemicals.

Burning these fuels produces many unwanted substances, such as smoke, and the gases sulphur dioxide, and carbon monoxide. Complicated chemicals called hydrocarbons – some of which can cause cancer – and acids and poisonous compounds are produced. Into the air in the United States are pumped every year 65 million tons of carbon monoxide, 23 million tons of sulphur compounds, 15 million tons of sooty and oily compounds, 12 million tons of dust, and 8 million tons of nitrogen compounds – and these figures are still increasing.

Smoke, sulphur dioxide and carbon monoxide are the main pollutants of the air. Smoke is made of very tiny particles of solid tarry material, which float in the air. Under special weather conditions the particles may mix with water vapour in the air and cause fog.

Fog is the biggest air pollution killer: in the famous London 'smog' of 1952 about 4,000 people died as a result of breathing the sooty fumes. The sooty particles stick in the lungs and cause severe coughing. For a person whose lungs are already strained the fog can be fatal.

In 1956 Britain introduced the first clean air laws. London air now contains 80 per cent less impurities than it did in 1961 and there is 50 per cent more sunshine in winter.

Most fuels contain small amounts of sulphur. When these are burned they produce a colourless gas, sulphur dioxide. Most of this gas mixes with water in the air and comes back to earth as very weak sulphuric acid. This eats into buildings and attacks fabrics like curtains in the home.

The third major pollutant, carbon monoxide is a deadly poison when it is concentrated. The automobile is the main source of carbon monoxide in the air. This colourless gas mixes with the hemoglobin of the blood to stop the body using oxygen properly.

Automobile exhausts not only contain carbon monoxide but also nitrogen compounds, lead and hydrocarbons. These hydrocarbons usually blow away. But under certain weather conditions they linger and cause smog of the kind regularly seen in places like Los Angeles.

The bright sunlight causes the hydrocarbons to decompose partially, producing a haze that stings the eyes and makes breathing difficult. One of the hydrocarbons, called benzpyrene, has caused cancer in experiments with animals. Lead also is poisonous. Many countries have now passed laws to control emission of automobile exhaust.

Industry and home heating also create huge amounts of carbon dioxide gas. The carbon dioxide already present in our air keeps the Earth warm by trapping the heat radiation (infra-red radiation) that our planet gives out. But if the amount of carbon dioxide in the atmosphere were to increase, the world's average temperature might rise, perhaps with disastrous effects on agriculture. The ice caps might melt, causing the oceans to rise and flooding many cities. Some scientists think the climate has grown slightly warmer in the last 150 years because of this form of air pollution.

See: *air, pollution.*

Find out by doing

Ask someone that smokes to blow cigar or cigarette smoke through a paper tissue. A stain should show on the tissue. It is caused by the tars in the smoke being trapped. Even a filter-tipped cigarette will have some of these pollutants in its smoke.

airship

A lighter-than-air gas-filled balloon that has an engine, steering equipment and accommodation for passengers and freight. Airships are also known as dirigibles or blimps. They are not used much nowadays but have had quite a varied history. They were used by the Germans to bomb the Allies during World War I. In 1929 an airship made a round-the-world flight carrying 61 passengers and crew.

Airships fall into two categories, non-rigid and rigid. The first attempted airship flights were made in non-rigid craft. These developed from the gas balloons that had been in use since the eighteenth century. The first problem to be overcome was to find an engine that was light enough for balloon ascents. Early engines were simply hand-cranked. But they did not generate enough power to make up for their weight.

It was the French engineer Henri Giffard who first produced an engine light enough. He fitted it to a balloon and made the first successful airship flight over Paris in 1852. Giffard used a steam engine that gave only three horse-power. And yet it weighed 350 lb. Electric engines were also used before the gasoline-burning internal combustion engine was developed.

Non-rigid balloons keep their streamlined shape by the pressure of lifting gas in the envelope. But the volume of the lifting gas in a balloon varies at different altitudes. This is because atmospheric pressure changes. A means had to be devised to keep the pressure within the balloon constant at varying altitudes. The answer was 'ballonets'.

These were compartments within the balloon envelope which, at ground level, were filled with air. As the balloon rose, the lifting gas would be inclined to expand. The air in the ballonets could be released into the atmosphere to allow for this. At a lower altitude the lifting gas would contract again and the ballonets would be pumped full by the driving motor or from the slipstream of the propeller.

Even so, the shape of the non-rigid balloon was hard to control when it was moving. Various methods were used to overcome this. A rigid metal keel was used. Very elaborate 'skeletons' of rigid girders and tension cables were tried. Eventually the rigid airship was generally accepted as the most efficient method of construction.

The most famous airships are the Zeppelins, named after Graf von Zeppelin, a German who had observed balloons in use in the American Civil War. He decided to use a number of balloons in a line within a rigid framework. This was covered with thin, lightweight fabric which gave a smooth surface.

Zeppelins were highly successful airships. About a hundred of them were used against the Allies during World War I. Only about ten were used for bombing. The rest were for naval reconnaissance.

As part of the Peace Treaty, Germany was required to give up its fleet. In 1924 the Goodyear

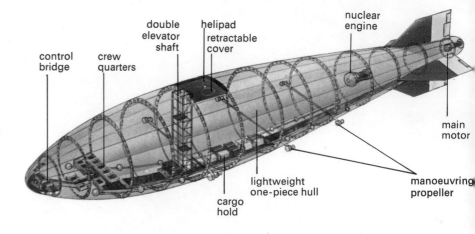

Modern design for a proposed airship. It uses helium instead of inflammable hydrogen, and has a helicopter pad for loading and unloading cargo

◁ The Zeppelin works at Friedrichshafen, Germany, in 1935. The huge skeleton of the airships was of lightweight alloy, and kept the ships rigid while travelling at speed

▷ In recent years airships have been made mainly for advertising purposes. But research goes on into their uses for transport and ocean survey work

▽ Final stages of airship construction. The fabric skin has been placed over the frame. The ship will be filled with hydrogen after being rolled out of the hangar

The R-100 crossed the Atlantic in 58 hours in 1930. The following year she was scrapped because of a disaster to the sister ship R-101

A non-rigid airship of 1902. Engines and pilot were carried on the 'gondola' slung beneath the gas-bag

tyre company began to build airships, and embarked on a most ambitious programme of development and construction.

The Goodyear airships were enormous and ingenious. The gas envelopes in each airship had a capacity of 6,500,000 cu ft. Filled with helium this would be capable of lifting nearly half a million pounds weight. They were nearly eight hundred feet long with a top speed of 72 knots. Distances of 6,500 miles could be undertaken in one hop.

These were powered by eight engines, each of 560 horse-power. The engines could be swivelled to give downward thrust for extra lift.

In earlier Zeppelins the engines were mounted in housings slung beneath the gas-bag. When an engineer had to carry out repairs on an engine in flight, he had to climb down on an exposed ladder, buffeted by the airstream. In the Goodyear airships, the engines were mounted inside the hull.

One of the most remarkable things about these airships was that they carried their own aircraft. Five small airplanes were carried in an internal hangar, and could be launched and even landed while the airship was in flight.

These military airships had to be used in all weather conditions, and sometimes were not easy to control.

The conditions and atmosphere in the car of a passenger airship were not unlike those on a luxury ocean liner. There were large, carpeted saloons and viewing chambers. In good conditions the ride was smooth and quiet and passengers had a wonderful, bird's-eye view of the world below.

Hydrogen and helium were the principal gases used for lifting. Hydrogen is the lighter of the two gases but it is also highly inflammable. Helium is not inflammable but was expensive to produce and vast quantities were required.

One of the most famous of the Zeppelins was the Hindenburg. It was the biggest of its type and was used for transatlantic crossings. Unfortunately it had to use hydrogen for lift, and in 1937 was destroyed by fire while mooring at Lakehurst in New Jersey.

Nowadays helium can be produced much more cheaply. If airships were to be revived, there would no longer be a fire risk from the gas in the envelope.

Aluminium was the lightest material available for Zeppelin frame-building. It was expensive. Nowadays it is readily available and much cheaper.

If airship designers had then had the benefit of what we know now, airships might have continued as an important form of transport. In fact many people today think that airships should be revived as a means of transport. See: *balloon.*

To think about

Do you think there is any point in reviving the airship? What would be the advantages or disadvantages?

albatross

A sea-bird of large wing-span. There are thirteen species of albatross, the best known being the Wandering Albatross, whose wings span nearly twelve feet.

Although the wingspan is vast, the muscles are fairly weak. Albatrosses are not strong fliers, but are very good gliders. They use air currents so efficiently that they can soar on slight breezes. Most albatrosses are found in the Southern Hemisphere, some in the North Pacific Ocean, but almost none in the North Atlantic. Possibly the total lack of wind in the Doldrums, a windless belt on the Equator, prevents them gliding any farther north.

Most albatrosses nest in the southern oceans of the world. They lay one egg, which may be incubated for up to seventy days.

Sailors used to believe that albatrosses were the spirits of drowned mariners, and for that reason it was considered very unlucky to kill one. This story was made famous in *The Rime of the Ancient Mariner* by Coleridge.
See: *birds*.

△ With its wingspan of nearly 12 feet, the wandering albatross can glide for many hours

▽ The wandering albatross probably breeds only once in two years, but the breeding season is long

albino

△ The iris of the eye in an albino is colourless. Blood vessels show through, making the eyes pink, as they are in this albino rabbit. Albinism is passed on by heredity, but it is likely that an albino's brothers and sisters will be quite normal. The albino girl on the right is with her sister

Any animal that lacks the normal colouring matter, or pigment, 'melanin' is called an albino. The absence of melanin can be seen in the skin, hair or feathers. Because the iris of the eye is colourless in an albino, the blood vessels show through, giving it a pinkish colour. Albinos also find bright light very painful.

Albino skin is unusually pink because skin melanin is missing. Albino people can be badly burned by sunshine because of this lack of pigment. They cannot develop a protective suntan without it.

Animals do not become albino. They are born that way. The only way albinism can occur is by being passed on from parent to young. However, albino parents do not necessarily have albino young.

In some countries albino animals are sacred. White elephants are worshipped in Thailand and white cattle in India. Experimental breeding has produced albinos among domestic animals such as rabbits and chickens.
See: *breeding*, *eye*, *heredity*.

albumin

When an egg is broken, you see surrounding the yolk a runny straw-coloured liquid. This is commonly called the 'white' of the egg. It is made very largely of the chemical called albumin. Albumin is one of the group of compounds known as proteins. These all contain nitrogen, and are very important as foods. They are found in all the cells of animals.

When egg-white is cooked it is no longer runny. It becomes firmer and changes colour. It really does become white. This is because the heat has changed the albumin molecules. The change is called coagulation. All proteins coagulate when they are heated. And they do not change back again when they are cooled.

There are many different sorts of albumin. The kind in egg-white is sometimes called ovalbumin. There is another kind in milk, called lactalbumin. The important one found in the blood is called serum albumin.
See: *egg*, *protein*.

Alchemy still flourished when Teniers painted this alchemist's laboratory in the seventeenth century. The two furnaces are its most important pieces of equipment

Paracelsus was a physician and his alchemical studies were mainly concerned with the medical uses of the substances that he worked with

alchemy

An early kind of chemistry that was largely concerned with trying to turn ordinary metals into gold. When this possibility was eventually disproved, alchemists turned their attention to other things, and the science of modern chemistry was born.

One of the most distinguished of the early alchemists was an Arabian called Jabir, who lived in the eighth century. He is often referred to by the Latin form of his name, Geber. One of the processes he described for making gold involved distilling water 700 times. This, he said, would make it white, brilliant, cold and no longer moist. He was wrong, and the whole elaborate process was a complete waste of time. But it was described absolutely seriously and was accepted, although probably nobody attempted to carry it out.

We do not know when alchemy started, but the earliest reliable records date from the time of Christ. It was seriously studied from then until the eighteenth century when it was discredited in the eyes of most sensible people. In this period it was mainly concerned with turning 'base' metals, such as lead and copper, into 'noble' ones, such as gold. This is called 'transmuting'.

Alchemists also tried to find or prepare the 'philosopher's stone'. It was supposed that this would transmute any metal it touched. Another of their dreams was to prepare the 'Elixir of Life', which would give eternal life to anyone who drank it.

'Alkahest' was a mythical liquid that would dissolve anything. Alchemists tried desperately to make it but do not seem to have considered what they would have kept the alkahest in, since it would have dissolved its container.

We now know that attempts to make gold by their methods are hopeless. Although we can transmute individual atoms using nuclear physics, it is not feasible to make gold in worthwhile quantities.

The early experimenters had strange ideas about the nature of metals. They thought all metals were made of the same matter, but that each had different properties.

Lead was matter with the added properties of greyness and easy melting. Heating lead 'destroyed' it by turning it into a red powder, which did not have these properties. Gold was the same matter, but with the added properties of yellowness and indestructibility.

The alchemists tried to remove the properties of lead and replace them with properties of yellowness and indestructibility. They believed they would then have gold.

Alchemists were also inclined to think that metals act like people do. It was thought that man is resurrected to a purer life after death. Gold was metal that had died and been resurrected in its pure form. If copper is dissolved in nitric acid and heated to dryness it forms a black powder. Alchemists said it had died and needed only to be resurrected as gold.

This religious approach to alchemy continued for a long time. The language of alchemy was used by people who were not alchemists to describe their religious beliefs. Religion has always used myths and fairy tales to describe mystical ideas, which are difficult to express in plain words. The language and ideas of alchemy were put to the same use.

Because of this, many texts that appear to be alchemical are really religious parables and have little to do with science.

The earliest texts about alchemy say that it started in Egypt. However, this may not be true. At that time, if someone wanted to put forward a theory he would look for some great authority in the past who had said the same, or nearly the same, thing. This would gain respect for his theory. If he could not find such an authority to back him up, he would just invent one. The early European alchemists may have invented their Egyptian links to lend dignity to their work. The Ancient Egyptians were certainly very clever, particularly at gold-plating and making alloys, or mixtures of metals.

◁ Even while alchemy flourished it was laughed at by many. This woodcut, probably by Holbein, satirizes the alchemist and his assistant

▽ An allegorical picture on alchemical subjects. In the foreground a man sowing seed represents the power of making gold. The corpse represents the 'death' of metals when dissolved. Behind, a resurrected body rises from the grave, to a trumpet call from an angel. This symbolizes the return of the metal, in the form of gold. The meaning of some other events in the picture is not fully understood

The Egyptians could make an alloy of copper and gold. To the alchemists, the result looked like gold. Therefore the Egyptian had created gold. He had transmuted the copper.

The Arabs were keen students of alchemy. In fact the word comes from Arabic. Geber, the Arab alchemist we mentioned earlier, is credited with a great many discoveries that may not have been his. He may have got the credit from some later alchemists who used Geber's name to give their ideas authority.

Geber's great contribution to alchemy was to define the nature of metals. He said that they were all combinations of mercury with different amounts of sulphur. He said that metals were formed underground by the blending of vapours of mercury and sulphur. If the alchemist could copy the natural process he would be able to make gold.

Although Geber's recipes for gold-making were incorrect, he did give the first clear and accurate account of how to make nitric acid. He also made 'aqua regia', a mixture that dissolves gold. Some of his drawings show very useful furnaces and stills.

Ramon Llull, a Majorcan who died in 1315, gave a perfectly clear description of how to make gold. It certainly would not work and yet he presents it as if he had done it. It may be that the experiment took so long that nobody ever managed to finish it. Another possibility is that his followers believed he was not talking about making gold metal but about some sort of mystical idea.

Alchemy attracted many swindlers. Chaucer's *The Canterbury Tales* describes one—as does Ben Johnson's play, *The Alchemist*.

However it also attracted the interest of eminent scientists. Isaac Newton (1642-1727) spent a great deal of time doing alchemical experiments.

Alchemy eventually died out when scientists began to understand the nature of matter and its construction.

See: *astrology, chemistry.*

alcohol

▷ Liquor fermenting in vats to form beer. The liquor is obtained from malt and barley by boiling it with water. Yeast, a kind of fungus, is added and it feeds on the sugar in the liquid. Ethyl alcohol is formed and carbon dioxide is given off, forming the froth seen here

▽ Molecules of the first four alcohols. Carbon atoms *(yellow)* are the 'backbone' of each molecule, to which hydrogen atoms *(green)* and an oxygen atom *(red)* are attached. The oxygen atom and the hydrogen atom joined to it are responsible for the most important alcohol reactions

The name 'alcohol' was once given only to the substance that makes drinks like wine and beer intoxicating. The word comes to us from the Arab chemists of more than a thousand years ago. They were the first people to boil wine and from it make droplets of a colourless liquid. This looked like water, but certainly was not water. For one thing, it would burn, with a flickering blue flame. It even tasted fiery.

Today we call the substance in intoxicating drinks by the special name ethyl alcohol. This is sometimes shortened to 'ethanol'. To a scientist 'alcohol' now means any one of many hundreds of other substances with certain chemical properties in common. Thus there is also the poisonous alcohol from heating wood, which is called wood spirit, or wood alcohol. The proper name for this is methyl alcohol, or methanol. Other examples are propyl alcohol, or propanol, and butyl alcohol or butanol.

Drinks containing ethyl alcohol have been made since prehistoric times. They are made by a process known as 'fermentation'. Single-celled plants known as 'yeasts', or the chemicals they make, are used in this process. These organisms act on the sugars in grain and fruit to produce ethyl alcohol and carbon dioxide gas. The ethyl alcohol remains in solution. The gas makes the liquid bubble. If they are distilled, alcohol in purer form is obtained. Chemical methods have to be used to make alcohol completely pure.

People use alcoholic drinks in moderate quantities to help them relax. In larger amounts alcohol can be a fatal poison. To avoid accidents and misuse, alcohol for other purposes is usually coloured and unpleasantly flavoured.

In the home, alcohols are found in many things. They are used in the making of perfumes, drugs and antiseptics. In industry they are useful for making other valuable substances and for dissolving oils, fats and plastics. Glycerol is an alcohol which is used in the making of explosives and Cellophane.

The alcohols are made up entirely from carbon, hydrogen and oxygen. They always contain the group of atoms called a hydroxyl, or -OH group, and this is why they are so similar. They can be grouped in a series according to the number of carbon atoms each molecule contains. The weight of the molecule increases as the number of the carbon atoms increases. Methanol, CH_3OH, is the first in the series, ethanol, CH_3CH_2OH, is the second, and propanol and butanol follow.

The alcohols with light molecules, such as ethanol, are clear liquids that mix easily with water. They have low boiling points and evaporate rapidly. They burn in air to give carbon dioxide and water, and they can be used in small 'spirit' stoves; they can also be used in automobile fuels to save gasolene. They have low freezing points. The alcohol called glycol is used as an anti-freeze in car radiators.

Alcohols with heavier molecules, like cetyl alcohol, $C_{16}H_{33}OH$, are oily liquids or waxy solids that do not dissolve readily in water.
See: *addiction, yeast.*

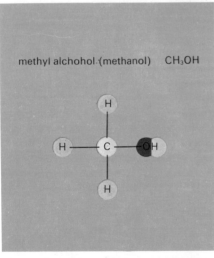

methyl alchohol (methanol) CH_3OH

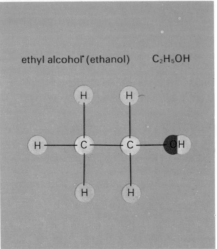

ethyl alcohol (ethanol) C_2H_5OH

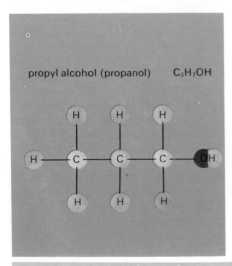

propyl alcohol (propanol) C_3H_7OH

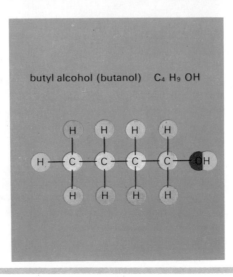

butyl alcohol (butanol) C_4H_9OH

algae

The simplest of all plants, algae are commonly seen in the form of slime on the sides of aquariums and as seaweed. There are more than 20,000 different species. All of them live in or near water.

Algae (the singular is 'alga') range upwards in size from the single-celled types, which can be seen only under a microscope. Some of these behave almost like animals, swimming about to find the best living conditions.

The type that appears as green slime on fish tanks is made up of strands. These are much larger than the single-celled algae, although still very small. The largest types are seaweeds found on most beaches and harbours. Kelp, for instance, grows to 150 feet.

Although algae are very dependent on water, they have a wide variety of living conditions. They can live in sea-water, fresh water, stagnant water and even in the moisture of tree bark. Some cling to rocks or stones and to the backs of other water-living creatures, such as clams and limpets.

Like most other plants, algae live by trapping the energy in sunlight. They do this by means of coloured pigments in their cells.

Botanists classify algae according to their colour: as bright green, blue-green, brown or red. The substances that give algae their colours are called pigments. All algae contain the green pigment 'chlorophyll' and the yellow-orange 'carotene'. Carotene gives carrots their distinctive colour and takes its name from the vegetable.

In brown algae these pigments are mixed with the orange pigment 'fucoxanthin'. In red algae they are mixed instead with 'phycoerythrin', and in blue-green algae with 'phycocyanin'. All of these pigments are used to absorb radiation from the sun.

The green and blue-green pigments absorb reddish light. Algae of these colours are found nearest the water surface where light of all colours can penetrate.

Brown pigments can trap blue and green light and this is found in algae at lower levels where only these light waves can penetrate.

The red deepwater algae can trap the last greenish blue light filtering through from the surface to the seabed.

The vital pigments are usually found in structures called 'chromatophores' in each cell. At the centre of each chromatophore there is often a dense bundle of protein and starch food-material known as the 'pyrenoid'.

Because algae live in water, there is constant liquid pressure on the cell walls. Some water enters the cells. This would tend to cause water-logging. However, most cells are equipped with a special compartment called the 'vacuole'. Water collects in this compartment, which then contracts and forces the water back through the cell wall.

The green algae form the largest and most varied group. There are 7,000 species, most of which live in fresh water. Single pear-shaped cells called *Chlamydomonas* are in this group. They have whip-lash tails, or 'flagella', with which they can move about.

Also among the green algae is *Spirogyra*, composed of tube-like cells joined end to end in strings. *Volvox* consists of single cells. Although they can live singly they always form colonies. More complex green algae include the sea lettuce, *Ulva lactuca*, and the pond weed, *Oedogonium*.

The green algae are thought to be the ancestors of all the green plants that now cover the land.

Blue-green algae are mostly found in fresh water. Millions upon millions of their cells form a hazy bloom near the surface of lakes in warm weather. The blue-green algae that are found in the sea form a large proportion of plankton. This is the diet of many fish and whales.

Red and brown algae contain the species that make up most of the world's seaweeds. Among them are *Laminaria* (kelp), *Fucus* (wrack), and *Chondrus* (Irish moss). But these groups also contain simple species, such as the brown 'diatoms' with their thick glass-like walls, and the thin red strands of *Asterocytis* sometimes found in fresh-water streams.

Algae reproduce in many different ways. The cell may simply split into two, making two cells where before there was one. Some cells produce as many as 16 daughter cells within the body and then release them. Some distribute spores that are like plant seeds and are left on their own to grow.

In other cases, cells known as 'gametes' are produced and come together to form the single

△ The best-known kinds of algae are the seaweeds that live in shallow water

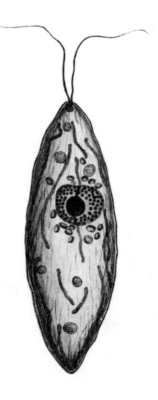

▽ This microscopic alga can swim by flailing the two flagella at the end of its body. The dark nucleus controls its activities

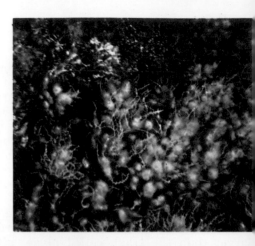

△ Examples of three types of algae. At the left is a red alga. This lives at greater depths. In the centre is a green alga, which can use the sun's red light. It belongs to shallow waters. At the right is a brown alga which lives at medium depths

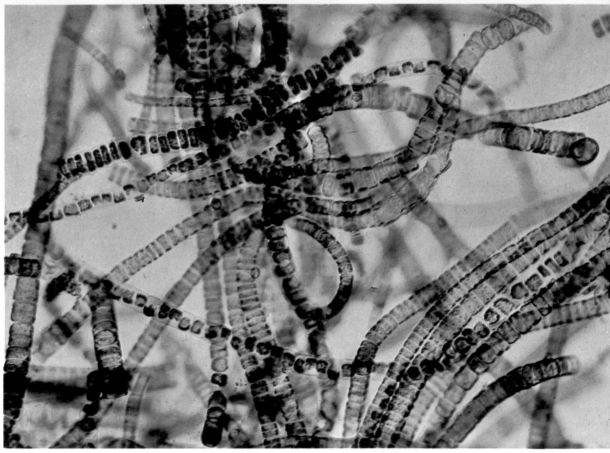

The long strands of this alga are actually colonies of many single cells ▷

cell from which a new plant will grow. This cell, called a 'zygote', is protected by a thick skin, which enables it to survive drought. After a drought passes the zygote can begin growth again. This type of reproduction is more common among algae living in very variable climates.

Algae can be a serious nuisance to man. They block filtration plants, make unpleasant smells and discolour the sides of swimming pools However, they are also very beneficial to man in many ways.

Seaweed harvesting in Japan is a multi-million dollar industry. The crops are used as manure, as food and in making medicine. Seaweed is not eaten much in the West, but in the East it is a sweetmeat and is used in soups.

Although seaweed is hardly used in Western cooking, an extract of algae is. This is called algin and it is an ingredient of ice cream mousse and sauces. Algin and alginic acid are also used to make photographic film, paint hand lotions, beer and rubber tyres.

There has been research into the possibilities of farming algae to provide food for man and animals. Crops were very rich but engineering snags sent costs soaring and the project was abandoned.

Algae have been fed to monkeys in space flights. The algae provided food, absorbed carbon dioxide in the space ship's atmosphere and gave out oxygen. The monkeys' breathing used up oxygen and gave out carbon dioxide, so this created a cycle.

This process may be developed for manned space flights.

See: *photosynthesis, plankton, reproduction seaweed.*

algebra

A branch of the science of mathematics. It is like arithmetic, but as well as using numbers it uses letters of the alphabet to symbolize numbers.

One reason for using symbols in place of numbers is that we often do not know what the number we are interested in is. We are trying to find out what it is.

Suppose a boy tells us that he wants to buy something costing £5 and he needs another £2. We could say this algebraically by writing $x + 2 = 5$. Here x stands for the number of pounds he already has. We can then go on to work out what number x actually is. Later we shall look at some ways of doing this.

Algebra can be thought of as a form of shorthand. For addition and subtraction we use the familiar signs $+$ and $-$. In arithmetic we use $\times$ as the multiplication sign. We avoid using it in this way in algebra, because x is often used to stand for an unknown number. To show that two numbers are to be multiplied together, we usually place them side by side with no symbol between them. For example, $2x$ means 2 multiplied by the number that x stands for. And ab means the number that a stands for multiplied by the number that b stands for.

For division we use the idea of fractions. $\frac{x}{3}$ means x divided by 3. If we need to show a number multiplied by itself several times we use small index numbers called 'exponents'. For example, x^2 means x multiplied by x. x^4 means $x\,x\,x\,x$; that is, four x's multiplied together. 2 and 4 are the exponents.

Here is an algebraic expression using some of the above 'shorthand': $x^2 + 2xy - 3y$. The symbols x and y stand for two unknown numbers. If, for example x stands for the number 3 and y stands for the number 5 the expression becomes: $(3 \times 3) + (2 \times 3 \times 5) - (3 \times 5)$ or $9 + 30 - 15$, which is 24. The brackets show which parts to work out first.

Algebraic statements

To make a complete statement using numbers we must have a 'verb'. We use 'equals' or 'is greater than' or 'is less than'. The signs for these verbs are $=$, $>$ and $<$. Using ordinary numbers, we can then write: $2 + 3 = 5$; $2 + 3 > 4$; $2 + 3 < 6$.

We can also use symbols instead of numbers. For example: $2x + 3 = 7$. This is an 'equation'. It says that twice the number that x stands for, with 3 added to it, is equal to 7. The statement is true if x stands for the number 2, but not true if it stands for any other number.

An equation is a statement that is only true for certain values of the unknown number. These values are called *solutions* of the equation.

An *inequality* is a statement like $2x + 3 > 7$. This statement is true for a range of values of x. It is true in fact for all values greater than 2. To solve an equation or inequality means to find the number or set of numbers that make it a true statement.

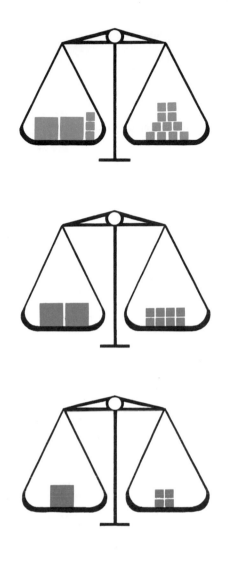

The two sides of an equation are like two equal weights. If they are changed in the same way, they remain equal. At the top, $2x + 3$ balances 11.

When 3 is taken away from both sides, $2x$ balances 8. When both sides are halved x balances 4

An equation can be thought of as a see-saw or balance. The illustration shows $2x + 3$ in the left-hand tray 'balanced' by 11 in the right.

If one side is changed the other side must be changed in the same way to preserve the balance. In the example: take 3 from each side; the equation becomes $2x = 8$. So $x = 4$.

In solving an equation the aim is to finish up with another equation that tells us at once what the unknown number is. This final equation has the unknown number on one side only. Nothing unknown must appear on the other side.

Arithmetic only makes statements about particular numbers. For example, $3 + 2 = 5$ is an arithmetical statement. But sometimes we wish to make a statement that is true for all numbers, or a wide range of them. For example, suppose we wish to say that $3 + 2 = 2 + 3$, and $4 + 6 = 6 + 4$, and so on for *all* possible pairs of numbers. We can do this with the single

If ordinary numbers describe a distance in a northern direction, negative numbers can be used for southward directions. Here the bars represent a boy who walks first 2 miles north, and then 3 miles. This brings him $2 + 3 = 5$ miles north of his starting point. If he then walks 2 miles south, he will still be 3 miles from base. And when he walks 4 miles south, he is then 1 mile south of his starting point, which is represented by -1

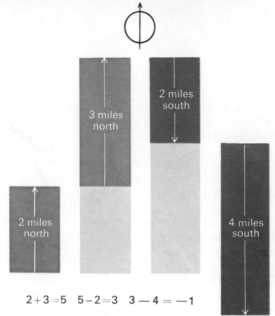

$2 + 3 = 5$ $5 - 2 = 3$ $3 - 4 = -1$

▷If positive numbers are used for the amount by which water in a tank is above its normal level, negative numbers show how far it is below normal. Then 3 represents more water than 2. But -3 represents less water than -2, **although 3 is bigger than 2**

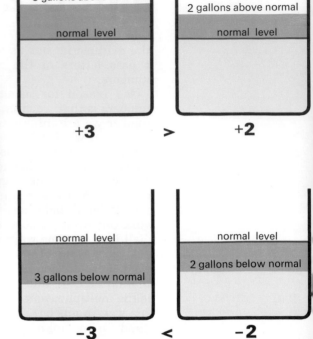

algebraic statement $a + b = b + a$, in which a stands for any number and b stands for any other number. We are saying that when adding two numbers together, it does not matter in which order we add them.

A very important example of a general statement in geometry is known as Pythagoras' Theorem. Let the length of the longest side of a right-angled triangle be called a. Let the length of the other sides be called b and c. The Theorem says: $a^2 = b^2 + c^2$. In words, this is: 'the square on the longest side is equal to the sum of the squares of the other two sides'. This is a **general** statement because it is true for every right-angled triangle. But it is not true for *any* three numbers. Two possible sets of solutions are: $a = 5$, $b = 4$, $c = 3$ and: $a = 13$, $b = 12$, $c = 5$.

Algebra has given us the power to discover – or invent – new kinds of numbers. The 'negative' numbers are examples of this.

Suppose that a boy walks 2 miles north from his home. We can write this distance as 2. If he walks another 3 miles north we can write $2 + 3 = 5$.

If he now walks 2 miles south we know that he will be only 3 miles north of his home. We write $5 - 2 = 3$. So 2 miles has to be subtracted when it is in a southward direction.

If the boy now walks 4 miles south, he will be 1 mile south of his home. We write $3 - 4 = -1$. The minus sign shows that the 1 mile is to the south. -1 is called a 'negative' number. Ordinary numbers are called 'positive' numbers.

Negative numbers could also represent, say, the number of gallons by which the water in a cistern is *below* its normal level. Positive numbers would represent the number of gallons by which it is *above* that level.

When the water in the reservoir is 3 gallons above its normal level there is more water than when it is only 2 gallons above normal. So we can write $3 > 2$.

When the water in the reservoir is 3 gallons below its normal level, there is less water than when it is 2 gallons below normal. So we can write $-3 < -2$.

Algebra can be applied not just to arithmetic but to many other parts of mathematics. One example is set theory.

A set is a collection of objects of any kind: apples, numbers, geometrical figures, and so on. They can be labeled with letters.

All the girls who are students at a particular school, considered together, are a set. Call this set G. All the students who happen to be in one classroom make up a different set, C. These two sets will probably overlap; if there are any girl students in the classroom they will belong to both sets.

We can join two sets together to make a larger set. The set of boy students, B, and the set of girl students, G, at a school together make the set of all the students at that school S. S is called the *union* of B and G, and in set notation is written: $S = B \cup G$.

When two sets overlap they are said to intersect. In the example above, the set of girl students, G, and the set of students in one classroom, C, overlap. The set of people who are members of both sets is called the *intersection* of the two sets. If we call this set Q we write $Q = G \cap C$. It is just the set of girl students in the classroom.

With the aid of symbols it is possible to perform calculations with sets just as we can with numbers.

Solving problems

Many problems can be solved using algebra. The first step is to construct an equation or an inequality that describes the problem in algebraic 'code'.

Suppose we want to find two numbers that add up to 12, and one of the numbers must be twice as big as the other.

First, let one number be represented by x

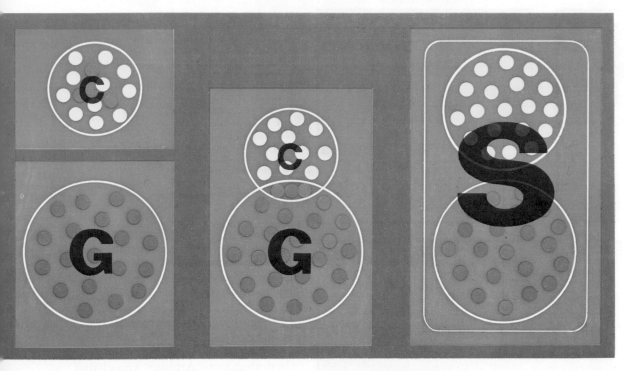

Sets can be made up in any way from any objects. Here G is the set of all the girl students in a school. C is the set of all the students in a classroom. These sets may overlap. All the girl students in the classroom belong to both sets. This is called the intersection of the sets. Two sets can be added to make a larger set. For example, the set of boy students and the set of girl students can be added to make the set S of all the students at a school

Then the other number equals $2x$. The equation says that they add up to 12; that is, $x + 2x = 12$. This is the same as saying $3x = 12$. Dividing both sides by 3 gives $x = 4$. So one number is 4. The other one is $2x$, which is 8.

Some problems lead to equations with two unknown quantities. For example: three pieces of wood must add up to 10 feet in length when laid end to end. Two pieces are the same length. Suppose they are each y feet long. Suppose the other piece of wood is x feet long. Then we can say: $x + 2y = 10$. Some possible solutions are: $x = 2$ and $y = 4$, or $x = 4$ and $y = 3$, or $x = 5\frac{1}{2}$ and $y = 2\frac{1}{4}$. The set of solutions has no end and the equation is said to be 'indeterminate'.

But suppose we know that one piece of wood must be 1 foot longer than each of the others, we can form another equation: $x - y = 1$. There are many solutions for this equation too; they include $x = 2$ and $y = 1$, $x = 4$ and $y = 3$, $x = 8$ and $y = 7$ and so on. However, there is only one solution that is the same for both equations: $x = 4$ and $y = 3$. A pair of equations solved together in this way are called 'simultaneous' equations.

The solutions to the two simultaneous equations can be shown on a graph as follows: for the solution $x = 2$, $y = 4$ of the first equation, mark a point in red whose distance is 2 units from the left-hand side of the graph, and 4 units from the bottom. Do the same for other solutions of the first equation, $x = 3$, $y = 3\frac{1}{2}$ and so on.

Then mark the solutions of the second equation with blue points. By joining up the points in each set, we get two straight lines, called the 'graphs' of the equations. Every point on the red line represents a solution of the first equation, every point on the blue line represents a solution of the second (see page 84).

There is one point which lies on both lines – the point where they cross. This represents the solution of the simultaneous equations, $x = 4$, $y = 3$.

Some statements are true for *any* numbers that replace the letters. These statements are called 'identities'. Here are some important ones:

$$a\,(b+c) = ab + ac$$
$$(a+b)^2 = a^2 + 2ab + b^2$$
$$(a-b)^2 = a^2 - 2ab + b^2$$
$$(a+b)\,(a-b) = a^2 - b^2$$

You can check these yourself by taking a and b to be any two numbers.

The rules that say how exponents must be used can be written algebraically. When x^2 is multiplied by x^3, we have:

$$x^2\,x^3 = (xx)\,(xxx) = x^5 = x^{2+3}$$

This is part of the general rule for multiplication: $x^a x^b = x^{a+b}$. This is expressed in words as: when multiplying, *add* the exponents.

Algebra is a very old subject. Babylonian tablets dating from nearly four thousand years ago discuss algebraic problems. Later the Greeks made great advances. They were interested mainly in geometry, and it influenced

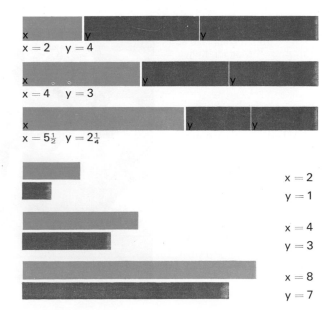

The equation $x + 2y = 10$ has many solutions. Three of them are shown here *(top)*. Three solutions of $x - y = 1$ are shown below

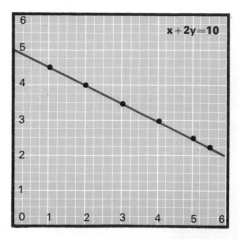

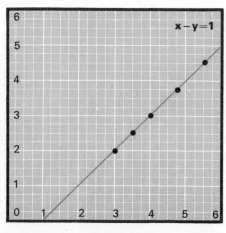

Each point in these graphs corresponds to some value of x and y. Its distance from the left side gives the value of x. The distance from the bottom shows the value of y.
(Far left) all points on the red line are solutions of $x + 2y = 10$.
(Near right) points on the blue line are solutions of $x - y = 1$.
(Below) only the values $x = 4$ and $y = 3$ are solutions of both equations

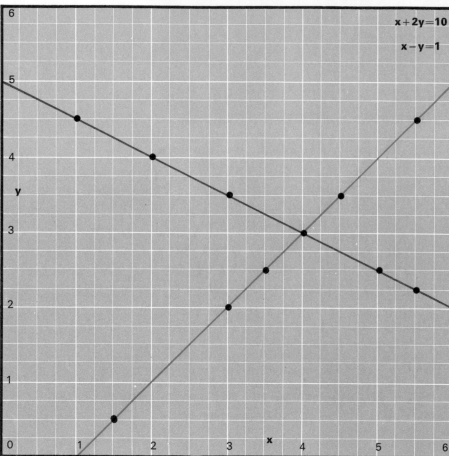

their algebra just as it influenced the rest of their mathematics.

There were great students of algebra among the Arabs and the Indians. The name 'algebra' comes from the title of a book by the Arabian mathematician al-Khwarizmi. It means literally 'joining together'. The subject of algebra flourished in Europe from the fourteenth century, thanks to Arabian knowledge.

Most of our modern algebraic symbols were in use in Europe by 1650. The letters x, y, z were used to represent unknowns by the great philosopher and mathematician Descartes. He was also responsible for the great advance of applying algebra to geometry in a way that the Greeks never dreamed of. For he introduced the graphs that made it possible to describe curves by means of numbers. And that meant that they could be studied in algebra, as we have seen above.

See: *arithmetic, graphs, mathematics, set theory.*

Find out by doing

Tell a friend to think of a number. Tell him to multiply it by 3; add 12; double the result; subtract 6; divide by 6; and subtract the number he first thought of. Then tell him that the answer is 3. (You can see that the result is always 3 by calling the starting number x and going through the steps of the calculation.)

Draw the graph of $y = x + 2$. Shade in the region that shows where $y < x + 2$.

alkali

Harvesting alkali salts from a soda lake at Magadi, Kenya

A chemical compound that can dissolve in water and neutralize acids. Alkalis are one sort of base. Bases are the chemical opposites of acids. The commonest are caustic soda and lime.

Alkalis usually have a soapy feel and a bitter taste. They are caustic. That is, they will burn the skin.

Alkalis are used in the industrial production of soap, glass, paper, textiles and many other things. Alkalis are one of the most important products of the chemical industry.

See: *acids and bases.*

allergy

At some time every year, certain people suffer from sneezing, running nose and watery eyes. They suffer from an allergy. It is usually called hay fever. Their bodies react badly to the pollen from plants and grasses that is blown around in the air in early summer. Some people suffer in the autumn, when there is tree pollen about.

Pollen is not the only thing that can upset allergic people. There are a great many commonplace things like dust and fur that can start allergies. And coughs and sneezes are not the only reactions found in allergies. Rashes and itches are common also.

The substances that produce allergies are called 'antigens' or 'allergens'. There are many different sorts. They include proteins from bacteria and pollens, and chemical substances from primulas and many other green plants.

People may also be allergic to foods. Seasonal fruits and vegetables (particularly strawberries), shellfish, chocolate, eggs and milk are often the cause of food allergies.

The body reacts to antigens by producing 'antibodies'. A different antibody is produced for each different antigen. When an antibody reacts with an antigen in the blood stream, the antigen is made harmless. However, if the antigen reaches tissue cells before it meets an antibody, it causes irritation in the cells.

The irritated tissue produces a chemical called 'histamine'. This seems to be responsible for many of the ill-effects of allergies.

There are many ways of treating allergies. An obvious one is for the sufferer to avoid contact with the substance to which he is allergic. This is often possible if the substance can be identified. It may be that the sufferer will have to avoid contact with the family cat or change his type of pillow if it is feathers that are the root of the trouble.

One means of identifying what substances a person is allergic to – his allergens – is called the scratch test. Small scratches are made in a row on the person's body. Tiny amounts of various suspected material like pollen and dust are placed in the scratches. If the skin around a particular scratch soon becomes red and swollen then the doctor knows which substance is the culprit.

Sometimes it is not possible for a sufferer to avoid an allergen. For instance it is not easy to get away from pollen in the air, even in cities. In this case it may be possible to treat the patient by giving him small doses of the allergen, gradually increasing the dosage. The hope is that he will become used to the allergen and not react so badly.

Another way is to prescribe drugs known as anti-histamines. These combat the histamine which is always released as part of the allergic reaction.

Antibodies also protect our bodies from attack by bacteria and viruses. They can prevent illnesses such as measles and mumps. Doctors can inject antibodies to immunize people against diseases. They take great care to make sure that these injections do not cause allergy.
See: *antihistamine, immunity.*

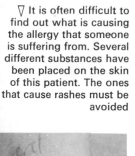

▽ It is often difficult to find out what is causing the allergy that someone is suffering from. Several different substances have been placed on the skin of this patient. The ones that cause rashes must be avoided

◁ Pollen grains as seen under the microscope. This is flower pollen. Many people are allergic to other kinds, such as that from grasses and coniferous trees. Opening pine cones, shown underneath, release clouds of pollen

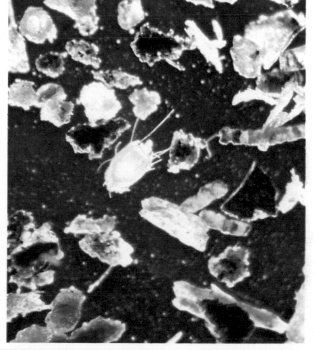

▽ A tiny creature that lives in ordinary house dust can cause allergies in some people. It appears in this highly magnified picture among dust grains. Hospitals are careful to keep wards dust-free

alligator

△ *(Top)* This adult alligator
is one of the many that
live in the Florida
Everglades National Park
(Above) A young Nile
crocodile. Its enemies
include birds of prey

△ All species of caimans
are inhabitants of the
Americas only. They are
smaller than alligators

▷ An alligator of the
Mississippi River

Alligators, caimans, crocodiles and gharials are
the survivors of what was once a very large
group of reptiles that included the dinosaurs.

The name alligator comes from the Spanish
el largato, which means 'the lizard'.

They live in water, eating insects, fish, mammals and each other. All are hunted for their
skins, to make shoes and handbags.

Alligators are found in America and China.
The American species is larger, reaching as
much as 19 ft from nose to tail. The Chinese
species grows to only about 4 ft.

American alligators can live for as much as
50 years. However, because they are hunted by
man, they rarely survive that long.

After mating, the female alligator builds a
mound of mud and vegetation in which she lays
her eggs – up to 80 at a time. As the vegetation
rots it gives out heat and this helps to hatch the
eggs. The young ones squeak loudly when they
hatch and the mother uncovers the nest to let
them escape. Baby alligators are eaten by many
animals and few eggs will survive to maturity.

There was a fashion for keeping alligators as
pets. This was not usually successful as they
soon grew too large.

Caimans are similar in appearance to alligators. They inhabit Central and South
America and grow to 20 ft, although the average
is 6-8 ft. They are aggressive and dangerous.

Crocodiles are slightly larger than others in
the family, reaching 23 ft. They are found in
Africa and Central and South America.

They are distinguished from alligators by
teeth in their lower jaws that show even when
the mouth is shut. In alligators these teeth
tuck into sockets in the upper jaw.

Their diet is much the same as the others' but
they are able to attack and eat larger mammals.
Crocodiles lurk in the water floating at the
surface with only nostrils and eyes above water.
They are easily mistaken for floating logs in
this position.

Crocodiles carry large stones in their
stomachs. This helps to weight them in the
water and compensates for the lifting effect of
the air in their lungs.

Birds often feed on and around crocodiles
basking in the sun. This is safe because when
they bask they are not interested in food. The
birds pick off insects living on the crocodiles'
backs, and even meat from between their teeth.
They act as living toothbrushes.

The term 'crocodile tears' has entered the
language, meaning hypocritical, or displaying
false emotion. This is probably because the
crocodile's jaws appear to be grinning. At the
same time tear ducts may be producing moisture
to lubricate the eyes. The crocodile seems to
grin while it cries.

The gharial and false gharial have very long
thin snouts and very sharp teeth. They feed on
fish but have been known to attack humans.
Gharial live in India in the rivers Indus, Ganges
and Brahmaputra. The false gharial looks very
like a gharial but is of a different family. It lives
in Borneo, Malaya and Sumatra.
See: *reptiles.*

alloys

It is impossible to 'mix' a solid lump of gold with a solid lump of copper. But if both metals are heated sufficiently, they will melt, and become runny liquids. Now it is possible to mix them, just as any two liquids can be stirred up together. When the mixture cools again, the result looks and behaves like a lump of solid metal. But what sort of metal is it? It cannot really be called gold, although it has a golden color. And it is certainly not just copper. It is what is called an alloy of gold and copper.

An alloy is a mixture of any two or more different chemical elements, at least one of which is a metal. Today, steel is probably the most commonly seen and used alloy. It is iron mixed with carbon and various other elements.

You might expect an alloy made of two metals to be rather like both of them, and have 'half-way' properties. Often this is so. But sometimes an alloy behaves quite differently from any of the metals in it. It has special properties of its own. This is what makes alloys so useful.

Pure copper is a soft metal. So is pure tin. Neither of them is really suitable for making tools. They would wear out and become distorted too easily. But if a mixture is made of copper and tin then the result – bronze – is a very hard alloy. Bronze was certainly one of the first alloys known to man. During the Bronze Age it was prized for making spear-heads, swords, cooking-pots and ornaments. Throughout the ages it has been used to make coinage. Bronze can be used to make tools and machine parts because it resists wear so well. And if a little phosphorus or silicon is added, the alloy becomes harder still. It can even be used to make piston rings.

Brass and pewter

Brass has also a long history. It is an attractive and useful alloy of copper and zinc. Pewter is mostly tin, with antimony and a little copper. The Romans also added lead, which makes the alloy softer. However, today the best sorts contain no lead. Gold and silver are rather soft metals when pure. So amounts of copper, nickel and zinc are usually added. The alloys are then hard enough to make coins and jewellery. They are also cheaper than the pure metals.

Tin, lead and bismuth all turn into liquids above 200°C. But if they are mixed in the right quantities, an alloy called Rose's metal results. This has a melting point of only 94°C. And with cadmium in the alloy, the result is Wood's metal. This melts at an even lower temperature – only 71°C. Alloys like this are used in switches for automatic water-sprinklers in buildings. If a fire breaks out, the metal soon melts, and the sprinkling system starts working.

Alloys containing mercury are called amalgams. But, unlike mercury, they are solid. They are hard enough to be used in dental fillings. Like mercury, they are bright, and silvery enough to make mirrors.

The most important types of alloy are those that contain iron. These are called 'ferrous' alloys. Pure iron is a useful metal, but if carbon is added, the result is steel, which is even more useful and versatile. By adding small quantities of other metals such as chromium, nickel, molybdenum or manganese, steel can be made stainless. Steels used in high-speed drills contain titanium, cobalt or vanadium. This makes them very tough. Alnico, containing iron, **nickel, aluminium, cobalt and copper, can be**

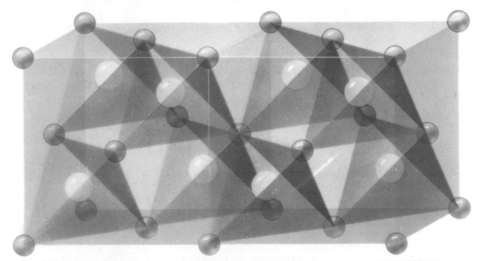

▽ When atoms of zinc *(red)* and selenium *(blue)* combine to make an alloy, they form this crystal structure. Alloys of some other metals have the same structure

smelted and cast to make lightweight permanent magnets.

Alloys are different from the original metal in them because the new atoms that have been added disturb the normal pattern of atoms in the metal. Every metal has atoms of a different size. They fit together to form crystals, and larger groups called grains. When different size atoms are mixed in, they distort the shape of the crystals and grains that form, and produce a different metal.

See: *iron and steel, metals.*

△ The surface of wrought iron seen through a microscope. The brown and yellow areas are two different alloys of iron with carbon, closely mixed together

To think about

Why would it be foolish to make coffeespoons out of Wood's metal?

alum

A chemical salt containing two metals, one of which is aluminium, chromium or iron. For example, potash alum is potassium aluminium sulphate. Potash alum occurs naturally and is used in the production of textiles, medicines, baking powder and dyeing.

When grown carefully in a laboratory alum will form a perfect crystal with eight faces

aluminium

A light-weight silver-coloured metal. Aluminium is the commonest element on earth after oxygen and silicon. About eight per cent of the earth's crust is aluminium in the form of various ores – bauxite, feldspars, micas, kaolin and clays.

Bauxite provides most of our aluminium. This ore contains aluminium oxide, alumina, combined with water. To get aluminium from this ore, the bauxite is crushed, washed and dried to get rid of any clay. Purified bauxite and hot soda lye are mixed and put into pressure vessels. The alumina present dissolves in the sodium hydroxide and becomes sodium aluminate. This solution is filtered to remove various impurities, such as iron.

When the filtered solution cools in a tank, crystals of aluminium hydroxide settle at the bottom. These crystals are collected, washed and heated to give pure alumina. Aluminium metal is extracted from pure alumina by an 'electrolytic' process – an electric current is passed through a molten mixture of alumina and a sodium salt, cryolite. In this process the final aluminium is between 99.6 and 99.85 per cent pure. The metal can be made even purer for special applications.

Biggest refiner

The world's total annual aluminium production is more than ten million tons. Jamaica is the biggest supplier of bauxite and the United States is the biggest refiner.

The aircraft industry is the biggest consumer of aluminium, because of its lightness and strength under tension. It cannot be exposed to high air speeds however, as it has a fairly low melting point (660°C) and air friction in flight can generate enormous heat.

Aluminium also resists corrosion. When the metal is exposed to the air its surface immediately oxidizes, forming a skin of aluminium oxide. This skin protects it from corrosion. Aluminium is also a good conductor of electricity, but the aluminium oxide coat makes it difficult to connect aluminium conductors into circuits. This problem can be solved by putting a thin film of copper on the aluminium, which shields it from the corrosive air.

Aluminium is widely used in manufacturing industries such as fashion, furniture and packaging. It is also used in a mixture with other metals to form alloys, which are easier to cast than pure aluminium.
See: *alloys, metals.*

Hot aluminium is rolled into bars. Every year more than 10 million tons of aluminium are produced throughout the world, largely for the aircraft industry

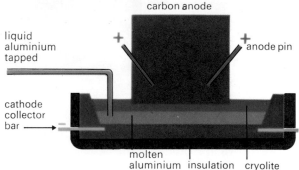

carbon anode
liquid aluminium tapped
+ + anode pin
cathode collector bar →
molten aluminium   insulation   cryolite

◁ Pure aluminium is obtained from alumina by passing an electric current through it. The alumina is mixed with a sodium salt called cryolite in a large vat. The current flows from a block of carbon, the *anode,* and is collected by metal bars, the *cathodes.* A pool of liquid metal forms and is drawn off

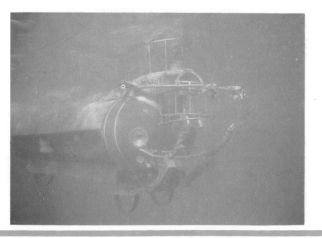

◁ This small experimental submarine, made entirely of aluminium, was named the 'Aluminaut'. The crew can perform work by remote control with the two mechanical 'claws' seen here

△ The first stage in the production of aluminium is mining the ore — bauxite. Depending on the other minerals present, bauxite varies in color from dark reddish brown to a creamy brown. The ore is found near the surface, in pockets up to 100 feet deep, so mining is usually of the open-cast type

◁ A later stage in the production of metallic aluminium is electrolysis of the purified alumina obtained from bauxite. Alumina is mixed with a sodium salt called cryolite and put into a series of vats. An electric current splits the alumina into aluminum and oxygen, and nearly pure metal can be taken from the pool that forms around the cathode in each vat. Here are shown rows of vats in a large aluminium producing factory in the States

Strong but very light, aluminium has many uses in construction. Here a helicopter made largely of aluminium is being used to manoeuvre girders made of the same metal

amber

A hard, clear brownish-yellow substance. It was formed from the resin produced by trees in prehistoric times. Resin, when it first flows from the bark of trees, is a thin, sticky liquid. In the air it gradually becomes thicker and thicker and finally hardens. Millions of years ago the forests in many areas of the world were so dense that the resin flowing from them built up into deep layers. As the years passed, the resin became buried in the earth and turned into amber.

Today lumps of amber are found deep in the earth in different areas of the world. A very rich source is the Baltic Sea, where pieces are washed ashore from layers of amber uncovered on the sea-bed. Sometimes amber contains the bodies of insects caught by the sticky resin when it formed.

Amber has always been prized, and used for making beads and ornaments. In very old times people thought that it was sunlight that had solidified in the sea. The Ancient Greeks called it 'electron'. It is from this word that we get our own words 'electron' and 'electricity', because when amber is rubbed with a cloth it becomes charged with static electricity. It will attract dust and small particles, such as pieces of tissue paper. It is a very good electrical insulator. See: *electricity*, *resin*.

Find out by doing

Rub something made of amber briskly with a dry cloth, and hold it near the back of your bare arm. What causes the tickling sensation?

Amber has long been prized for its value in the Baltic area, where this specimen came from

ameba

One of the smallest and simplest forms of animal life. An ameba consists of just one cell and lives in water. The largest ameba is called *Chaos chaos*. It sometimes stretches to 1/5 of an inch. Most amebas, however, can be seen only with a microscope. For this reason little was known about them until fairly recently, when microscope techniques were improved.

Creatures such as amebas, which come in the group called *Protozoa*, are thought to have been the first form of animal life on earth. *Protozoa* means 'first life'. They have remained unchanged for millions and millions of years. Other forms of life have developed from amebas.

At first sight, an ameba does not look as though it is living matter. It is just a small irregular blob of grey material, and it does not seem to move or do anything. However, if one watches very carefully, one can see that it does very slowly change its shape and move about.

This kind of movement does not look very lively. However, amebas have all the characteristics that biologists consider essential to life. They feed, grow, they have a form of breathing, and they excrete waste matter. They can move and reproduce. They respond to their surroundings.

In the middle of the grey blob of the ameba

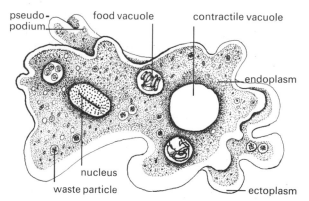

Certain features of the ameba are always visible. There are vacuoles containing food, and others containing water to be expelled. The nucleus controls all the activities of the animal. The soft endoplasm in which these lie is protected by the tough ectoplasm 'skin'

there is a darker speck of material called the nucleus. This is the control centre. It directs what the rest of the cell does. Although amebas are very small it is possible to cut one in half. When scientists have done this, they have found that the half with the nucleus continues to live in the normal way. The half that is without a nucleus, however, does not live long. It moves about for a while but is unable to digest its food. It dies after its stores have been used up. Without its 'brain' it cannot perform all the functions of life.

Outside the nucleus is the protoplasm, living matter that is found in all cells. In the central

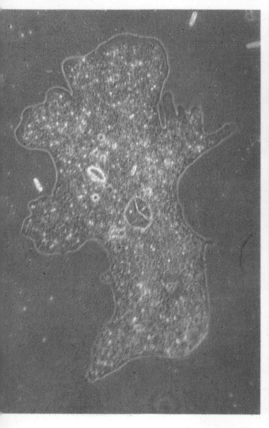

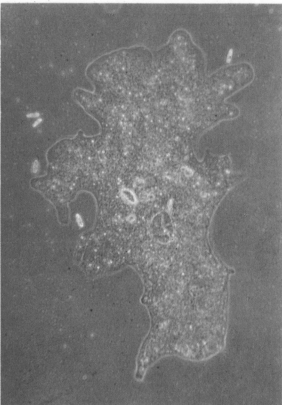

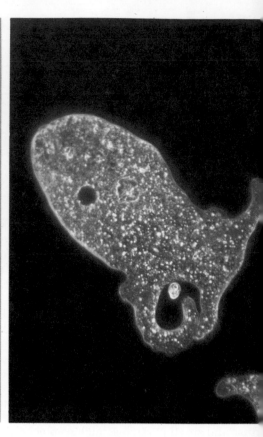

△ An ameba engulfs food. Two pseudopods form at its left side. They close round the prey. *(centre)* until it is encircled *(right).* Later the ameba will flow away, leaving what it cannot absorb

Amebas divide asexually. Each individual splits into two identical 'daughter' amebas

part of the cell this is watery, and is called endoplasm. At the edge of the cell it is more solid and glassy looking, and is called the ectoplasm. It is by changes in these layers of protoplasm that an ameba moves around, and also feeds itself.

When an ameba moves, a part of the ectoplasm at cne side becomes soft, so that the cell wall bulges outwards. The liquid endoplasm and the rest of the ameba's body then flow to fill this bulge. By repeating the process, the whole ameba can flow along. This is called ameboid movement. An ameba is constantly pushing these bulges out in all directions. They are called pseudopods, which means 'false feet'. If they do not meet a solid surface, they are pulled in again, and the ameba tries in another direction.

When the pseudopod touches a bacterium or a particle of food in the water, it flows around it. The food is thus taken into the endoplasm of the cell. Here the particle circulates until it has been digested. Any waste matter and excess water in the cell collects in a small bubble called a contractile vacuole. When it is full, the vacuole expels its contents through the cell wall and out into the water again. The white blood cells of the body are rather like amebas. They destroy bacteria by engulfing them in the same way as the amebas feed.

The ameba gradually grows in size. When it has reached a certain size it is ready to reproduce. The process of reproduction is very simple. The nucleus divides into two. Then the protoplasm separates to enclose each half, so that two identical new amebas are formed. This splitting is called binary fission. It is the simplest method of reproduction.

The best-known ameba, *Amoeba proteus*, is harmless, but others can cause serious disease if they get into the body. Amebic dysentry may be caused if certain amebas get into the gut.

The most harmful ameba

The most harmful type is called *Entamoeba histolytica*. It is a parasite. That is, it can only live on or in other organisms. If it is expelled from an organism, it forms a protective shell, or cyst. Inside this cyst it can survive extremes of temperature and dryness. Cysts can be blown about on the wind. If they land on food or drinking water, they may get back into someone's stomach. Then the amebas will break out of the cysts and start to live again. They will also cause dysentery in the person carrying them. Some cysts have been known to survive for fifty years. The amebas came out and lived again.

It is for this reason that it is important to keep food protected from air-borne cysts. Dysentery is very unpleasant and can spread rapidly if it gets into a main water supply or food distribution centre.

Some amebas have permanently hard shells. These are found mainly in sea water. The shells are gritty and one particular type is made into the drawing chalk used on blackboards. See: *protozoa.*

Find out by doing

Smear a small piece of damp soil across a glass slide, and search with a microscope for amebas among the soil particles. You will probably see many small swimming things, but look for greyish blobs that only very slowly change shape. Look for the pseudopods forming, and food particles being swallowed.

amino acids

Chemical substances, all containing nitrogen, that are the 'building blocks' from which proteins are made. Chemists have found 80 different amino acids in living organisms, but of these only 25 are common. Most of them have names ending in 'ine', such as lysine and leucine.

All living tissues contain protein. Plants and animals build their own particular types of protein by joining together different amino acid molecules end-to-end (see: *molecule*). This forms something like a chain with connecting links of different sizes and shapes. Although there are only 25 common different sorts of amino acid, it is possible to combine them in many different ways. The different types of protein that can be built up number thousands and thousands. The protein in chicken meat is completely different from that in beef or pork. Although the 'building blocks' are the same, their arrangement is quite different.

Two molecules of amino acid are able to join together, forming what is known as a peptide bond. When two amino acids join in this way, they form a double molecule, called a dipeptide. When many acids join together in a chain, the result is called a polypeptide. When polypeptide chains join together they make a protein molecule.

Animals are able to build up some amino acids from even simpler molecules, and can convert some kinds into others. However, there are amino acids that they cannot make for themselves, and that have to be supplied in the diet. These are called 'essential' amino acids. They are distinct from the 'non-essential' amino acids, which the animals can synthesize, or build up, as needed.

Essential for humans

For adults there are eight essential amino acids. These are isoleucine, leucine, lysine, methionine, phenylalanine, threonine, tryptophan and valine. Babies also need histidine. Cystine and tyrosine can, to some extent, substitute for methionine and phenylalanine respectively, and are called 'semi-essential'.

The protein in eggs is regarded as almost perfectly balanced. It has about the right amounts of all the essential amino acids. Fish, meat, milk and soyabeans are almost as good. Cereals such as wheat, rice and maize are an important source of protein, too, but they are rather low in lysine.

There is nothing in animal protein that a human being cannot equally well get from plant proteins. The main problem for people who eat no animal products at all is to get sufficient vitamin B12, which is rare in non-animal foods.

Lysine and methionine are sometimes added to pig and poultry feeds in order to improve the balance of amino acids. Additional amino acids are not usually fed to ruminant animals such as cattle and sheep. The reason is because these animals have bacteria in their stomachs which can make amino acids out of other substances.

When protein from food is digested in the stomach and the intestines, the digestive juices break it down into the amino acids from which it was built. The amino acids are absorbed into the bloodstream, and are distributed round the body. In the liver, some amino acids are changed into sugar, and other substances that can be used as fuel by the body. In other parts of the body the amino acids are linked together into proteins again. They are used to repair damaged tissues and build new ones, as well as to form hormones and other materials.

Origin of life?

Amino acids may have been present on Earth in the very early stages of its history. They may have joined up to form peptide chains. This is one of the processes which could have led to the origin of life.

Scientists have tried to re-create the conditions of those times in a number of laboratory experiments. Amino acids were formed. But exactly how life began is still a mystery.

See: *digestion, food, metabolism, protein.*

To think about

Say there were only two different amino acids, called A and B, and you had just two molecules of each. How many different ways could you arrange them? (AB, BAB, BAAB, etc). Each different arrangement would produce a different substance.

The number may surprise you. Now think about the number of different proteins that can be made using 25 amino acids, with as many molecules of each as you like. The number is infinite.

▽ How two molecules of amino acid join together. One molecule loses a hydrogen atom *(green)*, which joins to an oxygen *(orange)* and a hydrogen from the other molecule. The hydrogen and oxygen atoms that are lost form one molecule of water. The new, large molecule formed is called a dipeptide, and the link between them is called a peptide bond

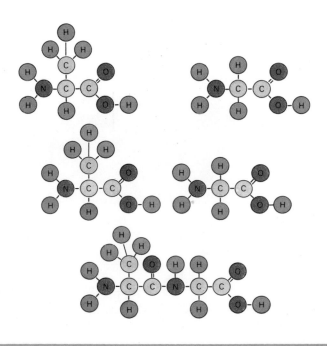

△ Each ammonia molecule
has three hydrogen atoms
(green) around one
nitrogen atom *(red)*

▷ Towers belonging to
an ammonia-making plant.
Ammonia is important in
making fertilizers, acids
and many plastics

ammonia

A colourless gas composed of nitrogen and
hydrogen. It has a distinctive smell and makes
the eyes watery and the nose run.

The liquid that is called 'household ammonia'
is of course not the gas itself. It is ammonium
hydroxide, ammonia dissolved in water. Ammonium hydroxide is a very strong alkali (see:
alkali), and is useful for cleaning in the house.

The gas is manufactured by two different
processes. In the most common industrial
method nitrogen and hydrogen are compressed
and passed over hot iron or platinum. The other
method is to collect the waste fumes from gas-
works. Ammonia is one of the by-products of
making coal gas.

Ammonia has been widely used as a cooling
agent (refrigerant) in refrigerators. It is easily
liquefied by pressure, and absorbs heat as it
evaporates again.

See: *fertilizer, gas, nitric acid, refrigerator.*

Ampère, André (1775-1836)

Ampère, standing, studies
the magnetic field of an
electric current with a
famous colleague, Arago

A French experimental physicist who is best
known for his pioneering work in the study of
electro-magnetism. Studying the relationship
between electric currents and magnetism, he
passed electric current along two parallel wires.
He discovered that, when the currents were
flowing in the same direction, the wires were
attracted to each other. When the currents were
opposite, the wires tended to move apart.

Ampère also demonstrated that the strength
of an electric current could be measured by
placing a compass needle near it. The stronger
the current was the more the needle would be
deflected. This principle is used in the ammeter,
an instrument which measures electric current.

A new science

As a result of these and many similar experiments he laid the basis of a new science which
he called 'electrodynamics'. It has since been
renamed electromagnetism. It forms the basis
of the technology that gives us electric loco-
motives and many of our domestic appliances.

Ampère expressed his most important discoveries in what is now known as Ampère's
Law. It states that when a current passes
through a wire, it creates a magnetic field. The
strength of the field depends on the strength of
the current, and the length of the wire. The
farther away a needle is from a wire, the less
effect there will be on it. The magnetic field
encircles the wire.

Ampère's name, like those of Watt and Volta,
has become a part of modern science. The unit
of electric current is named after him. It is
usually referred to as the amp. It is the amount
of electrical charge passing any point in a
conductor in one second.

See: *electricity.*

The magnetic field of
an electric current. When
no current flows *(near
right)* the compass needles
all point north. When the
current is flowing, the
needles point in the
direction of the new
field *(far right)*

amphibian

The word amphibian means 'a creature that leads a double life'. They are given this name because they lead part of their lives in water, and part on the land. The most common amphibians are frogs, toads, newts and salamanders. Their eggs are laid in water, and the young are able to breathe by means of gills, like fish. They also propel themselves in the water like fish, by means of tails.

As they grow up, most amphibians develop legs, and can walk on land and breathe air. In this stage of their lives they are more like reptiles than fish.

They are all cold-blooded animals. This means that they cannot regulate their body temperatures. They become as warm or cold as their surroundings.

Amphibians were the first animals to leave the water. They appeared on the earth about 300 million years ago. They are thought to have evolved in swamps, from lung-fish, which were able to breathe air and to slither on the mud by using their fins. They formed a very important step in evolution, because from them came the reptiles, even less dependent on water to live. After the reptiles came the more advanced animals, the birds and the mammals. We know from fossils that there were very many different kinds of amphibians in prehistoric times. Some of them were over eight feet long, which is much

bigger than any that are living today.

Amphibians are classified into two main groups: those which still have tails when they are fully grown, and those which have not. In the first group are newts and salamanders, and in the second, frogs and toads. There is also a third and rarely seen group of amphibians, called the caecilians, which have no limbs. They are burrowing worm-like creatures found in the soil in the tropics.

Adult amphibians lay their eggs, or spawn, in fresh water. Frogspawn is laid in masses, and toadspawn in strings. Newts lay eggs in pairs or singly. Each egg is in the centre of a globule of jelly-like material which protects it. The egg hatches into a larva called a tadpole, which breathes through gills and swims with wriggling movements of its tail.

As the larva grows, four legs develop. If the larva is going to become a frog or a toad, the tail gradually gets shorter and disappears. Newts and salamanders, however, keep their tails.

At the same time the outside gills disappear and lungs form inside. Now the creature can climb from the water and breathe air. This change from one way of life to another is called 'metamorphosis'. Although adult amphibians can breathe air and live on land, they must go back to water to breed.

Amphibians are divided into two groups — those that have tails in adulthood and those that do not. The spotted salamander *(far left)* and the crested newt fall into the first group. Newts lay their eggs singly or in pairs. Unlike most amphibians, salamanders mate on dry land. In the second group are frogs and toads. The bullfrog of North America *(bottom left)* lays as many as 20,000 eggs at a time. The midwife toad is peculiar in that the male assists in egg-laying and carries the eggs, wrapped around his hind legs until they hatch

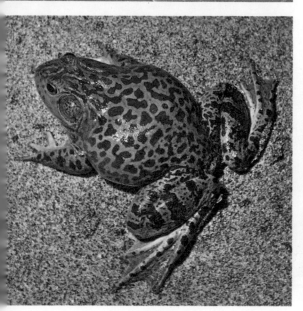

◁ The green tree-frog. Not all tree-frogs live in trees, although there are some that spend the whole of their lives up in the branches. These lay their spawn in the water that collects in the angles between trunk and branches, and the tadpoles hatch there and develop into adults. Note the special adhesive disks at the end of each finger and toe, a great help in tree-climbing

▽ The perfectly sloughed skin of the American red spotted newt, just like a discarded suit. Even we lose our skins, but only a few cells at a time, when we wash. In the case of many amphibians, the whole skin is shed at once. This is not part of the 'metamorphosis', or change of appearance, that amphibians undergo, but necessary so that the adult animal can increase in size

▷ The edible African bullfrog is one of the largest of the African frogs. It eats insects, other, smaller, frogs, and even small rodents. It has a loud snorting call, rather like that of a wild boar

▽ The tadpole of the European tree-frog. At this stage the back legs are developing, but there is no sign yet of front limbs. As the limbs do develop, so the tail is gradually absorbed, and finally disappears

◁The barking tree-frog, as its name suggests, has a harsh barking call. More remarkable than this is its ability to change colour to match its surroundings. Here a frog has just been lifted from the ground, and placed upon a green leaf. At the moment it still has a dirty muddy colour, with spots

▽ After some time, the frog's camouflage adjusts Now the creature has adopted a green colour, much more suitable for sitting on a bright green leaf, and the spots have very nearly disappeared. Many amphibians are able to change colour this way, if only slightly, as a means of protection

The growth of the salamander.
(Top left) Adults with a cluster of eggs attached to a branch under water.
(Top right) The eggs have grown into a recognizable shape but are still enclosed by the protective jelly.
(Above left) The salamander now resembles a miniature adult.
(Above right) The larva. It still has gills and cannot breathe air

The life cycles of different kinds of amphibian vary from this pattern. Some of them, like the hellbender and the mud puppy, do not leave the water. Several types of salamander never lose their gills. Still others are able to breathe through their skins, and do not need to grow lungs. A particularly interesting case is the axolotl, which sometimes spends all its life, and breeds, in the tadpole stage. In other circumstances it may 'grow up' into a spotted salamander, which looks quite different.

There are other unusual amphibians. Treefrogs lay their eggs in the rainwater that collects in hollows in branches. Some never come down to the ground. The midwife toad carries its eggs around in little pockets of ski on its back until they have grown into littl toads. The tadpole of the paradoxical frog grow to a length of ten inches. It then 'grows dowr again into a frog only three inches long. Th largest frog is the Goliath frog, the body o which may reach a length of 14 inches. Th largest salamander is the Japanese giar salamander, which grows to a length of five fee

In their early stages, amphibians are ve; etarians, but when grown they eat insects an other very small creatures. Many of them hav long sticky tongues, which they shoot out t catch their food.

See: *frogs and toads, newts and salamanders.*

anaconda

A giant snake found in tropical South America, east of the Andes. Anacondas are usually green with darker spots. They are water-loving animals and spend much of their time half-submerged, or draped across low branches overhanging water. There they wait for other animals, which they feed on. They kill their victims by squeezing the breath out of them.

Their jaws are loosely jointed so that they can swallow large animals. They usually catch birds and small mammals but can sometimes manage to kill and swallow young deer. Anacondas will occasionally attack caimans, which are similar to the alligator. After eating a large animal, they may rest for a week or more.

Of all the snakes, the anaconda has one of the most fearsome reputations. There are many stories of man-eaters up to 140 feet long. In fact, records of animals over twenty feet long are rare, and it is doubtful if any of the stories of man-eaters are true.

The anaconda, like the boa, to which it is closely related, is viviparous; that is, it gives birth to live young. As many as 40 may be born at one time, each between 1½ and 3 feet long. See: *snake*.

△ Anacondas are excellent swimmers
◁ This anaconda is probably only yawning but it is easy to see how it could swallow large animals

anatomy

The word 'anatomy' comes from the Greek words for 'cutting up'. Originally it meant just that – the cutting up of dead creatures to see how they were constructed. But today it means much more than that. It has come to mean the whole science of studying the structure of living things, whether animals or plants.

Today we use far more than just knives to study anatomy. We have microscopes and cameras to help us. We can use X-rays to see through the skin and tissues without cutting them. And we can even use radioactive chemicals to show up special parts of the body.

The human body is wholly covered by the skin. One way we can discover the shape, place, and working of the internal parts is to cut through the skin of a dead body. Careful cutting open of the skin, to show the anatomy beneath, is called 'dissection'.

The first important dissections were done not on human bodies but on dead animals. Study of the anatomy of different animals, pigs, dogs and monkeys, for example, was known to the Ancient Greeks. This sort of anatomy is called 'comparative anatomy'. Aristotle, one of the great scientists of Ancient Greece, was the son of a physician. About 350 BC he studied the internal anatomy of animals and fish. He described the stomach and intestines, the blood vessels and the internal sex organs. He is called the 'father' of comparative anatomy.

Fifty years later the first human dissection was carried out in full view of the people in Alexandria, Egypt, by the anatomist Herophilus. The body was that of a criminal who had been put to death. Herophilus made a special study of the brain and nerves. Another famous anatomist of ancient days was Galen of Pergamon. He dissected animals and studied the bones that make up the human skeleton. He lived in the second century AD.

From the time of Galen, through the Middle Ages, until the start of the sixteenth century, much anatomical knowledge was forgotten, because dissection was forbidden. Then the famous artist and inventor, Leonardo da Vinci, began to do animal and human dissections.

Modern anatomy really started with Andreas Vesalius. He went from Brussels to the University of Padua, in Italy, around 1530. He began scientific dissection on human dead bodies and carefully recorded what he found.

One hundred years later the English doctor William Harvey made his famous experiments to show how blood circulates through the heart and blood vessels of the body. This was the first link between knowledge of the parts of the body – anatomy – and the way in which they do their special work – called 'physiology'.

During the eighteenth and nineteenth centuries, more and more was discovered about the circulatory system. Scientists soon found out about the other body 'systems' that perform the body's tasks. Thinking and feeling were found to be governed by the 'nervous system'. This consists of the brain, the spinal cord, and all the nerves. The breathing in of oxygen and the breathing out of carbon dioxide are performed by the 'respiratory system'. This includes the mouth, nose and windpipe, and the lungs,

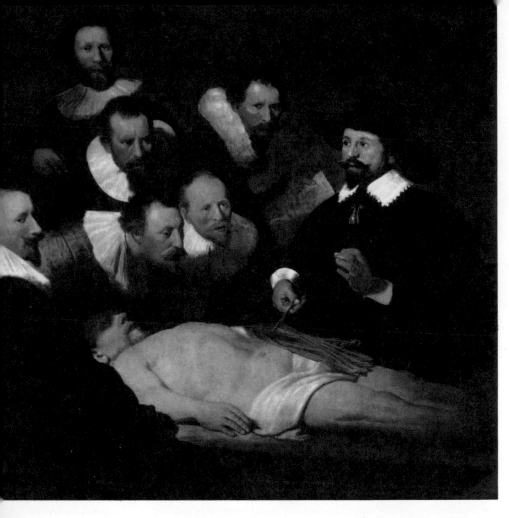

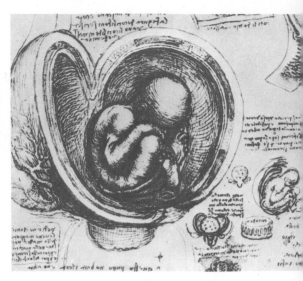

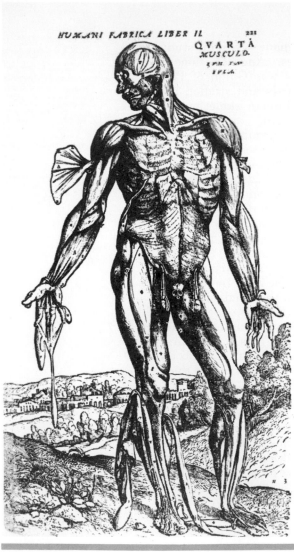

△ An anatomy lesson of
the seventeenth century.
The inner structure of a
dead man's arm is being
demonstrated by a famous
teacher of anatomy in
Holland, Nicolaas Tulp.
(Above right) Leonardo's
sketch of a child curled
up in its mother's womb
before birth. Leonardo's
excellent drawings were
based on his own
dissections

◁ A general view of the
human muscle system
made in 1543 by Vesalius,
who worked in Italy. His
skilful work and clear
drawings of his
observations made him
the first really modern
anatomist

diaphragm and ribs. This system acts as a pump
that draws the air in and out.

The 'digestive system' is responsible for
taking in food and digesting it in the stomach
and intestines. Food material can then be taken
up by the body's tissues. The 'reproductive
system' includes the sex organs. In the male
they produce sperm, and in the female they
produce eggs. When a sperm enters an egg, the
egg begins to grow into a baby. The mother's
reproductive system supplies the growing baby
with nourishment.

The body is supported by the 'skeletal system'.
This is the framework of bones and the muscles
and tendons that move them (see: *skeleton*).

Compare the anatomy of the human being
with the anatomy of other animals. There are
many systems and organs that look much the
same and seem to work in the same way. An
important feature of the group of animals called
vertebrates, which includes human beings, is
the presence of a jointed backbone. This is the
'vertebral column'. The bodies of the higher
vertebrates are all rather similar. They have a
thorax, or chest cavity, and an abdomen, which
is the cavity which contains the stomach and
intestines (see: *comparative anatomy*).

The study of the very fine structures of the
body is called 'microscopic anatomy'. This was
begun by the Dutch scientist Anton van
Leeuwenhoek in the seventeenth century. Today,
even more detail is revealed by using the huge
magnifying power of the electron microscope.

X-rays and radioactive substances are two
modern aids to the study of anatomy. X-rays
allow doctors to 'see' through the flesh of
patients. They can watch the movement of
organs like the heart or stomach during pump-
ing or digesting. The growing and joining up of
bones, both healthy and diseased, can also be
seen.

Liquids that contain a small amount of radioactive substance can be drunk, and then traced
in their movement round the body. Radioactive
iodine, for example, will travel to the thyroid
gland, and can give valuable information about
its working.

See: *physiology, surgery*.

anemia

A disorder in which the blood is 'too thin' to do its work properly. It may not contain enough red corpuscles or there may be something wrong with the corpuscles. The red corpuscles are the small cells in the blood that carry oxygen to the tissues from the lungs, and take away the carbon dioxide. The red substance in each cell, called hemoglobin, is responsible for carrying the oxygen and carbon dioxide. If there is not enough in the blood, the tissues do not receive enough oxygen for their needs. An anemic person is pale and tires very easily. He becomes short of breath quickly when he exerts himself.

Anemia will result if a large quantity of blood is suddenly lost from the body after an injury. It may also occur if blood is lost regularly from an ulcer of the stomach or intestine.

The most common form of anemia is caused by a lack of iron in the body. Iron forms a part of hemoglobin. If there is not enough iron, corpuscles are made that do not have enough hemoglobin. The result is 'iron deficiency anemia'.

In some disorders, red blood cells are destroyed in large numbers. This is called 'hemolysis'. The parasites of malaria, for example, and many bacteria, cause blood cells to break up. Some black people have a type of red blood cell that is resistant to malaria. But people with this type of blood have an increased chance of suffering from sickle-cell anemia – so called because red cells in the patients' blood are deformed into a sickle-like or crescent shape. See: *Africa, blood.*

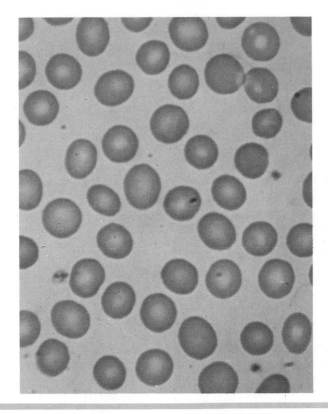

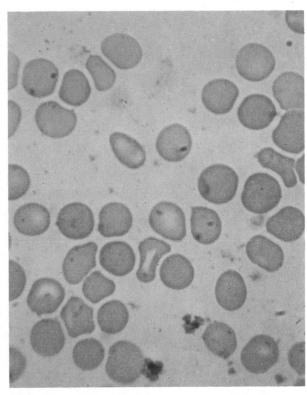

Blood as it appears under the microscope. At the near right is healthy blood, with its red cells normal. At the far right is blood suffering from lack of iron, affecting the shapes of the cells. The blood needs to contain iron in order to absorb oxygen

anemometer

An instrument that measures the speed at which the wind is blowing. There are several different kinds. A familiar one has three or four cups at the ends of metal spokes. These spokes are pivoted so that they can rotate. The wind spins the cups round. The speed at which they rotate depends upon the speed of the wind.

To measure the wind speed, an automatic counter can be attached. This will show how many times the cups spin in a minute. Or a small dynamo can be driven around, and the amount of electricity it produces can be read off a dial. The more electricity produced, the faster the wind must be.

In one anemometer, an electric current heats a metal wire. If the wind blows over this it cools the wire. As a result of cooling, the wire has a lower electrical resistance. By measuring the current it is possible to tell the wind speed.

If an anemometer is placed in a wind tunnel at known wind speeds the readings can be turned into an accurate scale. A rough scale of wind speeds was devised by a British admiral, Sir Francis Beaufort. The Beaufort scale ranges from 0-12. 0 is calm and 12 means hurricane speed.
See: *air, weather, wind.*

Find out by doing

Construct a simple anemometer using 3 knitting needles, a cork and two table tennis balls cut in half, as shown. If one of the cups is coloured you can easily count the number of revolutions per minute and devise a wind scale.

An anemometer that you can make yourself from table tennis balls and knitting needles. It stands in a tube mounted in sand

anesthesia

Medical doctors and dentists can perform all kinds of operations without causing pain. This is thanks to the discovery of chemicals and gases that take away the patient's power of feeling. These substances are called anesthetics.

When people suffer from headaches or toothaches, they can reduce the pain by taking tablets of aspirin or codeine. Touch, taste, and so on, are not affected. Substances that reduce pain but do not affect other sensations are called analgesics.

The first pain-killers ever used were wine, beer and opium, which do not work very well. In 1798, Sir Humphry Davy discovered that breathing in the gas nitrous oxide took away pain. In addition, it made him feel happy and nitrous oxide is still called 'laughing gas'. In 1818 Michael Faraday found that breathing ether also stopped any feeling of pain. The first doctor to perform a painless operation was Crawford Long in the United States in 1842. He used ether.

The credit for getting surgeons to accept anesthetics belongs to William Morton. He performed a demonstration operation with ether in Boston, Massachusetts, in 1846.

In 1847, the Scottish medical doctor James Young Simpson used another anesthetic, called chloroform, to make childbirth less painful. Five years later, Queen Victoria was given chloroform as she gave birth to her son. Once

the Queen had shown that anesthesia was safe and helpful, anesthetics were welcomed by the public.

All anesthetics work by preventing the action of the nerves that carry pain signals. There are four different kinds.

Surface anesthetics, such as lignocaine gel, may be rubbed onto the skin or mouth lining. Or, like ethyl chloride, they may be sprayed onto the skin. They take away feeling only for a very short time. They affect the endings of the nerves by freezing the skin or mouth lining. The surface anesthetic can be used to make injections painless.

Local anesthetics are injected through a needle, which passes through the skin. The chemical, such as procaine or lignocaine, spreads out near the place that the needle entered. Only the nerves in this region are stopped from working. This local anesthesia begins a few minutes after the injection and lasts for an hour or more. It enables a surgeon to perform small operations.

Another kind of anesthesia is *spinal* anesthesia. This time the injection is given in the middle of the back. The chemical catches the larger spinal nerves where they join the spinal cord.

Spinal anesthesia takes away all feeling of pain in the lower parts of the body. It can be used in operations on the lower parts of the body. It may also be used when a woman is giving birth to a child.

In *general* anesthesia the brain, and therefore

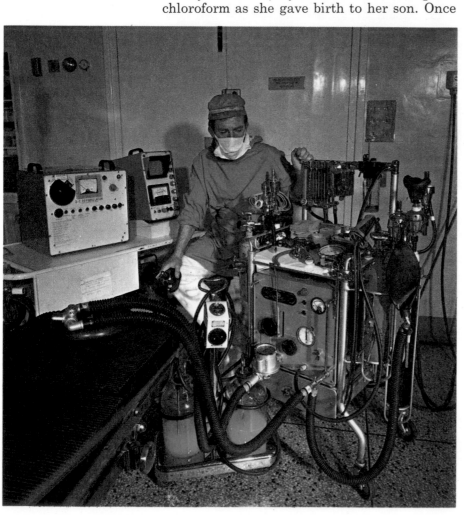

◁ An anesthetist with his equipment. The gas cylinders on his trolley contain nitrous oxide, the anesthetic, and oxygen. They are passed through the mouthpiece, which is also visible, in the anesthetist's right hand

△ Charles Jackson, an early experimenter, tried the effects of ether on himself. He had a long quarrel with William Morton over the discovery of ether's anesthetic action and the credit for it

the patient, is put to sleep while the operation is being performed. The sleep is deep enough to stop any pain. Major hospital operations usually require a general anesthetic.

As long as the patient breathes the gas, he stays asleep and feels no pain. The gases used in general anesthesia stop the thought and action parts of the brain from working properly. They are called the higher centres, and they are effectively asleep. The parts of the brain that keep the patient breathing and the blood circulating are called the vital centres. They go on working.

The medical doctor who gives the anesthetic is called the anesthetist, or anesthesiologist. He first makes the patient sleep by giving him an injection in a vein in the arm. He then places a mask on the patient's face and passes anesthetic gas through a tube into the mask. The gas might be nitrous oxide mixed with oxygen. The mixture is controlled by a machine operated by the anesthetist.

General anesthesia may be needed for only a short operation. The anesthetist can then give a simple injection into the arm vein. A drug like Pentothal can be given in this way so that the patient goes to sleep in a few seconds. The anesthetic lasts for five to ten minutes, after which the patient wakes up quickly. Broken bones can be put back in the right position without pain when Pentothal is given. This type of general anesthesia is called intravenous anesthesia. It was first used as recently as 1934. See: *drugs, nervous system, surgery.*

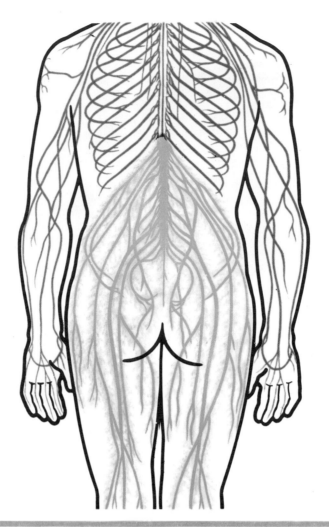

Nerves branch out to all parts of the body from the spine. When an anesthetic is injected into the spine, the nerves below that point lose their feeling and an operation on the lower part of the body can be performed

angiosperm

The most highly developed class of plants that bear seeds. The seeds grow inside a special structure called an ovary, which protects them. In the other class, called the gymnosperms, the seeds have no covering, and are exposed. All angiosperms have roots and stems and bear flowers. When the flowers die, the ovaries in which the seeds have developed turn into the fruit of the plant. Angiosperms form the largest and most important group of plants in the world.

There are two kinds of angiosperms. One kind produces only one seed-leaf, or cotyledon, from each developing seed. These are called monocotyledons. The much larger group of those that produce two seed-leaves are called dicotyledons.

Grasses, sedges, irises, tulips, orchids and palm trees are familiar examples of 'monocots'. Among the vast number of 'dicot' types are flowering plants such as roses and daisies. See: *botany, gymnosperms, plants.*

To think about

Which of the plants in your neighbourhood are angiosperms? And which of these are monocots and which dicots?
Clue: Monocots have parallel leaf veins and their petals are in multiples of three. Dicots have petals in multiples of two or five, and leaf veins in a network.

△ The white seeds of a pepper inside the ovary. *(Top right)* Petals in threes round a monocot's ovary. Below it, a dicot's ovary ringed by stamens, petals and sepals

▷ A typical angiosperm. The stigma above the ovary receives pollen brought by insects, which fertilizes the seeds. The plant's own pollen is made by the stamens round the ovary

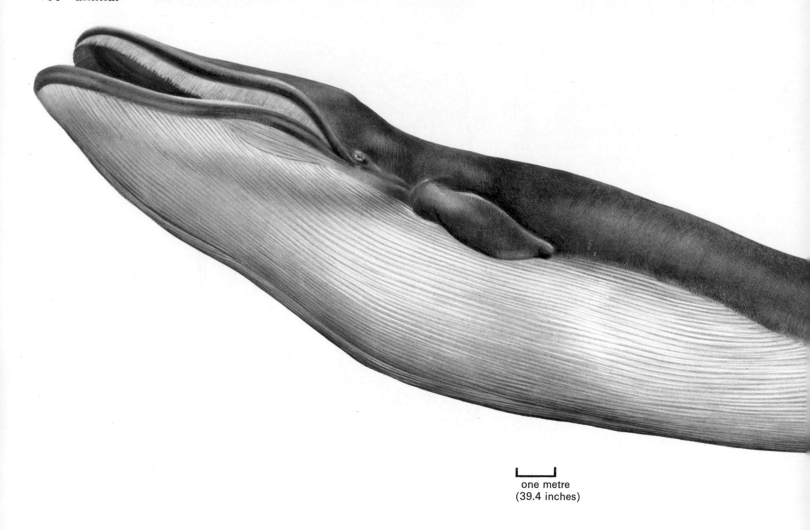

one metre
(39.4 inches)

animal

From tiny amebas to hundred-ton blue whales, animal life fills the world. What are the links between such very different things that enable us to call them all animals?

One thing that all animals can do is move. Some of them can move very fast indeed. The cheetah has been clocked at speeds up to 70 mph. But the barnacles on a beach are mobile too. As adults they do not move one inch from their position. But they have moving limbs inside their shells that they use for feeding.

Another thing that all animals can do is react to things around them. They have sense organs, which tell them what is going on in their environment (see: *senses*). This enables them to move towards food, home, or a mate, and away from danger.

All animals reproduce themselves; that is, they create more individuals like themselves (see: *reproduction*). Some very simple animals, like the ameba, simply divide to make two identical individuals. But most animals are of one sex or the other. The female produces eggs, which are fertilized by the male. These eggs grow into creatures that are of the same kind as the parents, but not identical to either of them.

Some animals have two sexes at once. Earthworms are like this. Each earthworm can produce eggs and fertilize another worm's eggs at the same time. Other animals have different sexes at different times of their lives. Oysters, for instance, all start life as males and later become female.

All animals must find food to eat (see: *food*). Some of them eat plants and are called herbivores. Some eat other animals and are called carnivores. The remains left behind when the carnivore has eaten all it wants are often finished by other carnivores called scavengers. Hyenas and vultures are scavengers. They also eat the bodies of animals that have died.

Some animals are parasites. They take nourishment from another animal without giving anything in return. Tapeworms and lice are parasites that can live in or on the bodies of human beings.

Animals feed in a different way from plants. Most plants take in non-living substances, including water and air. They build up sugars and starches from them. They need sunlight for this process, which is called photosynthesis (see: *photosynthesis*). Animals cannot do this. They

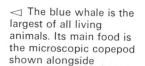

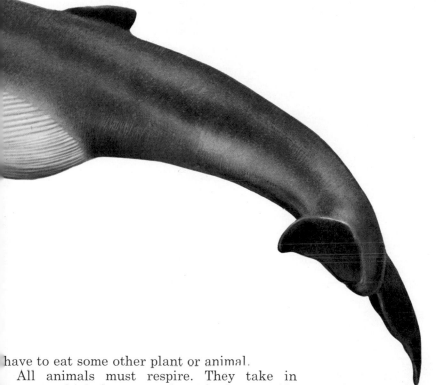

one millimetre
(0.04 inch)

◁ The blue whale is the largest of all living animals. Its main food is the microscopic copepod shown alongside

▽ Parasites live by taking nourishment from other living plants or animals. This leech is sucking blood from human flesh

have to eat some other plant or animal.

All animals must respire. They take in oxygen, which they use to burn food to provide energy (see: *breathing*). Carbon dioxide is produced by this burning, just as it is in an ordinary fire. The carbon dioxide is given out into the air or into the river or sea in which the animal lives. It is then taken in by plants. They need it for the process of photosynthesis. They make oxygen as a by-product of this process. So plants provide animals with the oxygen they need. In return animals supply the carbon dioxide plants need.

The oldest animal fossil known is about 800 million years old. It was a quite complicated animal and we think that simpler animals must have existed before it. The major divisions of the animal kingdom had been established as early as 500 million years ago (see: *fossils*).

Since that time, millions of new species have appeared and disappeared. Today about a million are known to scientists. Probably these are only a fraction of the total number existing.

Biologists classify animals into large groups called phyla (singular, phylum) according to how complex their bodies are.

△ Scavengers do not hunt for themselves. These vultures and hyenas have moved in to clean up after the hunter has left

▽ Carnivores, like this **cheetah, hunt very skilfully** and leave scraps for the scavengers only after their own needs are met

The animal kingdom

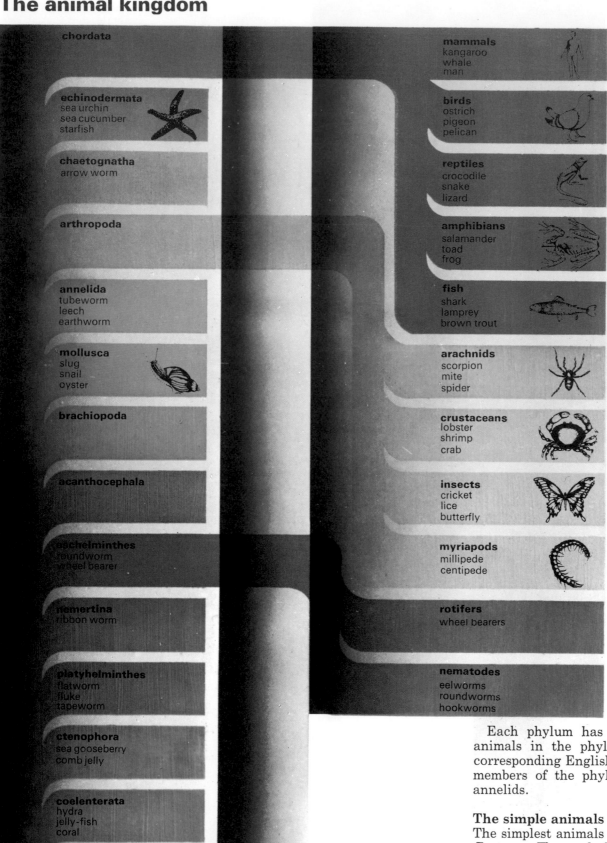

chordata

echinodermata
sea urchin
sea cucumber
starfish

chaetognatha
arrow worm

arthropoda

annelida
tubeworm
leech
earthworm

mollusca
slug
snail
oyster

brachiopoda

acanthocephala

aschelminthes
roundworm
wheel bearer

nemertina
ribbon worm

platyhelminthes
flatworm
fluke
tapeworm

ctenophora
sea gooseberry
comb jelly

coelenterata
hydra
jelly-fish
coral

porifera
sponge

protozoa
paramecium
euglena
ameba

mammals
kangaroo
whale
man

birds
ostrich
pigeon
pelican

reptiles
crocodile
snake
lizard

amphibians
salamander
toad
frog

fish
shark
lamprey
brown trout

arachnids
scorpion
mite
spider

crustaceans
lobster
shrimp
crab

insects
cricket
lice
butterfly

myriapods
millipede
centipede

rotifers
wheel bearers

nematodes
eelworms
roundworms
hookworms

This chart shows how the fifteen main phyla are divided into sub-phyla and further divided into classes. The chordata at the top of the tree contains the higher animals, including humans. At the other end are the protozoa, very simple, single-celled animals. The greatest number of species in any phylum is to be found in Arthropoda, which includes the insects

Each phylum has a Latin name, but the animals in the phylum can be called by a corresponding English name. For example, the members of the phylum *Annelida* are called annelids.

The simple animals
The simplest animals are placed in the phylum *Protozoa*. They only have one cell. The ameba is probably the best-known example (see: *ameba*). Some of them, like *Euglena*, are rather like plants, because they use sunlight to build up food in their bodies by photosynthesis. It is sometimes hard to decide whether they are really animals or plants. It may be that in the distant past all organisms were like this.
Slightly more complicated animals are found

Most animals have enemies of one kind or another, usually bigger, stronger animals on the lookout for food. Not all predators can be taken in by camouflage, so a more reliable form of defence — armour — can be lifesaving. The Carolina box-turtle is aptly named. In the space of moments, when a dangerous enemy is near, it can enclose itself in a box-like suit of hard horny armour. It pulls its head and limbs in under the tough shell, or carapace, leaving nothing showing. Even when turned over *(bottom)*, all it presents to an enemy is the underside of the 'box', just as tough as the top

△ Bugs or buds? Lantern y nymphs deceive their ird enemies, camouflaged with waxy furred tails

▽ Lizard or leaf? The leaftailed gecko looks most unappetizing in the guise of a dry, dead leaf

◁Another bizarre example of animal coloration is seen in the nymph stage of the South African insect called the mantis. Many animals camouflage themselves as inedible objects like dead leaves and twigs. The mantis, a beautiful pink at this stage, is hard to recognize as anything, unless it is a half-open tropical flower

▽ Found in many parts of the world are stick-insects, which really are very hard to see when they stay still. They have a colour like dead tree bark, limbs long and thin just like twigs, and even little projections on their backs and sides that look as though they could be thorns. When they do move, it is very slowly, to avoid attracting attention

▷The marine iguana lives only in the Galapagos Islands, and is a very interesting example of how animals have adapted during evolution. Its distant ancestors lived in the sea, but then came out onto dry land to live. Today the iguana is at home in the water again, although it loves to bask in the sun on rocks. It lives on seaweed, and can dive to great depths. Here a marine iguana emerges from the sea, to be confronted with a highly coloured crab. They are not enemies, and will ignore one another

▽ Besides being adapted to living in the sandy Namib desert in South Africa by means of its sandy coloured camouflage, the palmate gecko has webbed feet for running quickly over the sand. Here one of these lizards prepares to gulp down a dune cricket it has just seized. Note that the insect also has feet adapted for sandy ground

▷ Birds are the chief enemies of many insects. But they themselves have enemies they fear, whether larger birds of prey, wild cats — or humans. A superb example of protective colouring is seen in the Australian white-throated night jar. Crouching on the ground, it looks just like a piece of log. It 'freezes' into a very unbirdlike shape

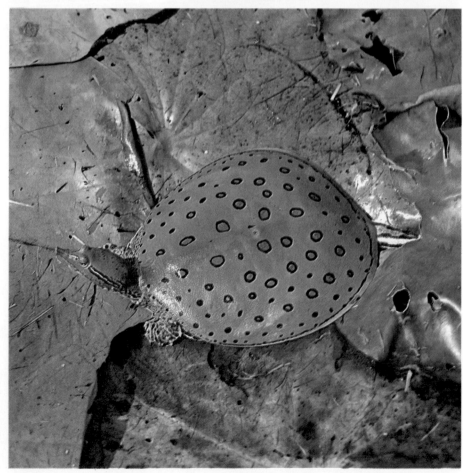

◁ The softshell turtle of North America spends most of its time on the muddy floor of riverbeds, and so has a muddy colour on its upper surface. The lighter coloured spots could be mistaken for stones, dead leaves, or even bubbles from rotting vegetation. An enemy looking down into the water would have a very hard job spotting the reptile

▷All mammals — animals that suckle their young — are related, however distantly. The Sunda Island gibbon, of the South China Sea, is a mammal, and so it is a relative of man. Here the similarity is not hard to see, although the immensely long limbs may seem comic

▽ A mammal, too, is the duckbill platypus of Australia. But who would believe that this could be related in any way to human beings? It must surely be one of the oddest creatures alive. It suckles its young, but they are laid as eggs, it has webbed feet, a tail like a beaver's, and a beak just like a duck's

The roundworms, which belong to the phylum *Aschelminthes*, are the simplest animals with an anus. This is an opening separate from the mouth through which waste is passed out. The roundworms are very numerous and live almost everywhere on earth. Most of them are parasites, and there are about fifty species that may live as parasites on the human body. The rotifers also belong to *Aschelminthes*. They are small animals with quite complex bodies, and with a 'crown' of hairs that can vibrate. This enables them to swim through the water. The current of water set up is also useful in bringing food to the animal.

The spiny-headed worms are closely related to the roundworms. They belong to the phylum *Acanthocephala*, and they are all parasites. Arrow-worms (phylum *Chaetognatha*) live in the sea and seem to be unrelated to other worms.

The brachiopods (phylum *Brachiopoda*) are animals with shells that live in water and resemble clams. In fact they are quite unrelated to true clams, which belong to the phylum *Mollusca*. Other molluscs are the snails, mussels, and the squids. The molluscs are one of the most successful of all animal groups. They include the giant clams, which burrow into coral reefs and can grow to six feet across.

Segmented animals

The phylum *Annelida* contains the segmented worms. The bodies of these worms consist of a series of sections linked together. The common earthworm is a dull-looking but very successful member of the phylum. Many of the sea-dwelling members are quite beautiful.

Primitive forms of the annelids have segments that are very similar to each other. More advanced creatures have segments with specialized functions. Many species have bristles on each segment for movement.

Early annelids may have been the ancestors of the next phylum *Arthropoda*. They have an armour of a hard substance called chitin. Like the annelids the arthropods have bodies divided into segments. The name arthropod means 'having jointed legs'. In addition to these limbs they have more developed muscles and nerves.

The phylum *Echinodermata* contains the starfish, sea urchins and sea cucumbers. They have a spiny armour on the outside supported by hard plates inside. They can move and grasp things with tube feet, which they pump up with water.

The phylum *Chordata* contains animals that have an internal support to their bodies at some time in their lives. This support is called the notochord. Some of the chordates have a notochord only for a brief period when young. They

ach animal species has eacted to its surroundings y developing special daptations. The bat (top) as extremely sensitive ars as a navigational aid. he very large pupils of s eyes enable the loris above) to see in poor ght

in the phylum *Porifera*, the sponges. Here many cells have come together, some with one task, some with another. For example, some of the cells keep water flowing through the body of the sponge. At the same time they absorb tiny plants or animals from the water. They then pass on some of this food to other cells. Some of the other cells simply have the job of covering and protecting the main body of the sponge.

The phylum *Coelenterata* includes the jellyfishes, sea anemones, and corals, as well as some other animals. Their bodies are built in two layers. The outer layer is called the ectoderm. The inner layer lines the cavity in which food is digested, and is called the endoderm.

Most of these animals kill or stun their prey with poisonous stings. There is another phylum called the *Ctenophora*, which is very similar. But they do not have stings, and catch their prey on sticky tentacles.

All other animals have a more complicated structure. In the early stages of their growth they have three layers of tissue. The muscles and some special organs of the higher animals develop out of the extra layer. The simplest of these creatures are the animals called 'worms'. Flatworms (phylum *Platyhelminthes*) are often parasitic. Bootlace worms (phylum *Nemertina*) live on the seashore and feed on smaller animals. These worms eject the food they cannot digest.

Animal species move in many different ways. ome, such as the tortoise, need not move fast — and cannot. On the other hand, the cheetah depends on its speed for hunting. This chart shows the different speeds animals can reach

| 10 | 20 | 30 | 40 | 50 | 60 | 70 mph |

All animals move in search of prey and mates, take in oxygen to burn the food they eat, and reproduce their kind. They have found countless different ways of doing these things, as the pictures on this page illustrate. The aquatic fly larvae *(near right)* are submerged and breathing through gills. The caterpillar pictured below them has cavities which show as dots along its side, and a network of tubes leading from them. These carry air to the points in the body where it is needed

For moths *(far right)* to reproduce, two of opposite sex must meet and mate. The hydra below them merely buds, like a plant, although it is an animal

The starfish *(below)* moves across the ocean bed by rising up on its arms. The grasshopper *(bottom),* has three pair of legs. The last pair are strongly muscled for jumping

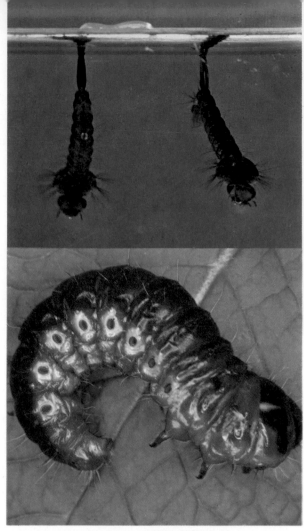

are often wormlike in appearance.

The most important of the chordates are the vertebrates, to which man belongs. Instead of a notochord they have a spinal column made up of bony sections called vertebrae.

The first true vertebrates were the fish. They had bony outside armour and a skeleton of cartilage. Cartilage is a much softer tissue than bone. Apart from the sharks, most fishes now have a skeleton of bone.

Most fish have scales protecting their bodies, but sharks have hard spiky projections called denticles. The eggs of most fish are fertilized by the male outside the body. Once again sharks are the exception.

Fish were the ancestors of amphibians. Amphibians have fish-like larvae, but the adults live on the land. Their lungs are poorly developed and they breathe partly through their skins. They have to keep their skins moist to do this. They have good sight and hearing.

Reptiles are similar to amphibians, but they have tough waterproof skins. They have proper lungs. They lay their eggs on land. These hatch into miniature adults without going through a larva stage. The huge dinosaurs of the past were reptiles. Today the group is made up only of turtles, crocodiles, snakes and lizards.

The mammals are included in the vertebrates. There are about 3,800 species. They are very active, and are usually covered with hair or fur. They can regulate the temperature of their blood.

The young of mammals are born alive, except in the case of the platypus and the spiny ant-eater, which lay eggs. The young animal is fed with milk from the body of its mother.

Mammals include herbivores, carnivores, and scavengers. Most of them are small. About a half of the mammal species are rodents. They have fast growing front teeth, which are kept short and sharp by gnawing. Another quarter of the mammal species are bats.

The giants of the mammals are the whales and elephants. The mammals closest to man are called the primates. They began with creatures rather like lemurs and bush babies. Today they include the monkeys, the apes and man.

Creatures like men appeared within the last million years. The species *homo sapiens,* which is his modern form, appeared very recently within the last 50,000 years. He has been especially successful. But he now threatens the environment he shares with all the other animals in the world.

The birds evolved later in geological time than the mammals. They are warm-blooded vertebrates, specialized for flight. Their feathers insulate them against cold. Birds all lay eggs which have to be incubated, or kept warm, till they hatch. Like mammals, they care for their young for the early part of their lives.

To think about

In what phyla do you think these animals belong?

tortoise	earthworm
clam	cat
salamander	ameba
jellyfish	moth

The biggest living thing is not an animal. Do you know what it is?

annual ring

Each year that a tree grows is marked in the trunk as a ring. To find out how old a tree is, count these annual rings.

A very young tree has a core surrounded by hollow cells. These cells, called the xylem, form tubes to carry the sap up the trunk. More cells grow each year. This forms a new annual ring which makes the tree trunk broader.

During the early spring, when it is warm and rainy, the cells grow fast. They are fat and there are many of them. In the summer, when it is hot and dry, growth slows. The new cells are small and packed tightly together. During the fall and winter, the tree does not grow. So each annual ring shows up as a broad ring of large light-coloured wood, with a dark edge.

Oaks, and some other trees that lose their leaves in the winter, have different rings. The spring wood is dense and dark. The summer wood is light and spongy.

In a good year, the tree will grow fast. The annual ring will be wide. If the spring is cold, if there is a flood, or the summer is too dry, growth will be poor. That year's ring will be narrow. In a country where the climate is the same all year round, the rings cannot be seen.

By counting annual rings, men have found

◁Light-coloured rings in this tree trunk show rapid growth periods. Dark rings occur in winter when growth slows or stops. They show how many winters the tree has lived through. This fish scale △ (greatly enlarged) also has age rings

trees that are over 3,000 years old, and they have also learned what the climate was like.

Scaly fish, like salmon and trout, also have growth rings on their scales which grow only in the warmer months. We can tell their ages in this way (see: *tree*).

ant

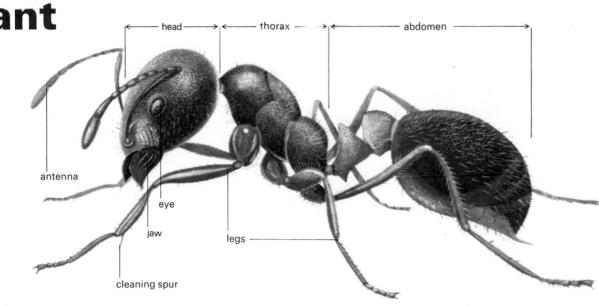

head ← thorax → abdomen

antenna

eye

jaw

legs

cleaning spur

△ Three castes of the fire ant. The largest one, at the top, is a queen. Her wings are almost entirely nibbled away. Below her is a soldier and at the bottom a worker. The worker is also shown enlarged

Ants have always interested men because, like us, they live together in complicated societies and co-operate with one another. Like bees and termites, they are 'social' insects, and the way they live is worth hours of study.

Over 6,000 species of ant are named, and about 10,000 species may exist. The species do not differ much in colour or shape as species of birds do. They differ mostly in behaviour. Termites are sometimes called 'white ants', but really they are not ants at all. They are more like cockroaches.

Ants looking like modern ones appeared long ago. Their first ancestors are not known. Probably they were originally tropical creatures. Most ant species today still live in the

tropics, but ants are found all over the world. They all belong to the family *Formicidae*. The burning acid that some ants spray or inject when they bite is called formic acid.

The ant has a body made up of three main parts. The head bears two feelers, called antennae (see: *antenna*). The mouth has several complicated 'mouth parts'. These include a tongue and the grasping or biting jaws, called the mandibles. The eyes are 'compound eyes.' They are large and include many separate small eyes.

The middle part of the body, the thorax, has three sections. Each section has one pair of legs. The ant, then, has six legs, like all insects.

The last part of the body is the abdomen. It

△ A queen ant — life size. The queen is the most important individual in the colony. She may lay thousands of eggs at one time

▷ South African safari ants, having raided a termite nest, carry off their victims in their jaws. These ants have a formidable reputation for their ability to kill and eat every living thing in their path that does not run away fast enough

△ A driver ant. These are frequently attracted to lamps at night. They do not sting or bite, although they are destructive

is joined to the thorax by a narrow waist. In winged forms there are two pairs of wings on the thorax, supported by powerful muscles.

Almost all ant species live in colonies. These range from a few ants to 100,000. They live in many different ways, but all form complex societies. A typical society consists of a queen and her offspring. The nest contains eggs, developing ants, female workers and males. The female workers are sterile – they cannot lay eggs. There are also fertile females, which will one day lay the eggs that begin new nests. Sometimes there are soldier ants as well.

Another specialized type is the doorkeeper. He closes the opening hole with his head and only lets ants enter. These different kinds of ant look different and do different work. The kinds are called castes.

The queen is very large and full of eggs. She stays deep in the nest and does nothing but eat and lay eggs. The workers feed and clean her. When she lays an egg, a worker carries it away. It is placed in a pile of other eggs. Workers keep turning and licking the eggs to keep them moist and clean. When a larva hatches out of an egg, it stays in the pile. It lives by eating some of the other eggs and grows.

Insects are covered by a hard shell-like cuticle. When they grow, they discard the old cuticle and grow a new, larger one. This is called moulting. After the first moult, the larva is carried to another pile. This is spread out so that workers can clean and feed each larva. The larvae are fed liquid from the mouths of the workers, and food brought from outside. Larvae that will become queens receive a special liquid from a gland on the worker's body. Worker ants lay eggs that they feed to the larvae and the queen.

After several moults, the larva becomes still, stops eating and spends several days changing into the form of an adult ant. This stage is called the pupa. In most species, the larva spins a silken cocoon around itself as it becomes a pupa. Workers carry the pupae to the warmest

and driest part of the nest. When they hatch from the pupa, the new ants are adult, but pale. They darken as they grow older.

Some of the eggs that the queen lays become workers or fertile females. The others become males. Females and males take longer to develop than workers do, and have wings.

The workers do all the work of the colony. They keep it clean, care for the queen and the young and guard the door. They hunt for food, take care of the food that is grown in the nest, prepare food that is brought in, and feed each other.

Once a year the male ants swarm. A mass of ants may be seen flying around a tree or one part of a path. The females then fly by and each finds a mate. After mating, the female is fertilized, or ready to produce eggs. She goes off to start a nest for her future offspring. The male dies.

Building nests

Ants live in many kinds of nests. A few species do not have nests. The most interesting of these are the army ants. These live mostly in South America, Africa and India. They are continually on the move, marching in columns and eating anything in their path. They even eat large animals that are wounded or tied up and cannot escape. Larvae and pupae are carried in the column by workers.

When the queen is ready to lay more eggs, the column stops. The ants find a hollow tree or a branch. Some grasp the tree. Others grasp the legs of these ants. As each ant hangs onto the legs and bodies of the ants around it, a mass of ants is formed.

Sometimes they hang like a curtain inside the hollow trunk. The queen shelters behind this. Other times she stays at the centre of a rounded swarm. Here the ants stay until the pupae have hatched into workers and the new larvae are ready to be carried.

Ants that nest underground dig with their mandibles or front legs. They carry the dirt away in their mouths. Each species forms

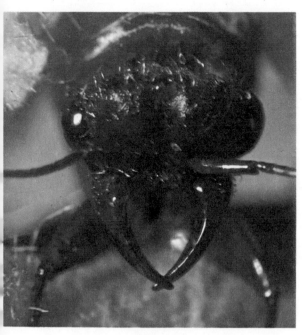

◁ The mouth parts of this winged safari ant are fearsome and when you consider in how many thousands ants swarm, you can imagine the extensive damage they do

▷ Wood ants keep 'herds' of aphids which they 'milk'. Here one can be seen obtaining a drop of honeydew from an aphid

▽ Wood ants also convey food by a chain system, each ant passing his morsel to the next one in the chain. The one on the left is passing to the one in the middle. Others to the right await their turn

different sort of nest. Some nests may go down nine feet and cover a circle ten yards in diameter. Above ground, some ants heap up dirt, then dig tunnels in it. Others build up walls and place roofs over them. *Lasius niger* builds tiny rooms with walls and domed ceilings less than an eighth of an inch thick. The ceiling of each room is supported by columns.

Ant hills cover the underground tunnels. The heap of dirt or grass and pine needles traps the sunlight. It is warmer than the surrounding soil and heats the nest. Wood ants make air holes near the top of their mound. They open them on hot days, make them smaller towards evening, and close them when it is cold.

Several species of ant make nests out of leaves. One rolls up a leaf and glues its edges together. Another, *Oecophylla*, uses an amazingly complicated method. The ants explore the leaves of a tree. One finds two leaves almost touching. It grasps one with its feet and the other in its jaws and pulls. More ants come to its aid. They may form a living chain of up to five ants. The end ones pull and use the middle ones as a rope.

When the leaves are close enough together, another ant brings up a larva. He carries it from one leaf to the other, back and forth. While it is being carried, the larva spins a silk thread. With this the ant weaves a curtain to hold the leaves together and make a shelter.

Ants eat many things, including seeds, insects, plants and dead animals. Soldier ants eat living animals. Some ants even eat other ants.

Many ants store seeds in their nest. Others chew dead insects and make them into a paste that can be stored or fed to the larvae. Ants that live in deserts, where it is often too hot and dry to go out, store liquids. Since they have no pots, they use ants for storage vessels. These ants, called 'repletes', drink so much that their abdomens swell up like balloons. They hang onto the ceiling of a chamber in the nest. When an ant is thirsty, it strokes a replete, which

▷ Although much smaller than their victim, these ants, by sheer weight of numbers, can overwhelm and dispose of him. Each will cut up and take off small pieces until the whole carcass is removed

gives it a drop of liquid.

Some ants keep 'herds of cattle'. These are aphids and other 'plant-lice'. Aphids are tiny insects that live on plants and suck their juices. Gardeners regard them as a pest. Aphids normally produce a drop of sweet liquid called 'honeydew' after eating. When an ant is taking care of them, the aphids produce their liquid only after the ant strokes them. A hungry or thirsty ant will go from aphid to aphid. He strokes each one, gets a drop of honeydew, licks it off, and goes on to the next.

Aphids seem to grow better when they live together with ants. Sometimes the ants carry them up to the tender young leaves. Ants often build shelters for their aphids. These may have doors too small for enemy insects to enter. They also keep the rain off. If a drop of syrup is put out, these ants will build a shelter around that too. The shelters are usually little mounds of dirt and twigs.

The gardening ant

The leaf-cutter ant, *Atta*, is a gardener. It grows a particular species of fungus inside its nest (see: *fungus*). The fungus produces swellings which the ants eat, just as people eat mushrooms. *Atta* cuts circles out of leaves and carries them back to the nest. Here it chews them, rolls them up and inserts them into the soil of its 'garden'. It brings in caterpillar droppings as fertilizer. It deposits its own manure on the garden as fertilizer too.

The nest of *Atta* is specially constructed to provide good growing conditions for the fungus. Around the outside of the underground nest there are air tunnels. Within, the temperature is quite warm. The air is damp and the carbon dioxide content of the air is high.

Starting a new colony is difficult. The *Atta* queen carries some fungus with her in her mouth on her mating flight. She digs a little hole and crawls into it. She plants the fungus there and lays her eggs. Queens of species that keep aphids inside their nests carry an aphis

clinging to their bodies when they fly away.

When the queen starts a nest, her wings drop off. Then the powerful muscles that moved them dissolve. The muscle turns into a liquid that she can eat and feed to her larvae. She also eats some of her eggs. When some eggs have hatched, the larvae live on eggs. Finally some larvae grow up into workers and can go out to get food. The first workers must grow up fast. They are quite small and are called minims.

Sometimes a queen takes workers with her when she leaves the nest. They help her to build a new one and feed her. Other queens take over an old nest. They kill the old queen. Sometimes they win the old queen's workers away from her. Then the workers forget to feed the old queen and she dies. The invading queen may take the larvae of the old queen and raise them as her own. Then they think they are hers and attack the old queen and her workers.

Ants find their way by the sun. An ant out hunting will keep the sun on one side as it goes and on the other as it returns. It keeps it shining into the same part of its eye. It also uses tall buildings or trees to guide itself. If it finds food, it lays a scent trail back to the nest. Ants have many glands on their bodies that give off different smells. They talk to each other by smells. The other ants are excited by the smell of the returned ant. They follow the scent trail to the food.

Ants are not always so busy as we think they are. At any moment, many of the workers are inside the nest, resting. Some species stay inside when it rains. In hot countries, ants go out early in the morning and in the evening, but in the middle of the day they stay inside their nest.

Probably most people think of ants as just insect pests. Certainly the kinds that sting or bite, or strip leaves from trees, are a nuisance. But most ants are harmless. Some are helpful because they kill other insects. And all of them are interesting to study.

See: *insects*.

Find out by doing

Build your own ant colony. Take a quart or larger glass jar. In the middle of it place a tall tin can. On top of this place a wet sponge or dish of water. Put the jar on a support in a pan of water, so the ants cannot escape.

Find an ant nest, dig down at least one foot, and place the dirt on newspaper. Look for the large queen ant. Put her in a jar. Collect about 100 ants in another jar. Take some soil from the nest.

Fill the space around the can inside your big jar with the soil, put the ants and queen in, and fasten the lid on tight.

Tie a sheet of dark paper around the jar. The ants will think they are underground and will dig tunnels.

Feed the ants with bits of bread, meat, honey, sugar water, vegetables and dead insects. Always remove unused food before adding new. Keep the sponge or dish moist. If the soil gets dry, use a dropper to dampen it.

Watch the ants in your colony. Use a magnifying glass. Try some experiments. Take one out for several days. See what happens when you put him back. Put some newly caught ants in. Watch what happens. Can you teach them to expect food at a certain hour? Try some experiments with a few ants on a table. How do they find their way? Try turning a sheet of paper after an ant has established a path across it. Does the ant still go to the same place or does he follow his old path on the paper and go the wrong way? Put one bright light by the table for several days. Then move it to another side of the table. Does this make the ants lose their way? You may have to put some crumbs or sugar out on the table to make the ants establish paths. Then you can see clearly if they go in a different direction. Sprinkle grains of sugar on the soil over one part of the nest, and watch carefully to see if ants carry off the sugar to make a store.

Large numbers of ants living together find cleanliness important. Try to watch those workers which have the task of dealing with refuse. Whereabouts in the colony do they put it? Is it left near where the young larvae hatch out or far away? What happens to dead larvae?

△ A cross-section through an underground ants' nest. The workers attend to all the chores of feeding and cleaning the colony

(Top right) A cross-section of a twig containing an ants' colony

(Above right) The door-keeper blocks the entrance with his head

(Right) He will clear the entrance for another ant but no other insect

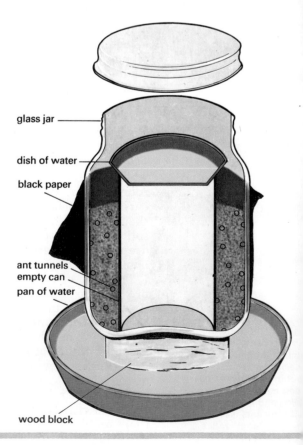

You can observe the social life of ants in a colony and also experiment with their reactions to changes in feeding patterns or lighting

glass jar

dish of water

black paper

ant tunnels
empty can
pan of water

wood block

Antarctic

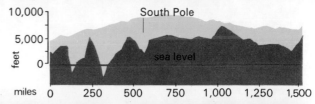

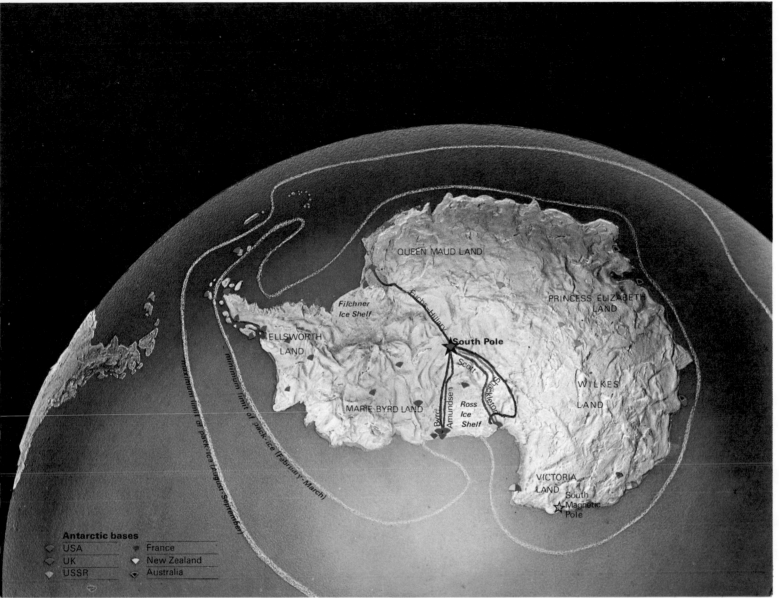

Antarctic bases
- USA
- UK
- USSR
- France
- New Zealand
- Australia

The Antarctic continent, vast and remote from any other land mass, has yet to be thoroughly explored and mapped. This is the most up to date available map. The diagram above the map is based on soundings made through the ice along a route across the pole. In places the ice is as much as 10,000 feet thick

This vast island-continent at the South Pole is permanently frozen under a thick layer of ice. Freezing winds sweep across it. Antarctica is probably the grimmest place on earth. Even the Eskimos of the Arctic could not live here.

The Antarctic continent has not yet been thoroughly explored and mapped. It probably covers an area of about 5,750,000 square miles. This is one and a half times the size of all fifty United States. The middle of the continent consists of a great plain. Near the centre of this is the South Pole. All around are lofty mountain ranges with peaks towering from 12,000 to 15,000 feet high. Some of the peaks, such as Mount Terror and Mount Erebus, are volcanoes. They are not active but could start erupting again.

Antarctica is thought to be about 6,000 feet above sea level. No one is certain, however, because the continent is covered with a sheet of solid ice. It is on the average about 5,000 feet thick. On top of the ice is a layer of snow several feet thick.

There may be rich deposits of coal and metal ores lying deep below the ground. But to reach the deposits would at present cost more than the value of the minerals.

The ice covering Antarctica is many times greater in area and several times thicker than any in the Arctic. The weather is also more constantly severe than it is in the Arctic. This is because the Arctic lies along the northern fringes of the European and American continents which send warm winds deep into the Arctic in summer. More warmth is brought by ocean currents. The Arctic snow melts in the summer, and the exposed land and water take up heat from the sun.

Antarctica is far from other land. It is surrounded by the Indian, Atlantic and Pacific Oceans. All the continents are too far away and are too small to influence Antarctica. Also, there are no warm ocean currents to reach the frozen continent. The great height of the land makes it colder still.

The summer temperature over most of the

Antarctica is the home of the penguin, the bird whose wings have evolved into flippers. Penguins cannot fly, and are even awkward on land. But in the water they are as adept at swimming as the fish on which they feed. Here a colony of Emperor penguins is seen against a typical icy Antarctic seashore

◁Captain Scott, the British Antarctic explorer, at the South Pole, standing by the tent left by Amundsen. In 1911 there was a race to the Pole. Amundsen, from Norway, reached the spot on December 11, beating Scott by a month, and returning safely. Scott and his party died on the return journey, beaten by the weather

△ Today scientific stations are built under the Antarctic ice. Modern equipment is used to drive huge tunnels and trenches to connect the different sections of an American base.
▽Specially designed to withstand the enormous pressures exerted by ice floes, an ice-breaker ploughs a channel through freezing Antarctic seas

△ An Antarctic ice shelf reaches the sea. The thick ice forms a flat landscape

▷ This is the sort of danger that faced a British trans-Antarctic expedition

▽An Antarctic survey expedition digs for geological specimens. Ancient snow samples can give information about polar climate and life thousands of years ago

Scientists struggle to catch a young seal. By attaching a depth recorder to its tail they hope to be able to measure the depth of the ocean to which the seal dives

continent seldom rises to freezing point and at the South Pole remains much lower. In midwinter the temperature falls to –60°C.

Because moisture in Antarctica is kept frozen, no rain ever falls. The air is dry, and so not even much snow forms. When snow does fall, fierce winds blow it in blizzards across the frozen wastes. Wind speeds of 50 to 100 miles an hour are common.

The only plants are a few algae, mosses and lichens (see: *algae, lichen, moss*). The Antarctic animals inland are mostly tiny wingless insects such as springtails and snowfleas. They are found in moss during the Antarctic summer.

Antarctica's coastline of 14,000 miles is an ice-covered wall of capes and cliffs. From the sea the continent slopes upwards to the plain surrounding the South Pole. The ice cap covering Antarctica moves very slowly outwards from the centre towards the sea.

Although there is so little life inland, marine birds and mammals swarm on the shores during the brief summer. Microscopic creatures called diatoms grow in the seas and stain the water yellow. They even colour the icebergs brownish. Enormous schools of shrimp-like creatures feed on the diatoms and other tiny organisms. All these tiny animals and plants are called plankton. This is the chief food of fish and whales.

Antarctic seals float about on the ice floes and dive for food. Sea elephants breed on the Antarctic coast in summer, and in many places there are large herds of sea leopards.

The most famous Antarctic birds are the penguins. Other birds which fish the Antarctic waters are albatross, skuas, petrels, and shags.

The Race to the Pole

Serious and scientific exploration of Antarctica began in 1901, when Robert Falcon Scott, a British naval officer, discovered King Edward VII Land. The first man to reach the South Pole was the Norwegian Roald Amundsen on December 14, 1911. He was followed 35 days later by Scott, who died with all his party on the return journey.

In 1958, the British Trans-Antarctic Expedition, led by Sir Vivian Fuchs, made the first overland journey across the South Pole.

Today Britain, Russia, America and Australia maintain stations in Antarctica for weather reporting and scientific research. In 1959, a number of nations, including America and the British Commonwealth, signed a treaty agreeing that Antarctica should be used only as a base for scientific research and that no military bases be set up on the continent.

Thanks to space satellites, the growth and melting of the ice cap throughout the year can be mapped easily. The Antarctic weather, which influences the rest of the world's weather, can also be observed from space. But there are still many scientific questions about the continent that can only be studied from Antarctic bases. Among the stations that are manned all the year round there is one, operated by the United States, that is located at the South Pole itself.

See: *Arctic, cold, geography, poles.*

To think about

If there are deposits of coal in the Antarctic, how can it have got there? Coal comes from trees which grew millions of years ago, but no tree could grow in the freezing Antarctic today. Do you suppose the climate has changed, or that the whole continent has moved south from a warmer part of the world?

anteater

▷ The Australian spiny anteater *(Tachyglossus achuleatus)* has a long leathery snout with which it turns over rocks. It can also dig into the ground at great speed

▽ The tamandua, *(Tamandua tetradactyla),* clings to branches with its claws and tail. Its tongue can stretch out ten inches to reach ants deep inside their nest

This is the name given to several species of mammal that eat mainly ants and termites. Their bodies are well adapted for this. They have strong curved claws on their forefeet in order to dig open the nests. They stick their long narrow snouts into the ants' nests and flick their tongues around to catch the ants on the sticky surface. As ants are so small and fragile, the animal has no need for teeth to crush them, and swallows them whole.

The great anteater lives in the forests of Central and South America. It is about two feet high by four feet long, excluding its long bushy tail. This is the animal we usually think of as an anteater. The female great anteater gives birth to one baby at a time, and carries it for its first months clinging to her back.

In the same group are two smaller tree-dwelling anteaters, the tamandua and the silky anteater.

The echidna or spiny anteater lives in Australasia. It is a marsupial and lays about one egg a year. The anteater keeps the egg in a pouch on its belly until it hatches. The adult looks rather like a porcupine. Its back is covered with long spines.

Two types of anteater live in Africa. The aardvark is about four feet long with a naked tail about two feet long and an almost naked body. Its front feet and claws are so powerful that it can dig amazingly fast. The scaly anteater, which lives in trees in Africa and South-East Asia, is covered with scales on its back and tail.

See: *marsupial.*

antelope

The eland is the largest of the antelopes. Its spiral horns grow to four feet. This type lives in West Africa but is thought to be dying out because of over-hunting and disease

Antelopes peacefully grazing on the broad African plain. A line of dignified antelopes approaching a water hole. A herd breaking up as the antelopes leap away from suspected danger. These are some of the most beautiful scenes in the game parks of Africa.

The word antelope comes from the Greek *antholopos,* meaning brightness-of-eye. Antelopes belong to the kind of mammals called ungulates, which have hoofs. Some ungulates, such as the horse, have an odd number of toes, and some have an even number of toes. Antelopes belong to the even-toed family. This includes cattle, sheep, goats, bison and buffaloes. All these animals have two-toed feet. They also have horns which grow when they are young and last all their lives. Deer are not antelopes. They have branched antlers which are shed and grow again every year.

The antelope walks on the nails of its third and fourth fingers. Its eyes are unusually large and bulging. This allows antelopes to look all around without moving their heads. Their ears are large and sensitive to catch the slightest sound of an enemy carried by the wind. All these organs help them to know when danger approaches. Then their long graceful legs carry them away fast.

Antelopes eat grass and leaves. Their front teeth are shaped for pulling up grass and biting it off. Their back teeth grind down the tough fibres. Their stomach has four chambers. Like cows, they first swallow their food, then bring it up to chew again. This regurgitated food is called the cud. Animals which do this are

The gerenuk is a shy, graceful antelope, fond of the leaves and young twigs of acacia bushes. By standing on hindlegs, and extending its giraffe-like neck, it can reach well over seven feet up into the foliage of trees and bushes. The gerenuk lives in the drier parts of southern Ethiopia. Somalia and Kenya

△ The suni is the smallest of the antelopes. Dainty and shy, it may not grow to more than a foot high, but can jump nearly ten feet.

▽Another graceful antelope is called Peter's gazelle. Its horns grow to a length of two feet or more.

▷The blackbuck, one of the fastest land animals, lives on the flat, open plains in India. Its horns have a spiral twist (*Below right*) The nyala is an ox-like antelope, found in Africa. Its diet is grass, leaves and fruit that has fallen from trees. The horns curve in and up

△ Only male waterbucks have horns — up to 3 feet long. This young bongo ▽ has yet to grow them

▽ Male impalas fight for leadership. But when the mating season is over, males and females form separate herds

called ruminants (see: *ruminant*).

The first antelopes probably evolved in North Africa. Then they spread all over Africa, into Asia and even Europe. The pronghorn of North America is a related species.

Today there are many different types of antelope. The duikers are small and live in the woods. Long twisted horns are carried by male bushbuck and kudus and by both male and female elands and bongo. The waterbucks and other large antelopes live near marshes.

The oryx, roan and sable antelopes are big and heavy. Their faces bear attractive white stripes. Wildebeests (gnu), hartebeests and topi are large animals with high, powerful shoulders and curved horns. The dikdik, with its slender straight horns, is a typical dwarf antelope. Goat-like antelopes called saigas live in Mongolia. Their noses have big puffy swellings, which filter the dusty air they breathe. The gazelles, impala and springbok of Africa are noted for their grace and speed.

Some antelopes herd together. Others prefer to remain alone. A few graze in pairs. Sometimes a male and a female antelope will stay together for life.

When they graze, antelopes do not harm the pasture as cattle do. Cattle bunch together. Their hoofs destroy the grass. They eat only the best types of grass. Antelopes eat all types of grass. They spread out. They do not stay in one place for long. They keep moving to find new grass as the season changes.

Most antelope species have babies once a year. They are born in the spring or at the beginning of the rainy season, when the grass begins to sprout. Large antelopes like the wildebeest carry their babies longer, and live longer themselves, than small ones like the dikdik. The calf is carried from four to nine months. It may run with the herd an hour after it is born. But often the mothers and calves form a separate nursery herd. Small antelopes live about ten years and large ones live up to twenty.

Antelopes feed at dawn and twilight, and rest while the sun is high and hot. They wake up often during the night. Even while resting, they are alert to danger. Running away from danger, they may reach fifty miles per hour. Impala can high jump eight feet and broad jump thirty feet.

Predators, animals that attack antelopes, include lions, leopards, wild dogs, hyenas and man. The oryx, sable and roan antelopes defend themselves with their horns but most others run away.

Many antelopes live within a territory which they mark with their own smell. For this they have glands on their faces and feet. The males fight to defend their territories. They also fight to win a female. The males rarely injure each other when they fight. The two animals prance around each other making threatening movements. Sometimes they butt each other. Rarely they lock horns and wrestle. After a while, one animal gives in and goes away.

Antelopes vary greatly in size and way of life. They are interesting animals to study and beautiful ones to watch.

See: *deer, hoofed animals.*

antenna

▽ There is an enormous variety of antennae in the insect world. This butterfly has long slender antennae ending in bulbous tips

▷ Feather-like antennae on this African moth are sensitive to touch

An antenna (*plural:* antennae) is a long, delicate feeler. Through it an animal can sense what is going on around it. Jointed-legged animals, the arthropods, have one pair of antennae. Crabs, crayfish and insects are arthropods.

Insect antennae are covered with tiny hairs connected to a nerve running to the brain. Each hair is so delicate that it feels the breath of air caused by heat, the movements of a nearby creature, or even sounds.

Flying insects regulate their wing-beats by the feel of the wind on their antennae. If it blows fast, they fly harder. If the antennae are covered, the insect will not move its wings. If one antenna is damaged, the insect flies crookedly.

When you move your hand towards a fly, it takes off. If it is on the other side of a pane of glass, it will not. The movement of air against its antennae frightens it more than the sight of your hand.

Bedbugs suck blood. When they are hungry, they look for warm bodies. A hungry bedbug in a jar will move its antennae towards the heat of a finger held against the glass. If its antennae are cut off, it will not notice the finger. Some insects taste and smell with their antennae. A wasp waves its antennae over jam before eating it. A hungry cockroach turns its antennae towards a piece of cheese. Arthropods' antennae keep them well informed.
See: *insects.*

anthropology

▽ The language of a tribe in Ecuador goes on record. This is one of the ways in which anthropologists trace cultural development

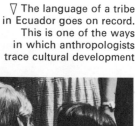

▷ A group of Iranian nomads on the move. Conditions are tough and they must always be looking for new sources of food as the old ones are used up. They carry all their possessions with them

Why are the Polynesians so much taller than the Eskimos? How do people develop such different tastes in food so that some people won't eat beef or pork or even wheat? Why do languages tend to occur in related groups? How did man begin to grow crops and make pots in which to cook his food? The science which tries to find the answers to such questions is called anthropology. This term comes from the Greek *anthropos*, meaning 'man' and *logos*

meaning 'study' or 'science'.

The study of man is a vast subject. Physical anthropologists study man's body. They started by studying bones found in prehistoric graves. They learned a lot about man's development. For example, ancient skulls have larger jaws than modern ones. This shows that ancient man ate coarser, harder-to-chew food.

The physical anthropologist also studies modern man. The type of hair, eyes, skin and

Different people, different foods. ◁In Mali, Africa, the market sells fruits and grain. In Holland (*below left*) cheeses are put on display and auctioned. Cheese is a food characteristic of people in northern countries

△ In Morocco, traders sit in the market-place selling local produce that people from other countries would not recognize. Everybody eats — but diets around the world show a great deal of variation

▽In Bangkok, people from the surrounding countryside bring their produce in boats and sell it in 'floating markets', characteristic of eastern countries such as China, Vietnam and Malaysia

Different people, different marriage ceremonies. In India△ elaborate veils and headwear are put on to mark the solemnity of the occasion

▷Colourful traditional costume for a wedding in Norway. The clothes are used only for important ceremonies such as marriages

▽In Japan, the couple to be married adopt special clothes. They show a blend of eastern and western influences

▷Traditional dress, too, for a wedding in England. The customs of a people are reflected in the way they 'dress up'

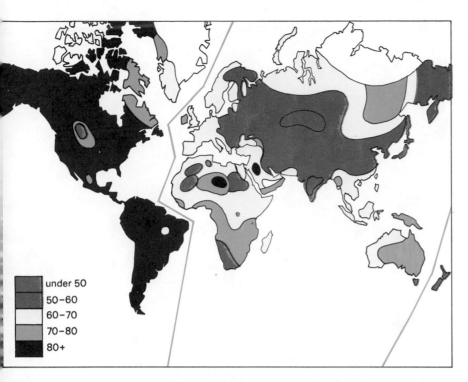

△ A culture within a culture. The Chinese community retains its traditions in Chinatown, San Francisco

△ An anthropologist's map showing the percentage of people with the kind of blood called Rhesus +. Such maps help us explain how different peoples are related, and how they have migrated in the past

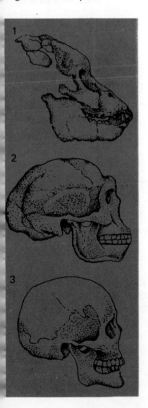

△ Anthropologists study the physical characteristics of man and his ancestors. These skull types trace man's development from
1) Proconsul through
2) Peking man to
3) modern man

colouring, and even blood type, shows where a race originally came from. Groups living far apart may be found to have a common origin long forgotten by the people themselves.

The size and shape of the body are now known to be related to climate. People who live in hot countries tend to be tall with projecting noses and long limbs. This provides more surface from which the body heat evaporates. In extremely cold climates the people are often short and rounded, with flatter noses. Their compactness conserves heat. This trend in shape can be seen in animals too.

Until man learned to change his environment, the person best able to adapt to the local dangers – hot sun, disease or wild animals – survived longest. He or she had more years in which to have children. The descendants of people best adapted to that locality soon outnumbered those of the weaker ones. In this way men living in different parts of the world developed into varied races. This trend has probably stopped by now.

Studying society

Learning how man has developed in the past may help to predict how he can adapt in the future.

Cultural anthropologists, also called ethnologists, study people's culture. This includes their language, how they work, how children are treated, education, religion, marriage customs and even what games they play. Today anthropologists work in teams. Each specialist studies one part of the culture.

Anthropologists find that societies differ greatly. In some societies children are watched strictly. In others they have great freedom. The roles of men and women differ. In many societies, men are expected to cry easily. In German, English and American society this is discouraged. The age at which children are

considered to be adults varies also (see: *adolescence*).

Each person's feelings, personality and ambitions are shaped by the culture in which he grows up. For example, many American Indian tribes frown on competition. Children feel that their school class is a team. To do better than others on a test or in a game makes a child ashamed. This emphasis on co-operation makes it difficult for many Indian children to compete in American society.

Marriage customs and the family also take many forms. In some groups the man moves into the house of the woman he marries and takes her name. In many countries the family includes grandparents, aunts and uncles and cousins. All the members of this 'extended family' may live in one house.

Today anthropologists also study the social customs in such societies as schools, factories, neighbourhoods and towns. Such studies can help us to understand the different ways in which people live together.

See: *races of Man*.

Find out by doing

Visit any special markets of the various national groups in your town. See what food and clothing stores there are to cater to particular nationalities.

If you have any friend whose grandparents or parents were immigrants to Great Britain, find out if their language is still spoken in the family. Do they know any of the folk songs from the old country?

To think about

Would it be a good thing if the world's cultures were to mix completely? What do you think the ways of life of primitive people offer them – and us – that modern life does not? (*For example, what kinds of things might a Brazilian Indian know about that we don't?*)

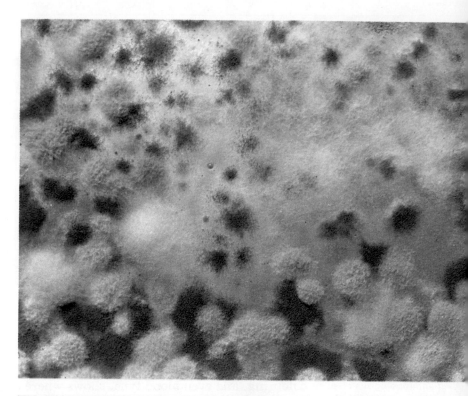

antibiotics

When a person gets an infection such as pneumonia or scarlet fever, the doctor often gives him an antibiotic. This is a substance produced by a living organism that stops other living things from growing. Penicillin is the one we usually think of first but there are many others. New ones are still being discovered.

Many diseases and wound-infections are caused by micro-organisms called bacteria. Before antibiotics were discovered there were few ways to prevent or cure these diseases. Antibiotics cure them so fast that they are called 'miracle drugs'.

Antibiotics are produced by micro-organisms so small that you need a microscope to see them. They tend to grow in clusters called colonies. The colonies are big enough to see.

The green or grey fuzz that grows on old bread, fruit and cheese in the kitchen is the colony of one type of micro-organism. This is called a fungus or mould.

The world is full of micro-organisms. There is not enough food, space or air for all. Some micro-organisms, usually moulds, have developed a special defence. They make a poison that prevents others from living too close to them. This poison is what we call an antibiotic.

Until the nineteenth century, no one knew what caused infections – the diseases that spread from person to person. Then, in 1860, the French scientist Louis Pasteur showed that some diseases are caused by bacteria. By the 1890s the bacteria that caused many diseases and infections were known. Doctors began to apply bacteria-killing liquids to wounds (see: *antiseptic*). But this did not prevent internal infections.

Two German doctors tried another approach. They used one bacterial species to fight another. The doctors, Rudolf Emmerich and Oskar Löw, showed that *Bacillus pyocyanus* produces a poison. They called this pyocyanase. This bacterium causes green pus in wounds. But when mixed with other bacteria, its poison kills them. They used pyocyanase on people with such diseases as typhoid, diphtheria and plague. Some got well. But others got sicker. The medicine was not safe enough to use on people.

Other scientists kept on looking for antibiotics. They found many. But some did not cure disease in people. Others harmed the bacteria, but harmed the people too.

Then, in 1928, Alexander Fleming discovered penicillin. He was studying *Staphylococcus*

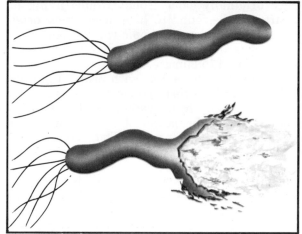

△ Two fungi grow side by side on a culture plate. The darker mould is *Penicillium* from which the antibiotic penicillin is made. The lighter one is *Aspergillus* which is harmful to man.
◁ The upper bacterium is healthy but the lower one has been attacked by an antibiotic. One way that antibiotics work is to attack the cell wall
▽ The left group of cells is normal. They grow lengthwise and then split to reproduce. The right group attacked with penicillin, cannot split normally

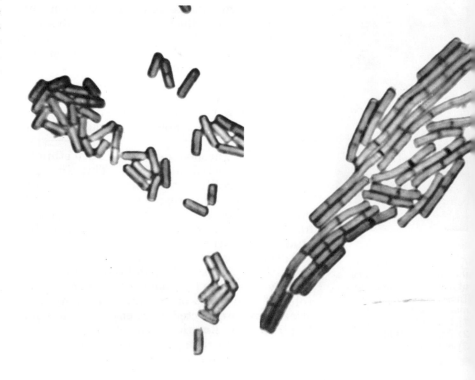

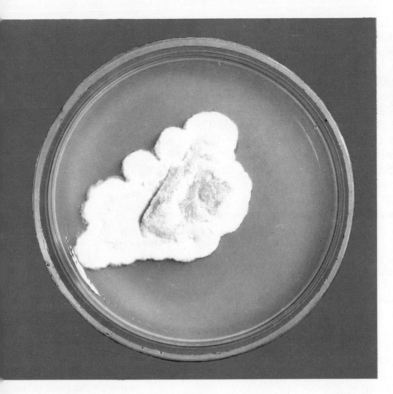

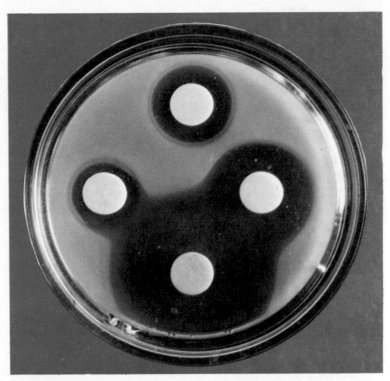

...ureus, a bacterium that causes many infections. He grew the bacteria in small glass plates, called petri dishes. The bacteria grow and multiply on top of the dish until it is covered with a golden creamy layer. One day, Fleming found that a few cells of mould had fallen on to a dish. Around each cell was a clear area where the bacteria were not growing.

He did not throw the plate away. He kept it, watched it and thought. The mould was producing an antibiotic. He grew more mould and collected droplets of liquid that it made. He tested this liquid and got good results. The mould was *Penicillium notatum*. Fleming named his new drug penicillin. He published his results in 1929. But he did not know how to produce large amounts of penicillin in order to treat many people.

During the 1930s, a substance used in making dyes was found to kill bacteria. This was sulphanilamide. The 'sulfa' drugs were made from it. They cured many diseases. Antibiotics were almost forgotten. But sulfa drugs were difficult to use. Sometimes they harmed the patient, though usually only slightly.

Mass-produced antibiotics

In 1939, two scientists in England, Dr Howard Florey and Dr Ernst Chain, tried to produce large amounts of penicillin. The problem is that, as a fungus grows, it uses up all its food and air. It produces waste products that collect and harm it. Engineers helped the doctors to solve these problems. They designed methods to keep bringing new food and air and take away waste products. By 1943, penicillin could be produced in 1,000 gallon tanks. Then a new species of *Penicillium* was found that makes 200 times more penicillin than Fleming's species does.

Penicillin cures many diseases, but not all. The search for antibiotics continued. Some of these are still produced commercially by growing colonies of micro-organisms. Others are now produced by man-made processes.

Antibiotics work in various ways. Some kill the bacteria. Others simply stop them from multiplying. One way antibiotics do this is by interfering in the making of cell walls around the new bacteria. Then the body can kill the bacteria.

Antibiotics do not work against viruses. These organisms cause the common cold, flu, measles and mumps and other diseases. Scientists are looking for a cure for viral infections. (See: *virus*.)

A major problem in using antibiotics is that bacteria become resistant to them. Then they are useless. There are two types of resistance. Resistance to penicillin builds up if small doses are given. It can be avoided by giving such large doses of penicillin that all the bacteria are killed at once. But resistance to streptomycin can occur all at once. It is not predictable.

Strangely enough, people who take antibiotics for a long time may develop new infections. The reason for this is really quite simple. Our bodies are full of micro-organisms. They all compete for food. If an antibiotic kills off the strongest ones, the others have an opportunity to grow. Often the new infection is caused by a fungus (see: *fungus*). Fungi are often unaffected by antibiotics that harm bacteria.

Scientists are constantly studying how antibiotics work. This helps doctors to use them more efficiently.
See: *drugs, disease*.

Find out by doing

Ask the older members of your family if they know of old cures for illness that use moulds in any way. (For example, using old bread).

(*Left*) The mould *Penicillium notatum* from which the antibiotic penicillin is extracted. Its ability to kill bacteria was discovered accidentally. Fleming left a bacterial culture he had been using on a window ledge. After a few days he noticed spots of *Penicillium* mould had formed, and that around them no bacteria were able to grow

(*Above*) Doses of penicillin in four different concentrations are placed on circles of paper on a bacterial culture plate. The effectiveness of the doses can then be compared by the sizes of the clear areas round them

antihistamine

An antihistamine is a drug that acts against the effects of histamine. Histamine is a chemical made by the body. When a person gets hay fever, too much histamine has been made. Touching or eating certain substances may cause a running nose, sneezing, wheezing, 'nettlerash', itching or pain. This is also caused by the body producing too much histamine. Antihistamines relieve the symptoms. No one knows why so many tissues produce histamine. Scientists are still studying this puzzling question.

Antihistamines were first discovered by a French scientist in 1937. They do not stop the histamine being made. They do stop the body reacting to it.

A person taking an antihistamine will feel some side-effects. These are effects caused by the medicine, but not really wanted. The most important one is sleepiness. After taking an antihistamine it is difficult to think and react quickly. Studying is difficult and driving may be dangerous.
See: *allergy*.

antiseptic

Antiseptics are chemical solutions that kill germs – bacteria – or stop them from multiplying. They are used to get rid of bacteria from the skin and things like clothing and furniture.

Antiseptics help to prevent diseases from spreading. Infections and infectious diseases are caused by germs. Germs include bacteria, viruses and fungi. But generally only bacteria are killed by antiseptics.

The air, all objects, and all animals, including human bodies, are full of germs. Most of these germs are harmless, and many are even useful to us. A few on the skin do not matter, but if the skin is scratched or cut, they can infect the wound. The body can fight harmful germs, but needs some help if there are too many.

The cells inside our bodies are delicate and can be harmed by strong chemicals, so antiseptics are used only outside the body. Really strong antiseptics, that would even harm the skin, and can be used only on things like table tops and floors, are called disinfectants.

We owe our knowledge of infection to many men, including Joseph Lister, Louis Pasteur, Ignaz Semmelweis and Robert Koch.

Some antiseptics destroy germs. Others only stop them from growing and multiplying. One bacterium can multiply into one thousand bacteria in just three hours. Some types of germ produce hard cases round themselves, called spores. Antiseptics cannot kill germs enclosed in spores. An antiseptic does not sterilize, which means to kill absolutely all germs, but it can greatly reduce the number of germs.

Soap is a weak antiseptic. Surgeons scrub their nails, hands and arms thoroughly before performing an operation. There must be as few germs as possible in the operating room. Germs in an operation can cause disease and prevent proper healing.

Alcohol, in a 70 per cent solution, is one antiseptic the doctor cleans your skin with before taking a blood sample, or giving an injection.
See: *antibiotics, bacteria, fungus, virus.*

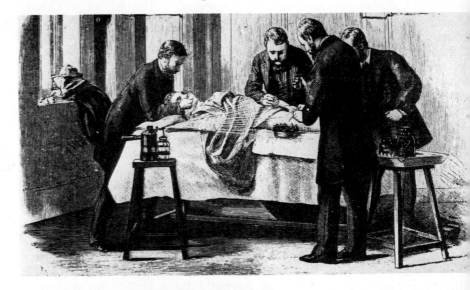

▽ In the first attempts at antiseptic surgery Lister used carbolic acid as an antiseptic. The carbolic spray on the stool to the left was intended to create an antiseptic atmosphere around the operating table Lister first used this technique in 1865

▷ A surgeon carefully washes his hands in antiseptic soap before touching anything in the operating room — even the taps which are turned on and off for him by a nurse. He wears a face mask to trap germs that may be carried by his breath

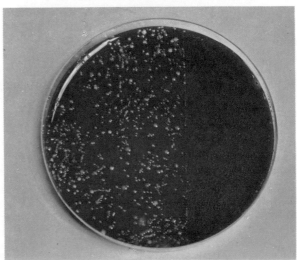

◁ A fly has walked across this plate. But beforehand the plate was partly treated with antiseptic. You can see where the germs from the fly's feet have been able to flourish and where they have been killed by the antiseptic

appendix

Many people who have had appendicitis wonder what the appendix is for. Many doctors do too. Its purpose is not known.

The appendix is a worm-shaped sac, and is correctly called the 'vermiform appendix'. It is about 2 to 6 inches long and as thick as a pencil. It opens out of the caecum, the top end of the large intestine.

There are two theories about why we have an appendix. It may be all that is left of a large pouched caecum, like those found in some grass eating animals. These animals cannot digest the cellulose in plant tissue. Certain microorganisms – bacteria – can. Masses of these bacteria live in the caecum of grass-eating animals and help them digest their food. As our early ancestors changed their form and evolved into modern man, they no longer ate grass. There was no longer a need for a pouched caecum, and it slowly disappeared. Perhaps our

appendix is all that is left. Organs that have lost their usefulness often do not vanish entirely, and are called 'vestigial organs'.

The other theory is that the appendix is an important, specialized organ. It may influence the muscular action that pushes food down the gut. It may secrete hormones. It may fight infection.

Sometimes the opening of the appendix into the gut becomes blocked. Then the appendix hurts and becomes infected. This condition is called appendicitis.

The symptoms of appendicitis are pain, loss of appetite and vomiting. The pain is usually felt near or above the umbilicus (belly button or navel). Sometimes it is felt lower, on the right side. It continues for hours. If appendicitis develops, the appendix must be removed by a surgeon.

Because we do not know for certain what use the appendix is, surgeons only remove it when they are quite sure the operation is necessary. See: *digestion*.

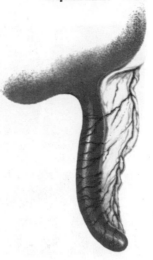

△ An inflamed appendix. It could very rapidly become worse and even burst. Surgery is usually performed as soon as the condition is diagnosed

aquarium

Bright coloured fish swimming among beautiful plants in crystal clear water. That is the ideal aquarium. Is it very difficult to make? Mistakes in keeping fish are made because their needs are so unlike ours. But if you follow a few simple rules, your aquarium should be successful and a source of pleasure.

The tank is important. It should be rectangular and shaped so that the surface area of the water is large. This allows the water to take in oxygen from the air. Fish breathe in this dissolved oxygen through their gills. They breathe out carbon dioxide gas, just as we do. A large surface allows the carbon dioxide to escape from the water into the air. So the tank should be long and broad. If it is not, the fish will not be able to breathe.

The tank should be glass. The metal support should not touch the water, because poisonous substances might dissolve out. Soaps, detergents and other chemicals are also poisonous.

Setting the scene

The gravel, plants and water must be carefully chosen too. Gravel should not contain limestone or chalk, as this harms the fish. Coral is pretty but contains too much lime to use in an aquarium. Gravel should not be too fine. Plant roots need coarse, loose gravel particles to grow between. Wash the gravel well in hot running water in a basin before using it.

Plants supply a little oxygen through photosynthesis. By this process they make oxygen and also use up carbon dioxide. But plants do not make enough oxygen to balance the breathing of the fish. Plants are used mostly for their looks. Fish can hide behind them and lay eggs on them too. Put the plants towards the back of the aquarium, behind the fish, then they will not swim out of sight.

Which plants will grow well in your aquarium

depends on the light and temperature. You can experiment with several types to find which ones look best. If the light is strong, the best might be: fanwort, waterweed or water thyme. In less light good ones might be: tape grass, eelgrass, arrowhead, floating fern or water sprite. Cryptocorynes need even less light than these.

If you use tap water, let it sit for several days in a shady place. Put a cover over it raised about an inch on corks or pieces of wood. The cover prevents dust falling in, but allows air to circulate. This lets the chlorine that was put into the water to purify it evaporate. If the tap water in your neighborhood is very 'hard', it may need special treatment. Hardness means that the water contains calcium salts which can be bad for the fish.

△ A small ornamental aquarium. It contains a variety of decorative fish and is equipped with heater, thermometer and aerator. The water plants, apart from being decorative, help to maintain the supply of oxygen in the water

(Far left) An angelfish swims in a freshwater tropical tank. The coiled element of the heater can clearly be seen within its protective glass case. Beside it bubbles of air rise from an aerator

(Left) A cold water aquarium which requires no heater. It has, however, a gravel filter which cleans the water. This type of tank is suitable for the goldfish and catfish seen here. The waterweed *Elodea densa* is a good oxygenator

If you boil the water, then let it sit for several hours, harmful calcium salts will settle out on the bottom of the container. Add some of this cooled, boiled water to the other water. If you add water later to replace any that has evaporated, include some boiled and cooled water. Water that fish have lived in is called 'conditioned'. It contains products that help the fish to live and grow. Unlike those of other animals, fishes' waste products are not harmful. Feed your fish very little for the first two weeks. By then the water should be clear and should remain so from then on.

Dirt that must be removed includes uneaten food and dead fish. Snails may eat some of the extra food. It is better not to give the fish too much food.

Do not move the tank after you have put the water in. It is very heavy and may leak afterwards. Too much sunlight will heat the water. This will lower the amount of oxygen dissolved in the water. If the fish stay near the surface and gasp, there is not enough oxygen in the water. This could happen on a hot, sunny day. Artificial light is just as good as sunlight. The plants need about 8 hours of light a day.

Too much sunlight will also encourage the growth of the plants called algae. They form a scum on the water and grow inside the glass, so that it is hard to see the fish.

The temperature must suit the type of fish you have chosen. It must not vary. A room that is warm in the daytime and then drops more than 5°C or 10°F at night will not do.

Overfeeding is the most common reason why fish die. Fish only need food three times a week. Watch them eat it and do not give them more than they can eat in ten minutes. Fish like variety in their meals. So give them chopped meat or worms, lettuce and hard-boiled egg-yolks sometimes. Packaged fish food is good for routine feeding. The fish also eat plants and animals that live in the water. These living

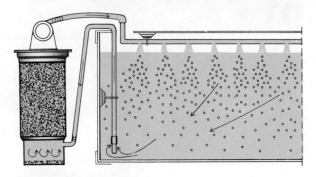

◁ A combined filter and aerator. A pump draws water from the aquarium into the lower chamber and up through the filter. Any debris or waste matter is trapped there. The clean water is then carried to sprays above the tank. The water is aerated as it is sprayed. Some fish need aerated water

things are too small to be seen without a microscope. Living food may be bought and given to the fish once a week. Snails or some catfish may help to keep the tank clean. They eat extra food, algae and dead plant leaves. But they cannot eat all the food if you continually give your fish too much for their needs.

What kind of fish?

Sea fish of course need salt water and for most tropical fish it must be warmed. An electric heater that fits inside the aquarium can be bought. Another useful gadget is an aerator. This bubbles extra air into the water. A beginner should start with fish that can be kept at room temperature. These include goldfish, minnows, some darters, sunfishes, suckers, sticklebacks, gars and mud minnows.

Perhaps the guppy is the best fish to start with. It does not need specially heated or aerated water. It bears living young. Other fish that are almost as adaptable as the guppy are: platyfishes, swordtails and black mollies. Tetras, corydoras, catfishes and danios will live together peacefully with guppies and platyfishes. Other types of fish may fight and injure each other when kept together.

There are many kinds of strange and beautiful fish that live in tropical waters, but only a few are suitable for keeping in tanks. They are the ones that can live in water that is not

An aquarium on a very large scale — one that you can walk around. In this 'dolphinarium' in Hawaii the activities of dolphins (not fish but mammals) can be observed through the glass sides of a huge 'vision tank'

water. Tropical fish do not need so much. For tropical fish allow half a gallon for each inch of fish.

You should also have a small aquarium for baby fish. If you have both male and female fish, the females may lay eggs. The eggs will settle on the plants, and look like tiny pearls. Put the part of the plant to which the eggs are attached in the other aquarium. Otherwise, the fish may eat them. When the young fish hatch, feed them tiny amounts of hard-boiled egg yolk, crushed into fine bits.

If a fish gets sick, it should be removed immediately into another aquarium. This may prevent the other fish from catching its disease. Examine it with a magnifying glass. Perhaps it has parasites on its body. Think whether you have put any new or dirty object into the tank. This may have poisoned it. Even the dirt or soap on your hands could be harmful.

What will happen to your fish if you go away on holiday for two weeks? It is better not to ask a friend to feed them. If he has never taken care of fish, he will feed them too much. It is better to feed them a little more than usual for the week before the holiday. Be sure that the plants are healthy and the aquarium clean. Healthy fish can live for two weeks by eating the plants and the tiny animals that live in the gravel.

If you follow these suggestions and ask in your pet shop for advice, your fish should be healthy. Your fish will entertain you. You will learn a lot from your aquarium about the plants and animals that live in the rivers and seas. See: *fish*.

△ One of the most popular of the tropical freshwater fish is the guppy. Also known as millions fish, the male is brightly coloured, the female less so.

▽ Another tropical freshwater variety is the 'kissing gourami' of Indonesia. It grows to 30cm in the wild, less in the aquarium. Only the males 'kiss'

moving, and can eat different foods from their natural ones.

The tank must be large enough for the number of fish you want to have. Overcrowding kills almost as many fish as overeeding. When fish rise to the top of the tank and gasp, it often means that they are too crowded. There is not enough oxygen for all of them. For goldfish a safe rule is to allow 2 gallons of water for each inch of the fish's body, not counting its tail. Many other types of fish also need this much

▷Gobies are among the smallest of the fishes, most being less than three inches long. Even the 'giant goby', found in the Mediterranean, is only nine inches when fully grown. The gobies are almost all colourful and good aquarium fish

▽ Butterfly fish are usually highly coloured. Their colours are used for recognition, and to warn off intruders. These fish are very possessive, and jealous of the 'territories' that they establish for themselves

Archaeopteryx

A reconstruction in the British Museum of what the Archaeopteryx must have looked like

Scientists were able to build the model on the basis of information gained from this fossil discovered in Germany

One hundred million years ago, in the Jurassic geological period, lived the earliest known bird, the Archaeopteryx. The name means 'ancient winged creature'.

We only know of five Archaeopteryx fossils. They were all found in Germany. In summer 1981 another fossil was said to have been found in Colorado.

There are many features that birds and reptiles have in common. Probably they are descended from a common ancestor. The Archaeopteryx illustrates this. It was about the size of a crow. It had teeth like a reptile. Its backbone was flexible like a reptile's. Its tail was long and reptilian under its feathers.

Its breastbone was small. This is normal in reptiles, which crawl. Birds need a large strong breastbone. Their wings are moved by powerful muscles which pull against it. With its weak breastbone, the Archaeopteryx could not have flapped its wings hard. It could not have flown very well. Its wings were rather too small.

Birdlike features are seen in the animal's large eyes, wing-like front limbs and feathers. Also, its brain was larger than a reptile's. The bones of the wing had flexible joints, as in a reptile. There were three 'fingers', with claws.

The Archaeopteryx had long, strong legs for running and claws for perching on a branch. It was probably warm-blooded like a bird. Its interesting combination of bird-like and reptilian features provides evidence that birds and reptiles come from a common ancestor. See: *birds*.

archeology

Archeologists removing remains from an ancient burial ground that was discovered by construction workers on their building site. These may tell a great deal about previous civilizations

How did the primitive tribes of Europe live, work and wage war two and a half thousand years ago? Who built the ancient cities of Ur and Nineveh in the Middle East? What did the pyramid-builders of America eat and drink, and what kind of homes did they live in? Where did the statue-builders of Easter Island come

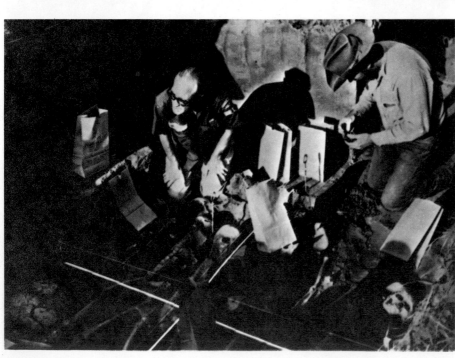

from? There are no written answers to these questions. It is the job of the archeologist to try to answer questions like these by studying all the traces that a people has left behind.

The most important clues are often the objects that were made by man. These are called artifacts. People used to be buried with their favourite or most useful possessions. They also drew pictures of their houses and possessions inside their graves. Graves are rich sources of artifacts. Food clothing and wooden things usually rot, but clay pots and metal tools last longer. In a dry climate many things may be preserved for centuries.

Archeologists spend a lot of time digging. Villages were usually built by a road or a river, and there may still be towns there today. So to find the old village sites it is necessary to dig. Recent artifacts lie near the surface and cover older ones. A site that has been lived on for centuries will have layer after layer of houses and tools with the oldest at the bottom.

A site can be dated by its depth. The amount of radioactive carbon in the things found also shows how old they are. Annual rings in the wood of tools or house walls help to indicate the age by showing an especially dry or cold year (see: *annual rings*). As many sites are studied, the climate of the region in the past becomes known. The people's techniques and styles in tools also date them. We can tell by the

The treasures of the past that archeologists have discovered are often in danger of destruction, and must be moved to safe places for preservation. In Egypt, the temple at Abu Simbel, thousands of years old, was carefully taken to pieces and moved so that a new dam could be built, and a valley flooded

△ ▽Archeology underwater.
Divers explore sunken
wrecks and bring to the
surface objects of ages
long since gone, clues
to Man's forgotten past

▷Young archeologists
in Somerset plot the site
where the legendary King
Arthur is thought by
many to have had a large
and splendid castle

remains of people's clothes and their methods of cooking and lighting how recently they lived. An archeologist notices whether they used stone or metal tools. Their cooking pots may be crudely made, beautifully made but not baked, or baked hard and painted with elegant designs.

The positions of things are important. Artifacts moved from their site lose much of their meaning. Everything found is carefully recorded, marked on a chart and labelled before it is studied.

There are many scientific aids that modern archeologists use. Metal-detectors, for example, help to locate buried coins and jewellery at a depth of several inches in the ground.

What he finds teaches the archeologist about the people who lived in the site. People do not change much. By studying ancient people, we can learn more about our world, and how we earned our ways of doing things. See: *anthropology*.

Find out by doing

With a group of friends, try to visit an archeological site where excavation is going on. Ask whoever is in charge to show you what has been found, and the way that work proceeds.

If you can obtain an aerial photo of nearby countryside, try to identify local crops, and perhaps old pathways and disused roads which used to cross them, show by colour differences.

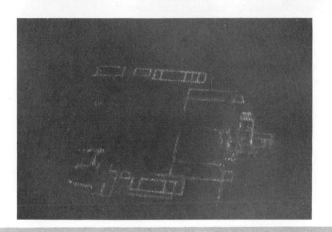

X-rays reveal the history of a sword. *(Top left)* A piece of the sword blade as it appeared to the naked eye. *(Next)* An X-ray shows two faint images, one on top of the other. The designs were of a Roman centurion on one side and on the other *(above)* an eagle. The sword is about 1,800 years old *(Left)* Aerial photography shows a grass pattern indicating an ancient relic. At ground level this would not be noticed

Archimedes (287-212 BC)

'Give me a place to stand and I can move the world.' When the Greek philosopher Archimedes exclaimed this, he was not merely boasting. He had discovered the principle of the lever. With a long enough and strong enough lever, a man can lift any weight.

Archimedes was born in Syracuse, Sicily. He studied in Alexandria, Egypt, for a time and then returned to Syracuse.

Levers had been used before Archimedes' time. But he showed why they work.

A lever is a long rod that turns upon a support called a fulcrum. A crowbar is a lever. Its turning point is the bend just before its tip. A see-saw is a lever too.

Archimedes realized that a small weight far from the fulcrum will balance a heavy one close to it. He discovered that there is a law that describes this. The weight times the distance on one side of the fulcrum must equal the weight times the distance on the other side. For example: a 1 pound weight 10 inches from the fulcrum balances a 10 pound weight 1 inch from the fulcrum. The lever that would let a man move the world would have to be very long!

One of Archimedes' greatest discoveries came about when a goldsmith tried to cheat the king of Syracuse. The king ordered a new crown in pure gold. He suspected that the crown he received contained gold mixed with silver. He asked Archimedes to find out.

At first Archimedes did not know how to do this without damaging the crown. Then, one

day, as he sat down in his bath, the water overflowed.

At that moment he realized that an object submerged in water displaces its own volume of water. This gave him a method of measuring the volume of any object, no matter what shape.

Archimedes' next step was to weigh the crown. Then he took a block of pure gold of exactly the same weight. He submerged both

▽ Archimedes' screw. As the shaft of the screw is turned the spiral carries water to the top of the tube. The water has been raised from one level to a higher one. This is still in use as a means of irrigation, more than 2,000 years after it was first invented

in jars containing measured amounts of water. The crown displaced more water than the gold. So it contained a lighter, bulkier metal.

This led to the principle of physics that we call today 'Archimedes' Principle'. It was well-known that whenever an object was lowered into water the object was pushed upwards. The further into the water the object was lowered, the greater the upward force, until the object was completely immersed. The upward push could be measured by weighing the object in air, and then in the liquid.

Archimedes stated that the upward force must be equal to the weight of the water displaced by the object. This is the famous law now called Archimedes' Principle. The Principle enables us to understand how ships float.

The upward force will not be enough to stop the object sinking if it is made of solid stone or metal, for example. But if it is made of something light, like wood, or a hollow vessel, the upthrust will send it to the surface.

Archimedes also made many discoveries in mathematics. He had the good fortune to be

highly admired in his own time. His discoveries are valuable thousands of years after his death. See: *boats and ships.*

Find out by doing

Find a kitchen measuring jug marked in fluid ounces. Fill it to a mark about 2/3 deep with water. You can find the volumes of various heavy objects – stones, pieces of iron, etc – by placing them in the jug and making a new reading of the water volume.

Take an empty pill container with its top screwed on. It will float in the water in the jug. Partly fill it with sand, shot, ball bearings or coins until it just begins to sink. You can find the volume of the container by reading the change in water volume. Now weigh the container, with its contents, on a kitchen scale.

You will find that the weight of the container is equal to the weight of the water it displaces. (One pint of water makes 20 fluid ounces, and weighs 20 ounces). You can also try the experiment shown in the diagram (far left). You can buy a spring balance from your hardware store, or borrow one from a friend who goes fishing.

△ At the left, the top spring balance shows that the object weighs 5 lb. When it is dipped into a basin that is full of water, some of the water is displaced and overflows. On the right, the lower balance shows that this displaced water weighs 2 lb. So the upward force on the object is 2 lb. It now seems to weigh 3 lb

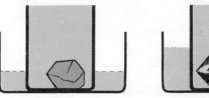  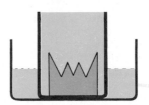

Pure gold occupies less space than the same weight of silver, as the overflowing water shows. The king's crown was gold mixed with silver, and was bulkier than pure gold

Arctic

The American Robert Peary after his expedition to the North Pole in 1909. He was the first man to get there

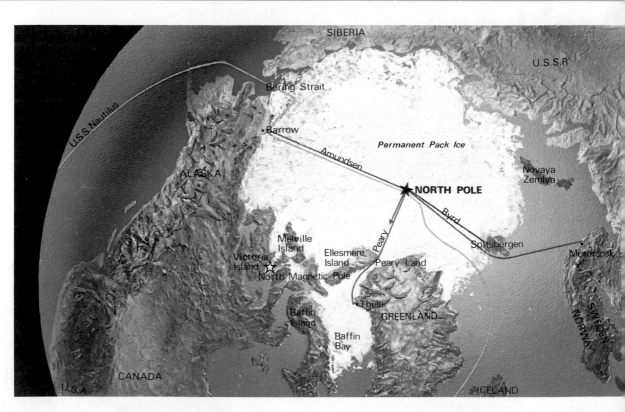

At the frozen northernmost part of the Earth lies an ocean of ice. From its shores the great land masses of the Northern Hemisphere spread to the south. Within and around this sea are islands and shores inhabited by countless plants, animals and a few hardy men. This is the Arctic.

There are several ways of defining the limits

of the Arctic. It could be called the area within the Arctic Circle. This is an imaginary line. Within this circle at least one 24-hour day and one 24-hour night occur during the year. That is, there is at least one day in each year in which the sun does not set, and one in which the sun does not rise at all.

A better definition of the Arctic might be the

area beyond the last trees. As you climb a high mountain, you come to the timberline. Above this it is too cold and conditions are too severe for the forest to continue. The same thing happens as you go north. Only a few stunted trees are able to survive, in the most sheltered valleys.

The centre of the Arctic consists of an ocean which is about four times larger than the Gulf of Mexico. Between Greenland and Europe, it opens into the Atlantic Ocean. Between Alaska and the USSR, the Bering Strait leads into the Bering Sea and the Pacific Ocean. There are many islands off Siberia, near Greenland and, especially, between Greenland and Canada.

The centre of the Arctic Ocean, and for several hundred miles around the North Pole, is a mass of thick ice. Much of the rest of the ocean is covered with drifting ice up to 100 feet thick. On top of the ice lies snow blown by the wind into deep drifts.

During the Arctic winter at the North Pole the sun does not rise above the horizon and there are six months of darkness. Then during the summer the sun does not set, and shines even at midnight. This is why the Arctic is known as 'the land of the midnight sun.'

The weather in the Arctic is not nearly so cold as in the Antarctic. The mildness of the Arctic climate is due to warm currents in the air and water. The average winter temperature in the colder parts of the Arctic is about −37°C. In the warmest parts, the coast of southern Greenland, Iceland and the European coast, the average temperature is about −7°C. In many parts of the Arctic during summer hot spells, the temperature is around 27°C.

On most of the Arctic lands, the ice melts in the summer. Much of the land is tundra. This is flat sand covered with moss and heather. The soil layer is thin and only the top few inches thaw. Below, the ground is permanently frozen. This is called permafrost.

There are special difficulties in building on tundra. The foundations of a building go deep into the permafrost. The heat from the building

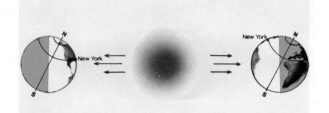

△ A midsummer night in the Arctic has no sunset
◁ Every 24 hours the Earth turns once. In summer, people near the North Pole can see the sun all the time, and have a 24-hour day. In winter they never see the sun. Outside the Arctic, day and night have varying lengths

makes the frost in the soil melt. The soil becomes soft and the building sinks slightly and tilts over.

Plants grow very slowly in the tundra. The marks left by machines such as tractors will last unchanged for many years. For this reason, Man must be especially careful not to cause damage to the environment in the tundra.

△ Laplanders, who are native to the Arctic region, round up a herd of reindeer, also native. Reindeer at one time supplied nearly all the Lapps' food and clothing needs

Cold and inhospitable as
the Arctic regions may be,
there are plants and
animals that can survive
the climate. In the spring
there are delicate and
brightly coloured flowers
blooming in many places
where they can take root.
(*Right*) The pasqueflower,
(*below*) saxifrage, and
(*below right*) the alpine
poppy, all flourish.
(*Bottom*) The Arctic fox,
in a splendid coat that
gives both protection
from the cold and a
good camouflage from
enemies and prey, is
well adapted to Arctic
conditions.
(*Facing page*) Caribou
gather on a hillside,
protected from the
biting winds that sweep
across the countryside
in the Arctic regions.
People from the north of
Canada herd these animals
much as ranchers do in
America with cattle.
Caribou are closely
related to reindeer,
and, like them, live off
the sparse vegetation,
including the lichens that
grow on trees and rocks
within the Arctic circle

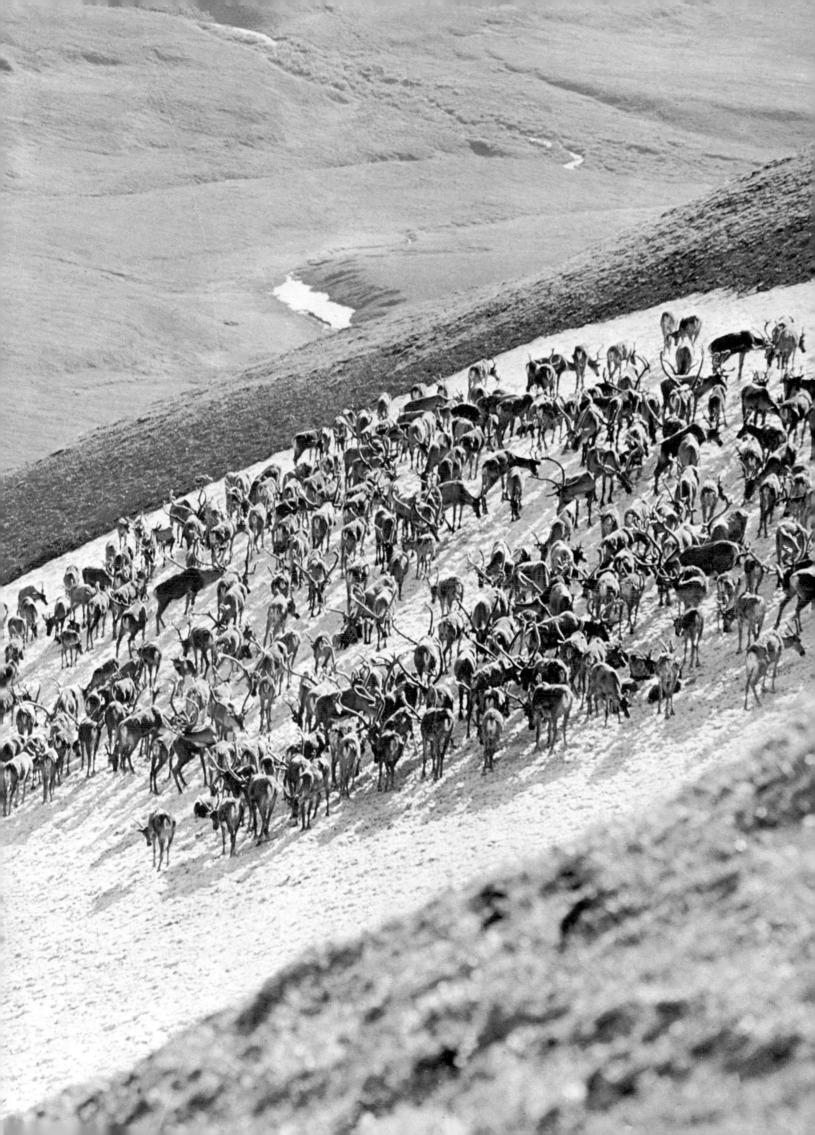

A polar bear pads across the polar ice cap. They cover hundreds of miles of ice, land and sea in search of food

An American atomic submarine surfaces from below the polar ice cap. This visit took place 60 years after the first expedition there by Peary

There is some mountainous grassland in the Arctic, always partly covered with snow. Plants begin to come up and flower while the snow is still on the ground. For a short time in July, the tundra is a mass of flowers. There is a continuous cover of mosses, grasses, tiny flowering plants and dwarf bushes. The curious plants called lichens flourish, clinging to the rocks (see: *lichen*). Most Arctic plants are small.

Many animals live on the Arctic land including the polar bear, caribou (reindeer), arctic wolf, arctic fox, weasel, hare, lemmings and other small animals. Birds include the ptarmigan, gyrfalcon and snowy owl. The musk ox lives in the North American regions.

There are no frost-free caves. So the animals do not hibernate – that is, sleep through the winter. Many more birds migrate to the Arctic in summer. Many fish live in the streams. Insects are numerous and flies and mosquitoes are a nuisance in summer.

The Arctic Ocean is rich in animal life. More animals live in the water than on the land. Mammals include several kinds of whale, many kinds of seal, and walruses. Fish live here also, but there are not so many as in sub-arctic waters.

Except for the blue fox and musk-ox, Arctic mammals grow white coats for winter. The colour is an excellent protection. They are hard to see against the white snow drifts. The white colour also helps to preserve the animal's body heat (see: *absorption of light*).

The people native to the Canadian Arctic and Greenland are the Eskimos. They have spread out over an immense area. Yet they are remarkably similar in physical type, language and culture. They have wide faces with high cheekbones, noses that do not stick out much, and a fold of skin that hoods over each upper eyelid. Their features are called 'Mongoloid'. The people of Siberia look similar, but belong to several different groups.

Arctic peoples live by hunting, herding and a little agriculture and trading. The Eskimos used to depend mostly on the sea. They wer once famous for their skill in handling thei canoes, called kayaks. In Siberia, the peopl are mostly wanderers. They follow their herd of reindeer across the tundra. As Europea traders, whalers and government control hav moved north, more of the Arctic people hav settled down. Many of them now live in villages and run farms.

There are enormous mineral deposits in th Arctic. These include coal, iron, copper, an other minerals. Towns have grown up along th barren coasts to serve the mines. Many o deposits exist there also.

Greenland was colonized by the Norwegian in 986. But contact was lost in the 15th century It was rediscovered in 1578 when Europea explorers began to look for the 'Northeaster Passage'. They had hoped to find a route t India across the North Pole. Later, when fu trapping and trade developed in North America men searched for a 'Northwest Passage'. I 1728, Vitus Bering showed that Asia and th American continent were separated by sea. I 1878-9, the first boat sailed from Europe, alon the coast of Siberia and through the Berin Straits.

The first man to reach the North Pole wa the American, Robert Peary, who travelled b dog-team in 1909. The first men to fly over th Pole were Richard E. Byrd and Floyd Bennett in 1926. In 1958 two US nuclear submarines the *Nautilus* and the *Skate*, cruised around unde the ice and even came to the surface at the pol

Find out by doing

Airlines now regularly fly over the Arctic. From maps or from airline offices, find out how much distance is saved by going over the poles rather than over the Atlantic or Pacific. (For example, between Anchorage and Stockholm, or between London and Los Angeles).

To think about

Why do you think life is so much more abundant in the Arctic than in the Antarctic?